"A brave, bold book that nails it: if we want jobs for our kids, we have to stop thinking of ambition as unCanadian and competition as not nice. *How We Can Win* is a roadmap to the future."

> Arlene Dickinson, bestselling author of *Persuasion* and CEO of Venture Communications

"A breath of fresh northern air that has cleared my view of the future, and what we need to change to succeed together."

> Chris Hadfield, astronaut and bestselling author of *An Astronaut's Guide to Life on Earth* and *You Are Here*

"A critically important book for anyone who cares about the future of the Canadian economy. The incredibly raw story of how Tony Lacavera started WIND—trying to shake-up the Canadian telecom industry—should be mandatory reading for all Canadian entrepreneurs, and for anyone else who is trying to weather this country's business and cultural ecosystem. Not only is *How We Can Win* a courageous telling of the hard truths we need to hear, it is a real page turner."

> Michele Romanow, a Dragon on CBC's *Dragons' Den* and co-founder of Clearbanc

"Canadian entrepreneurs have the talent to build amazing companies. *How We Can Win* shows what the challenges are, why people give up and go to Silicon Valley, and how to get them to stay. Because if we can't, we are in big trouble."

Ted Livingston, founder and CEO, Kik

"An entrepreneurial David who has fought many Goliaths, Tony Lacavera understands what it takes to compete and win, and in this excellent book he shows us how we can shift our economy into innovation-led SUPERGROWTH mode."

Michael Serbinis, founder and CEO of League

"This book is about innovation, entrepreneurship, technology, public policy and management—illuminated beautifully through story-telling and policy insights. But its overall message is one of urgency: the world economy is evolving quickly, and competing nations don't have the luxury of waiting for later to sort things out. Competition policy *is* innovation policy. Culture matters. Capital and talent are mobile. In *How We Can Win* Anthony Lacavera and Kate Fillion shine a light on Canada, but leaders and citizens of all countries will benefit from reading this book. Except, perhaps, for those in countries that are already ahead—the United States and China. The irony is they will likely read the book anyway. In fact, they'll read it first. And perhaps that's the point."

Ajay K. Agrawal, Peter Munk Professor of Entrepreneurship, Rotman School of Management

How We Can Win

And what happens to us
and our country if we don't

Anthony Lacavera
and Kate Fillion

Random House Canada

PUBLISHED BY RANDOM HOUSE CANADA

Copyright © 2017 Anthony Lacavera

www.penguinrandomhouse.ca

Random House Canada and colophon are registered trademarks.

Library and Archives Canada Cataloguing in Publication

Lacavera, Anthony, author
     How we can win : and what happens to us and our country
if we don't / Anthony Lacavera and Kate Fillion.

Issued in print and electronic formats.
ISBN 978-0-7352-7259-0
eBook ISBN 978-0-7352-7261-3

     1. Entrepreneurship—Canada. 2. New business enterprises
—Canada. 3. Success in business—Canada. 4. Canada—Economic
Conditions—21st century. I. Fillion, Kate, author II. Title.

HC115.L15 2017   330.971'07 C2017-903366-2

Canada-US trade map on page 49 reprinted by permission of its creator,
Trevor Tombe.

Text design by Five Seventeen

Printed and bound in the United States of America

2 4 6 8 9 7 5 3 1

Penguin
Random House
RANDOM HOUSE CANADA

For my incredible family and friends,
and the extraordinary community at Globalive
that has challenged the status quo

—ANTHONY LACAVERA

For Rudy Talarico,
who inspires kids to win
on the basketball court and in life

—KATE FILLION

Contents

INTRODUCTION

In 2007, I set out to build a new telecommunications company in Canada. Nine years later, I sold WIND Mobile for $1.6 billion. Most people—especially our investors, who got back six times what they'd put into the company—considered it a successful exit. I made a lot of money too. But to me WIND was, in some key respects, a failure. I didn't start a company just to make a profit. Like most entrepreneurs, I also wanted to make a difference.

Many Canadians are deeply skeptical about business, viewing it as a less than noble calling. But the entrepreneurs I know are pretty idealistic. They want to make the world, or at least their corner of it, a better place. That's why astronomically successful entrepreneurs, men and women who are millionaires many times over, volunteer their time at incubators and accelerators, mentoring the next generation and funding start-ups. Upstarts with quirky, niche businesses also truly believe they're changing the world. The 22-year-olds who build a new gaming platform or create an app for construction site managers aren't engaged in a cynical exercise to rip people off so they can laze around all day playing beer pong; they're passionate about gaming or construction, fanatical even, and sincerely believe they're making other people's lives better.

My own lofty goal was to shake up the telecommunications market so that all Canadians, regardless of which carrier they used (though of course I hoped they'd choose WIND), got better service for a lot less money. When I started WIND, three major carriers controlled telecommunications in this country; they had some of the lowest customer satisfaction rates yet some of the highest fees on the planet. I used to go bananas when I got my cellphone bill. The cost was usually way higher than whatever plan I'd signed on for, due to all the hidden charges and confusing overages—and exponentially higher than what Americans were paying.

It was obvious to me that a challenger would be able to disrupt the market in ways that would be good for consumers, good for the industry as a whole and, ultimately, good for the country. Even way back in 2007, when the ability to send and receive e-mails on a mobile device still seemed borderline miraculous, it was clear that wireless was going to be as important to the twenty-first-century economy as the railway had been in the nineteenth century—and it was equally clear that Canada was not ready. Because our country is so big and our population density so low, we faced network construction challenges that smaller countries such as South Korea and Singapore, both global leaders in connectivity, did not. Our telecommunications infrastructure was fragmented; outside major urban centres like Vancouver and Montreal, connectivity wasn't great and it was also relatively slow. However, no one was rushing to upgrade Canada's infrastructure. When an oligopoly controls an industry—and in Bell, Telus and

Rogers, we have an oligopoly—there's little pressure to innovate. Why bother, when building better networks costs a fortune and reduces shareholders' dividends? What's the hurry, when customers have nowhere else to go?

A little competition would change everything, I thought. A fourth, lower-cost carrier would force the incumbents to slash prices. I was right about that, temporarily, anyway. When WIND began operating, prices dropped across the board. And when we announced that we wouldn't charge a "system access fee"—an absurd, made-up charge that didn't relate to the provision of any actual services—Bell, Telus and Rogers, and their wholly owned subsidiaries Fido, Solo, Koodo, Virgin Mobile and the rest, stopped charging that "fee" too.

But I also thought that having more players in the wireless market would revitalize the telecommunications landscape in ways that would kick-start the creation of new businesses and help make Canada more competitive, and there I was wrong. The Canadian telecommunications infrastructure is still subpar and access to it is still overpriced, and that's not just bad for people who like to stream movies on their phones. It's bad for businesses that rely on the Internet—which is pretty much every business these days, though the impact on high-tech companies is most severe—and therefore, ultimately, really bad for our economy. A crucial part of the infrastructure for the knowledge economy, something that needs to be the equivalent of a beautifully paved six-lane highway, is still, in a lot of parts of the country, more like a dirt road. Nor did WIND usher in an attitudinal shift, emboldening entrepreneurs to dream big and try to build businesses capable of disrupting the oligopolies that dominate so many sectors of our economy, from banking to energy. Unwittingly, we may have done the reverse, providing a cautionary tale about the futility of trying to challenge the status quo in Canada.

Why didn't the advent of a fourth carrier have a bigger impact? The simplest explanation is that WIND was not, in the end, a strong-enough challenger to break the oligopoly's stranglehold on telecommunications and force fundamental change. I wasn't a perfect CEO and I definitely made mistakes, but the biggest one was underestimating the barriers to competition in Canada, not just in telecommunications but in almost every sector of our economy. Some of these barriers are cultural, historical and intangible, while others are structural, regulatory and glaringly obvious. Some are the product of the way our capital markets function, others are related to the way our government operates. Some spring from the power of oligopolies and the way our business elites interact to protect the status quo; others can be traced back to our education system and how we learn to think about our own prospects and capabilities. But the net effect is the same: if we can't compete, with each other and with the rest of the world, there's a ceiling on growth in Canada.

The consequences go far beyond the fate of a single company or even an industry, and right to the heart of what kind of country Canada will become in the twenty-first century. A major transformation of the global economy is under way. Amidst considerable uncertainty, two things are very clear: the rules of the race to the future are radically different than they were during Canada's first 150 years, and we are up against countries that already have a big lead on us because they got started earlier or because they have advantages we don't have, or both. Simply to catch up, we *must* embrace competition. If we want to win, we have to do even more: let go of some cherished egalitarian ideals and focus our energy and resources on those sectors, companies and people that have the very best chances of succeeding. If all this sounds a little too aggressive and unCanadian, consider what's at stake: our way of life.

Already, our children's prospects are considerably worse than ours were, not only because of trends originating outside our borders but also—largely—because of what's happening inside them. Our population is aging and we generate less value per hour of labour than workers in many other countries in the Organization for Economic Cooperation and Development (OECD). Our economy has not diversified beyond natural resources, our GDP growth is shrinking, and our infrastructure is inadequate. Our trade with the most important emerging markets is declining, and we have failed to build the kind of multinational companies that create jobs and power an economy. Fluctuations in the price of oil have made most Canadians aware of at least some of these trends, but many don't seem to understand how little time we have to course-correct.

And if we want to preserve Canada's well-deserved reputation for tolerance, decency and equality of opportunity, we have to course-correct. The values we hold dear—the shared beliefs that most clearly and positively define what it means to be Canadian—don't come cheap. Our social safety net absolutely depends on prosperity. How long could we continue to provide high-quality universal health care if some of our largest companies were disrupted by new technologies and the corporate tax base was destroyed? How welcoming could we afford to be to refugees if the price of oil plummeted, or if the United States began imposing new tariffs on our exports? How good would our universities and colleges be if their funding was cut dramatically?

I'm not an economist. But looking at Canada's prospects through an entrepreneur's lens, it's clear that the way we think about, approach and incentivize competition in general and the creation of new businesses in particular is a big problem. Our resistance to competition, and the dampening effect that has on innovation, helps explain why more than 300,000 of our best and brightest now work in Silicon Valley, creating lots of jobs, wealth and tax revenue—for the United States. To ensure Canada's future prosperity, we need to hang on to our most talented and innovative people, the ones who will add the most value to our economy, whether they're software developers or teachers or farmers. And we also need to attract immigrants of a similar calibre, as many as we can get.

That won't happen until we change the way we do business in Canada. I say *until*, not *unless*, because I'm an optimist. But I also don't think there's another option. If we don't make some fundamental changes to the way we think about and approach competition, we can stop worrying about the future. We won't have one.

CHAPTER 1

Exhibit A

B ecause I know it best, and because it is such a bright, shining example of Canada's competition problem, I'll start with the telecommunications industry. From banking to broadcasting to oil and gas, our economy is dominated by oligopolies, but in telecommunications, power is unusually highly concentrated. Three big carriers, Bell, Rogers and Telus, control about 92 percent of the wireless market.

In 2007, they controlled even more: 94 percent. And in many major cities, consumers really had only two choices, not three. Telus didn't aggressively pursue market share in the East, and Bell didn't aggressively pursue it in the West, as though the companies had decided, in quintessentially Canadian fashion, to split the golden goose eggs politely rather than squabble over them. There was plenty of wealth to go around: in 2006, wireless revenues were $12.7 billion, up more than 15 percent over the previous year. RIM and mobile e-mail, the beginning of the mobile Internet, large-scale adoption of cellphones—those were heady days, and because the Big Three had already swallowed up all the smaller carriers such as Microcell and Clearnet, there were no competitive pressures.

What consolidation meant for consumers was that prices climbed year after year. As one OECD report after another confirmed, Canadians paid more for wireless than just about anybody in the developed world. Michael Geist, the Canada Research Chair in Internet and e-commerce law at the University of Ottawa, summed up the situation this way: "The Canadian wireless market is hopelessly behind the rest of the world with limited competition, higher prices, and less choice."

Canadians are accustomed to paying more for a lot of things, from candy to cars. We tend to think of higher prices as one of the trade-offs we make for living in a country with universal health care and a strong social safety net: sure, stuff costs more, but we are also getting more, in the grand scheme of things.

That wasn't the case with wireless. Higher prices didn't translate into better service or an awesome network or much of anything else except really high profits for the Big Three. Canadians were paying top dollar for access to a telecommunications infrastructure that was actually declining relative to other countries', according to the International Telecommunications Union. Each year, the Union publishes a development index that measures the state of wireless networks and information and communications technology (ICT) around the world. In 2002, Canada was in ninth place, but by 2007 we'd plummeted to nineteenth—the steepest drop of any country ranked in the top fifty. (By 2016, we'd slipped to twenty-fifth, below countries such as Malta.)

The long-term economic implications are really troubling. Wireless is the foundation of the digital economy, permitting not just individual communication but machine-to-machine communication—the Internet of things—and the creation of new businesses.

Smartphones, smart homes, smart cities, smart businesses: all of these depend on wireless. But as the wireless age was dawning, Canada was already at a disadvantage compared with other developed countries. One reason we haven't caught up is that the bar is constantly being raised. The pace of technological change is accelerating while, simultaneously, demands on the network are increasing, as more and more devices—not just phones but appliances, home security systems and now semi-autonomous vehicles—are connected to the Internet. When you think about how cities of the near future will be set up, complete with sensors communicating the location of every pedestrian in every intersection to every autonomous vehicle in the area, you begin to understand how strong wireless networks need to be. Unless you're constantly upgrading, improving and innovating, there's no chance of keeping up and creating a competitive infrastructure. Governments can and do intervene to ensure those kinds of investments are made; the South Korean government, for instance, made technology in general and broadband access in particular a huge focus in the mid-nineties, and today the country leads the world on the ICT development index. But in countries like Canada, which rely on market forces to push wireless development, competition in telecommunications is the main driver of innovation. If no one's really competing, incumbents don't have to rush to make investments that will eat into their profits. They can take their time, which is what happens in Canada. Investments do get made, but the Big Three are not in any big hurry to make them, and it often seems as though they act in unison (two of them, Telus and Bell, actually share a single network).

Nor is there an incentive to expand globally. Though the Big Three are awash in cash, they do not seize investment opportunities outside Canada. Sprint was on its knees during and after the economic crisis in 2008 and could have been purchased on the cheap, but the oligopoly collectively passed on an investment opportunity that would have created jobs for Canadians and wealth for our country. Bell, Rogers and Telus were doing just fine right here at home, so why take a risk.

All of which explains why the Canadian government deliberately set about trying to create more competition in wireless. A lot of European countries, notably the UK, had done the same thing, holding auctions where some portion of the spectrum was set aside specifically for new entrants to encourage the emergence of strong challengers that could shake up the industry. In late November 2007, Jim Prentice, then the industry minister, announced that advanced wireless spectrum would be auctioned off the following May. "We are looking for greater competition in the market and further innovation in the industry," he said. "At the end of the day, our goals are lower prices, better service and more choice for consumers and business. That is why we are setting aside a portion of radio spectrum exclusively for new entrants into the wireless market." Bell, Rogers and Telus would be allowed to bid on only 60 percent of it, leaving 40 percent exclusively for new players.

There's a lot of mystification and jargon in the wireless industry— purposely, I suspect, to confuse consumers to the point where they just throw up their hands, stop asking questions and pay their bills. The basic concepts are not really that complicated. All wireless communications signals travel invisibly through the air on a spectrum of radio frequencies. When you're on a call or watching TV on your mobile, you're doing it via some sliver of spectrum. Think about your car radio: when you're listening to 99.9 FM, you're tuned to a station that broadcasts at 99.9 megahertz. Turn the dial to check out a different station and you tune into another frequency.

At its core, a cellphone is really just a radio, but it's able to tune to a much broader set of frequencies, simultaneously, so it can communicate a lot more information with the network than a radio that receives just one narrow band at a time. As with radio stations, wireless operators acquire licences granting them exclusive use of specific frequencies in particular geographical areas, so they aren't all trying to transmit signals over the same frequencies in the same markets at the same time.

Initially, the government doled out spectrum licences for free to the companies that became Bell, Rogers and Telus, in much the same way that, in the nineteenth century, homesteaders were granted large parcels of land. The idea in both cases was that the pioneers would create value on the real estate they'd been gifted. Wireless operators delivered, big time, building lucrative empires on their slices of the spectrum. But the spectrum is finite, and by 2007, what was left for wireless usage was incredibly valuable, and all the more so because the government was preparing to sell the equivalent of prime beachfront property—spectrum that could, in a few years, be used for fourth-generation LTE networks and, by 2020 or so, for 5G networks. (While 3G is good enough for downloading web pages, 4G is what you need to watch videos and 5G is what will power the Internet of things.)

The wedge of spectrum opened to new players would amount to less than 14 percent of the total mobile spectrum in use after the auction, but Bell, Rogers and Telus apparently felt that even 1 percent was too much. They'd strenuously lobbied the government throughout the consultation process leading up to the announcement of the auction, arguing that set-asides—remember: standard practice in OECD countries—were unnecessary and unfair. Telus insisted that the market was already "vigorously competitive"; Rogers, a major beneficiary of government largesse in the past, characterized newcomers, who'd be paying through the nose for spectrum licences, as "all time corporate welfare bums."

You might think that Canadian consumers would have been up in arms, lobbying the government just as strenuously for more competition. That's what happened in the United States when a spectrum auction was announced at about the same time. A quarter of a million Americans wrote to the Federal Communications Commission (FCC) urging the government to set up the auction in a way that would result in more affordable and accessible Internet access. The story unfolded rather differently in Canada: exactly four consumers volunteered their views during Industry Canada's consultation.

At the time, it seemed to me that consumers' complacency didn't really matter because the government did the right thing anyway. However, new applicants had only three months and a few days to get their finances in order. The deadline for applications for the May auction was March 10, 2008; bidders looking to get licences in anything more than a few small markets were required to put down deposits of hundreds of millions of dollars.

I didn't have that kind of money, but I thought I could raise it. Since 1998, I'd been building companies on the fringes of the $36-billion telecommunications industry, starting with fixed-line operator services for hotel chains. Because the incumbents were slow to innovate, opportunities were plentiful. One of my companies brought prepaid calling cards to Canada; another, Enunciate, which I co-founded with two former Bell executives in 2000, was the first to offer automated, no-operator-required teleconferencing; a third start-up, One Connect, brought Voice over Internet Protocol (VoIP) communications to small and medium-sized businesses. In 2004, Globalive Communications, the holding company for all these businesses, was named the fastest-growing company in Canada by *Profit* magazine and, for the first time, made Deloitte's annual list of Canada's best-managed companies (we've been on it ever since).

I did not do all this on my own, of course. I had exceptionally able co-founders in all my businesses, and many people helped Globalive to grow, especially Brice Scheschuk and Simon Lockie, who joined the executive team in 2003 and 2005, respectively, and quickly became my close friends. Though Brice's title was chief financial officer (he became our CEO in 2015) and Simon is our chief legal officer, it's perhaps more accurate to say that they were—and still are—my most trusted business advisers. Together, we'd been pretty successful. Nevertheless, in 2007, Globalive was a complete nonentity compared with Bell, Telus and Rogers. We didn't have our own facilities or fixed-line infrastructure; we had to lease capacity from the incumbents, who were very unhappy that regulations compelled them to do so. Although we were far too small to pose a competitive threat, they had started to make it more difficult for us to get access by, say, dragging their feet on implementing new circuits and filling work orders. It was a little like having a landlord whose idea of dealing with a leaky roof is to tell you to put a bucket on the floor: you have no choice but to grin and bear it, especially if you can't afford to buy your own place.

By 2007, it was clear that wireless was the future. The barriers to entry, however, were extraordinarily high: you needed not only spectrum, which is wildly expensive, but also enough capital to construct a massive network of cell towers and to build a retail operation. So when the government announced the set-aside, effectively removing the most significant barrier to entry, it was a game changer. Finally, Globalive had an opportunity to own infrastructure and build a new business in a booming industry. I issued a press release announcing that we would participate in the auction.

Not one news outlet bothered to call to find out more. No one believed we had the resources to participate. To be fair, they were right, but I was confident we could raise enough money to register for the auction. This wasn't because I'd ever raised hundreds of millions of dollars before; to purchase Yak, a discount home phone and Internet service provider, in 2006, Globalive raised $65 million, and it was incredibly difficult and painful. Still, I was sure

I could find investors who would see the spectrum auction the same way I did, as a once-in-a-lifetime opportunity to create a new national carrier. The market was already big enough for a fourth player—most US cities have four to six providers—and growing every year, and the government was rolling out the red carpet for newcomers. The core team at Globalive wrote up a business plan laying out a ten-year horizon, and in December 2007, I hit Bay Street, looking for investors.

The timing wasn't ideal for a big project with a short fuse. Everyone was winding down for the holidays and a lot of decision makers simply weren't in the office. Those who were gave me a seasonally appropriate reception: frosty, though sometimes there was a touch of good cheer, given that I was laughed out of more than one boardroom. Some people were scared off by my ambition. Their attitude was, "This is *Canada*. You can't raise $600 million to start a new business." Others, who knew the telecommunications industry well, cited the history of carnage: "AT&T lost $6 billion in Canada, Sprint lost well over $1 billion—if they couldn't break the oligopoly, you don't have a prayer." Some dismissed me outright as crazy, while others complimented my audacity, then dismissed me as crazy.

One big problem was that most Canadian investors just aren't all that comfortable with technology investments. Professional investors are extremely sophisticated and aggressive when it comes to assessing risk in mining, oil and gas, and other natural resource plays; this is one of the best places in the world to seek financing in those sectors, because they are so well understood. But in other areas investors tend to be both more wary and less patient—they want liquidity and fast exits. I was pitching a long-term investment, the kind where, before you can even think about generating revenue, you have to construct something on the same order of complexity as a hydroelectric grid. I needed backers who would be comfortable parking their money for at least ten years.

So I was fishing in a very small pond—more like a puddle, really. The CEOs of our biggest companies tend to belong to the same clubs, support the same charities and hang out in the same enclaves in Muskoka in the summer. By and large, they look out for each other, which is really touching unless you're running around looking for financing for a disruptive company. Many of the potential investors I approached already had, or wanted to have, strong business and/or social ties to Bell, Telus and/or Rogers, and weren't about to endanger them, especially not for a 33-year-old upstart on what more than one person told me was a "suicide mission."

Our plan had been to line up investment and then leverage it to woo a strategic partner with significant operational experience in the industry, someone who could provide advice and guidance, not just money. By January, when I hadn't raised one dollar, it was time for Plan B: look for a strategic partner with really deep pockets. It was clear that only a telco would be patient enough and confident enough in the outcome—and in the value of my experience—to wait for a return. To find one, we'd have to look outside Canada. Typically, an investment banker would be hired to coordinate an international search, but we didn't have that kind of time. The deadline to register for the auction was just two months away. So we went old school, cold-calling wireless companies all over the world. There's a publicly available ranking of telecommunications companies, from a massive one in China right down to a tiny network in eastern Europe, and we started working our way through it, calling the main reception number of companies that looked like good potential partners and asking to speak to someone in the business development team. Usually we didn't get a return call, so we'd repeat the process until we actually got someone on the line. Though most of the people we spoke to passed on the opportunity quickly, they were definitely more interested than any Canadian investors I'd met.

In February, we reached Michael O'Connor, the lead business development officer at Orascom Telecom (OT) in Cairo. Egypt's Orascom conglomerate was founded in 1950 by Onsi Sawiris and grew into a group of highly diversified companies—cement, technology, hotels and resorts—run by his three Western-educated sons. Naguib, the eldest brother, founded and ran the telecommunications arm of Orascom, which at that time had about 125 million subscribers around the world, primarily in developing countries such as Pakistan, Algeria and Bangladesh. But OT was dwarfed by Orascom Construction, run by Nassef, the youngest brother, which builds office towers and even entire cities. What makes the Sawiris family's extraordinary global success even more extraordinary is that they are Coptic Christians, a small minority in a predominantly Muslim country, and no strangers to prejudice. In the sixties, the Egyptian government nationalized Orascom's assets and Onsi wasn't allowed to leave the country for six years. The family rebounded—spectacularly: in 2008, *Forbes* estimated their net worth at $36 billion.

Michael O'Connor was Naguib's right-hand man at Orascom Telecom and, luckily, he hailed from Peterborough, Ontario, so he knew all about Canada's cozy oligopoly in telecommunications. It didn't take much to persuade him that the spectrum auction was an intriguing business opportunity, and after a few phone calls with Brice, Simon and me, he arranged for me to have a fifteen-minute meeting with his boss in Cairo. When I tell Canadians this story, they're usually dumbfounded: why would a modern-day pharaoh meet with a nobody from Welland, Ontario? To me, the question is a perfect reflection of the lack of confidence and ambition that is crippling our ability to participate in the global economy. Sure, I was a nobody, but it wasn't outrageous to think an international telecom giant might be interested in backing a new, made-in-Canada business. Three facts made the investment appealing: average revenue per user per month (ARPU) in Canada was sixty dollars, much higher than just about anywhere else in the world; all three incumbent carriers charged roughly the same prices, suggesting a major opportunity for a competitor; and wireless penetration was just 75 percent, relatively low for a developed country.

To outsiders, the picture was clear: here was a chance to bust up a bloated, stagnant oligopoly and corner a healthy share of a growing market in a stable democracy. Already, Vodafone, with investments all over Europe, had expressed interest, and I was pretty far along in talks with Novator, which owned and operated wireless companies mostly in the Baltic States and Poland. Orascom Telecom, the twelfth-largest mobile network provider in the world in terms of subscribers, also had good reason to be interested. In 2007, Naguib had sold the telecommunications network he'd rebuilt in Iraq, and was actively scouting for a new place to invest his "war chest," as he'd told CNN in late December. He'd ruled out many of the emerging markets he usually favoured—already too crowded with players—and wanted someplace "where I can go in and make a difference and create immense value, just like we did with Iraq, and even add to" that war chest. From my perspective, Canada fit that bill. In developing countries, OT's average ARPU was only about five dollars; relatively speaking, Bell, Telus and Rogers were charging—and pocketing—a fortune. A fourth carrier could charge less and still do very, very well.

But there was a catch. In 2008, foreign investment rules in Canada were particularly strict for telecommunications companies. Essentially, foreigners had to be willing to give their Canadian partners complete control over the investment. That might have been palatable if I'd had a big track record in wireless (I didn't, my telecommunications expertise was in fixed line) or if I were contributing the lion's share of the money. My plan was to put in $10 million total—huge money for me personally, but nothing compared with what I was asking for from investors.

Trying to persuade people to bankroll a company they'll have no say over is an extremely difficult sell, as you can imagine, so I prepared for meetings with potential foreign investors very, very thoroughly. Early in my career I'd learned the hard way that preparation is everything. While I was still studying computer engineering at the University of Toronto, I joined a start-up that built websites; soon we had clients like Deloitte and BMO and an office in the Scotiabank tower. Since everybody in town was clamouring for a website, I thought we were masters of the universe. I was twenty-two, and my idea of preparing for a meeting was swaggering into someone's office and saying, "Sure, we'll build you a website. The deposit is $50,000, sign here." When IBM and the big system integrators came in and started not only building websites but creating e-commerce platforms, prices dropped and arrogant punks were annihilated. We hadn't diversified or built the kind of relationships with clients where we understood their needs well enough to pivot.

Failure is an excellent teacher. I learned a lot from that experience about the value of studying for meetings, whether with customers or investors, so you go in with a solid understanding of the other party's background and needs. You can't get that from a quick Google search, particularly if you're completely unfamiliar with the cultural context, as I was when it came to Egypt. I'd been to Morocco once on holiday, but had never been anywhere else in North Africa and never done business in a Muslim country. So I approached the meeting with Naguib as though it were a final exam on Arab culture, reading two books on the subject, plus everything I could find on Orascom, the Sawiris family and Naguib himself. There was a lot, because the family is iconic in Egypt—like rock stars, the brothers are referred to by their first names only—and Orascom was the country's first multinational company and is still one of its largest private sector employers.

The OT headquarters are housed in two gleaming towers the Sawiris brothers built on the banks of the Nile, which are also home to other multinational companies, a high-end mall and Naguib's own palatial penthouse residence. When I got off the elevator and stepped into the lobby, the aesthetic was cool, modern and familiar, but the soundtrack was lively and polyglot—I heard snippets of Arabic, German, French and English conversations—and it became obvious that a lot of people were ahead of me in a very long line to see the CEO. The timing of appointments was notional, apparently, and no one seemed in any rush. Except me: I hate wasting time, so I asked if there was a room I could use while I waited. Once installed in a small, windowless space, I rehearsed my fifteen-minute presentation out loud, start to finish, for more than two hours, as the time of my appointment came and went.

When I was finally ushered into his office, I was incredibly nervous and launched right into my presentation, which I still remember word for word: "Mr. Sawiris, thank you for meeting me. I've followed your career with great admiration, you're obviously one of the world's leading entrepreneurs. I'm an entrepreneur in Canada, tiny by your metrics, but I've had some success in telecommunications and fixed line—"

He stopped me. He didn't want to hear my presentation. "Tell me about yourself," he commanded.

Knocked off script, I stumbled along, rattling off the first things that came into my head: I'm Italian-Canadian, grew up in a small town in Ontario, didn't have any advantages in terms of connections and didn't come from money, but built a telecommunications company from scratch. That could only have taken a minute or two, but it felt like a year. It was clear that Naguib had zero interest in looking at the detailed deck I'd prepared, so I segued directly to my conclusion: "Now I have an opportunity to buy some wireless frequencies. I don't know much about the wireless industry, but I do know about the Canadian market, and I'd like to partner with you to leverage my knowledge and what I've built so far, and to leverage your global perspective and your capital, to build a competitor to the incumbent operators in Canada."

I was relieved to get that out and was opening my mouth to supply more details when Naguib stopped me again. "You said you're tiny. How tiny?"

"Well, I started from nothing, but now my sales are about $120 million, Canadian."

He looked at me for a moment, then asked, "Monthly? Or quarterly?"

"Annually."

"You really *are* tiny." His tone was matter-of-fact, not condescending, but it was clear the meeting was over. Instead of goodbye, though, he said, "Let's have dinner tonight."

And then I was back in the lobby. Maybe nine minutes had passed, total. I had no idea what had just happened.

But that evening I joined him for dinner at the Four Seasons, an Orascom-built hotel, which turned into a three-hour event where we talked about everything under the sun. Except telecommunications. Naguib was different than he'd been in his office—warm, engaging, extremely personable—but one thing was the same: he was in complete control of the conversation. He talked a bit about himself, telling me that he'd grown up in Germany after Nasser nationalized his father's company, so German became his second of five or six languages. We spoke in English and then for a while in French—he went to university in Switzerland, so his was better than mine—and he told me how much he loved techno and dance music, even flying DJs in from Europe to perform at nightclubs he owned in Cairo, though he had to be careful because some powerful people in Egypt didn't approve of his taste or his hobbies. He was vocal about both his faith, which is strong, and his hope that Egyptian society would become more secular, more welcoming not just to Coptic Christians but to liberal Muslims who didn't believe women should be forced to cover themselves to walk down the street.

Mostly, though, he wanted to know about me. What's your family like? What school did you go to? What do you do for fun? "Tell me everything there is to know," Naguib instructed. So I did.

I told him about my dad, a small-town lawyer who became a judge and is still my best friend, and the first person I turn to for advice, because he can see a situation from all sides and always tells it like it is. And yet he always has my back. At a critical moment early in Globalive's development, he invested in the company—a vote of confidence that meant even more to me than the capital he provided, which helped keep us afloat. Naguib, better than most people, understands the importance of family, and he smiled when I told him about my mom, a high-school teacher with high standards and zero tolerance for arrogance. Character is everything to her, and if she thinks I've done something that endangers mine, she doesn't hesitate to let me know. Both my parents were alarmed when I told them that I wanted to start my own company, and urged me to consider working for a big, established company after I graduated. We had a nice, secure, middle-class life—didn't I want that for myself?

They didn't put their collective foot down on my entrepreneurial ambitions, though, because they knew that once I'd made up my mind to do something, there was no stopping me. This didn't mean that I was always right; at the dawn of the cellphone era, I'd forged ahead with a doomed business predicated on the notion that the world would always need pay phones. But once I've committed to something, as my parents figured out early on, only complete failure will convince me to change direction. My mother likes to tell people about the time I was six years old and propped a ladder up against the fence in our backyard so I could climb over to the neighbours' yard. When she caught me doing this, she pointed out that I might fall off the ladder and break my neck, and ordered me to stop. I did. But over the next two weeks, whenever she wasn't looking, I surreptitiously dug a trench underneath the fence and then turned my hand to dismantling the thing altogether. I can't remember why I wanted to get to the other side so badly, but I do remember feeling it was intolerable to let anything stand between me and my goal. Bullheadedness may be genetic, because my sister is the same way. By far the smartest person I've ever met—though two years younger, she leapfrogged up to my engineering class at the University of Toronto, where she finished near the very top (I did not) and went on to get an MBA and a law degree in record time— she is now Google's chief litigator. God help anyone who goes up against her in a dispute over intellectual property or anything else. Growing up, I don't think I ever won an argument with my sister.

Talking so much about my childhood made me self-conscious, but each time I tried to turn the conversation back to Naguib, he asked more questions. What are your passions? When did you start working? What sports do you like? Which is how I wound up talking about playing hockey in high school, reminiscing not so fondly about how the coach used to scream at me because I was always cruising around the blue line ready to pounce on a loose puck, completely neglecting my defensive responsibilities. I also told him about my first real job: desk clerk at a perpetually over-booked hotel in Niagara Falls, where I learned how to deal with irate customers because just about every night in peak season, people showed up with confirmed reservations and I had to tell them there was no room at the inn—but, lucky break! it just so happened that there *was* room at one of our more expensive sister properties. And I talked about finally getting my pilot's licence in 2007, fulfilling a lifelong dream.

I'd never had a business meeting with someone so uninterested in talking business. Throughout the evening, I struggled to understand why such a powerful person had any interest in my life. Ten years later, I get it, and I find myself asking the same kinds of questions Naguib asked me when I'm deciding whether to invest in an entrepreneurial venture. He taught me that the most important thing in business partnerships is to understand you're partnering with people, not sources of capital; whether your personalities and strengths mesh or clash usually determines whether the partnership succeeds or fails.

When dinner was over, Naguib said simply, "I like you and I'd like to partner with you."

That was Thursday night. On Monday morning, a huge crew of his people showed up in Toronto to do due diligence on Globalive, and we started planning how we'd build Canada's fourth wireless carrier.

In March, Globalive registered to enter the auction with a deposit of $230 million. No one was expecting us to show up with $50, much less $230 million, and I think it's fair to say people in the industry were shocked. Regional operators such as Vidéotron and Shaw also showed up with sizable deposits, but they wanted to strengthen their existing networks and weren't looking to build a truly national business. I was.

The auction was a bonanza for the federal government, which raked in $4.8 billion at the end of the day. Globalive alone paid $442.5 million for licences that would give us access to a pool of 25 million potential subscribers; though we didn't manage to secure anything in Quebec, we emerged as the new entrant with the best claim to be Canada's fourth carrier. Mobilicity and Public Mobile were the other new entrants, but they had relatively cautious financial backers and, consequently, wound up with many fewer licences. Because we had a highly experienced strategic investor with a much longer view, we were better funded and therefore able to get off the ground faster—even despite Industry Canada's exhaustive, six-month review to ensure that WIND was compliant with the government's foreign ownership regulations.

Most OECD countries permit foreign investment in telecommunications as a way of introducing competition and strengthening networks. The Canadian government had recently been urged by its own blue-ribbon panel of business leaders (headed by Bell's former CEO, Lynton "Red" Wilson, no less) to follow suit, so long as foreigners did not launch or acquire telcos that controlled more than 10 percent of our market. Nevertheless, at the time of the spectrum auction, Canadian restrictions still strongly discouraged foreign investment: at least 80 percent of the voting shares in a telco had to be held by Canadians, and there was also a much vaguer rule that a company could not otherwise be controlled by non-Canadians.

Therefore, between September 2008, when we paid for our licences, and March 2009, when we actually received them, Industry Canada conducted an extensive investigation into every aspect of WIND's ownership structure. They requested several changes—for example, they wanted more independent Canadian directors on our board—and we complied, readily, not least because each change wound up increasing Globalive's power vis-à-vis Orascom. However, the end result was never in question, at least not in my mind, because WIND was not controlled by Naguib and never could be, because of the way we'd set up the company. So while the review dragged on, and the clock kept ticking on our loans, we started building cell towers and hiring staff. By the time Simon and Ken Campbell, WIND's CEO, finally went to Ottawa to collect a phonebook-thick stack of yellow licences, we were almost ready to launch.

———

One of the biggest advantages of a strategic partnership is that you don't just get money, you also get mentorship from people who really know what they're talking about. I'd been thinking we'd build a brand from the ground up, but people at Orascom pointed out that it would be much cheaper and faster if we licensed a brand from one of Naguib's existing operations. WIND is a huge wireless brand in Italy and also popular in Greece, and was already familiar to Canadians with ties to those countries. Licensing the brand meant we didn't have to come up with a name or a logo, or think through the cosmetic aspects of our retail stores: colour scheme, fixtures, shelving, countertops and so on. That decision saved us many months, and freed us to focus on figuring out what Canadians really wanted.

We decided to ask them directly, by creating a website where people could share the good, the bad and the ugly about their wireless experience. We didn't spend a single dollar advertising wirelesssoapbox.com—we didn't have to, because it went viral. Canadians started posting their wireless bills, saying, "Look how I got ripped off this month." People vented about all the fine-print charges—system access fees, 911 fees, device set-up fees, unlocking fees—and the astronomical data roaming charges, the highest in the world. Some people uploaded transcripts or tapes of their customer service calls, and ranted about getting the runaround from agents who kept them on the phone for hours but couldn't answer their questions or deal with their complaints. That site gave us a ton of market intelligence, for free. Canadians wanted fair pricing with no tricks or hidden charges, along with a next-generation, faster network and a better customer experience. They helped us figure out what WIND would stand for: integrity, transparency and innovation.

As we got started, we felt tremendous pride and excitement about what WIND was going to offer: bills written in plain English, with no hidden costs, and Canada's first unlimited data, calling and texting plans. The shared sense of mission in a start-up can seem cultish to outsiders—it's just a company, after all. But to those on the inside, it's never "just a company" or "just a job." It's an all-consuming cause. Everyone in a start-up has sacrificed something—a pension, or stock options, or just the certainty of knowing the company will still exist six months down the road—and, as a result, is that much more passionately committed to success. At WIND, the people who had kids tended to be fuelled by a particularly strong sense of outrage: their teenagers' phone bills were a major pain point. Many of our senior people had walked away from jobs at the Big Three carriers because they wanted to make a difference in the industry; listening to the collective disappointment and outrage on our wireless soapbox doubled their resolve. My role was basically to campaign non-stop, reminding everyone that everything we did had to relate to our commitment to integrity, transparency and innovation. If we add this equipment, will it deliver on our promise of innovation? If we adopt that billing system, how will it promote transparency?

In the meantime, there was static from the Big Three. Bell, Telus and Rogers are very successful companies run by very smart people, and they'd gobbled up all the smaller fish in the pond. I'm sure the idea that the pond was about to be repopulated was a little irritating. But the sniping was weirdly personal—according to the rumours that got back to me, I was, despite having started a dozen successful businesses, an arriviste, a lightweight, a playboy—and weirdly disproportionate to the threat we posed. We were playing David to not one but three hulking Goliaths; no one, including me, thought WIND was going to put any of them out of business. We aimed to be a fourth carrier, not to knock out an incumbent. Our goal was not to be the fastest, biggest or even cheapest, but to build a company that provided good value for money by offering lower-cost wireless and more attentive customer service.

Although I wasn't so naive as to imagine the incumbents would welcome us with open arms, I didn't expect them to dispute our right to exist. But they did. While the Industry Canada review was still going on, Telus sent a letter to the Canadian Radio-Television and Telecommunications Commission (CRTC), suggesting that they too might want to look into WIND's ownership structure. Industry Canada regulates the spectrum, but the CRTC regulates telecom operators. Both use the exact same test to determine compliance with foreign ownership rules, so we figured we had no worries. Right?

Wrong. The CRTC elected to conduct its own review and, in a highly unusual move suggested by Telus, decided for the first time ever to make its review public, which, not coincidentally, meant that Telus, along with Bell and Rogers, could participate. I knew we were in serious trouble when the Globalive contingent—Brice, Simon and me, plus a handful of lawyers—showed up in Ottawa for the hearing and found ourselves facing an army of lawyers and telecom executives, while dozens more, who hadn't been able to squeeze into the room, milled around outside. Oddly, given that they were supposedly "vigorously competitive," they seemed awfully chummy and were all singing from the same song sheet: WIND is a shell company for a foreign interest. Why, they chorused, did we have an Egyptian investor instead of red-blooded Canadian backers? I told the truth: Canadian investors were not willing to take on the oligopoly, for reasons I was beginning to understand all too well.

Not a single consumer advocate or group showed up in our defence, which is extraordinary since we knew from our wireless soapbox experiment that a lot of Canadians were fed up with the status quo. But at the hearing, we stood alone to argue our case in a roomful of lawyers whose job it was to protect the status quo.

The essence of the complaint against WIND was that Naguib was actually running the show, which was comical. Quite apart from the fact that the company had been painstakingly structured to keep him at arm's length, Naguib was number sixty on *Forbes*'s list of the world's wealthiest billionaires, with an extraordinary art collection, opulent homes in London and Paris, and a fleet of private planes (and full-time pilots—all Canadian, interestingly enough). Aside from running OT, he served on the boards of huge global businesses and had a mind-boggling catalogue of complex investments all over the world. In terms of his overall portfolio, WIND was a rounding error. Yes, he held 65 percent of WIND's equity, but mostly in non-voting shares. He was not sitting in Cairo masterminding our expansion or plotting our marketing campaign or deciding where to build cell towers. We actually had been having a difficult time just getting his attention. Naguib's style is to make big bets, like introducing wireless in North Korea (which didn't work out so well: the government refused to let him repatriate his earnings), and then delegate responsibility, often to very young executives. Of course he checks in on his investments, but he's the opposite of a micromanager. He did not, for instance, come to Ottawa for the CRTC hearings, though he did join via satellite at one point. To get a few minutes with him, I'd fly to Cairo and might wait a day or two—he was that busy, but also that trusting. He wouldn't have invested in a company he had so little say over if he hadn't believed we were fully capable of running it.

When the CRTC ruled on October 29 that WIND was not controlled by Canadians and therefore could not operate, I was floored. I couldn't accept the decision, because it made no sense. The federal government had held an auction with the explicit goal of decreasing the power of the oligopoly, yet had now ruled in a way that reinforced its power. They'd taken our $442.5 million and approved us, then unapproved us, and we couldn't do anything about it. Usually, a review of this nature is a back-and-forth, as it had been with Industry Canada: the government probes and questions, and the company explains, elaborates and proposes solutions. But the CRTC had deliberated without communicating with us, even to ask follow-up questions. It soon came out that, among other things, they had completely misunderstood our board nomination process. When the decision was announced, the CRTC gave us no hints as to what we needed to do to address their concerns, because they would not or could not divulge how, exactly, we'd fallen short in their estimation.

We had about 600 employees and 35 retail locations ready to open, with more in the works. In total, we had sunk about $800 million into WIND. And now we were hemorrhaging millions of dollars a week because we could not launch. Ottawa insiders were as bewildered as we were. The most popular theory was that we were casualties of an ongoing turf war between Industry Canada and the CRTC, and it was pointed out to us repeatedly that many of the top people in the latter organization got their start at Bell, Telus or Rogers.

I will never forget having to call Naguib to explain that although one arm of the government had taken our money and issued licences, another arm would not let us use them. I was actually embarrassed to be Canadian at that moment. I was certain he was going to blow up and say, "We're done, WIND is dead—and I'm suing your government." But Naguib was used to "rough places," as he called them, and had tangled with governments in Zimbabwe, North Korea, Iraq and Syria. While he was appalled that in the so-called developed world, public servants could be pitted against each another to protect an oligopoly's gold mine, his instinct was that WIND must be on the right track if the incumbents felt so threatened by our existence. I think he took the oligopoly's resistance as a personal affront, and in a sense it was. The fact that he was Egyptian seemed to arouse suspicion and disdain; one oligopoly executive tweeted about "King Tut," while another prominent Canadian telecom executive joked about camels on a call with industry analysts. Naguib is a proud Egyptian but also an American citizen and a member of the International Advisory Committee to the New York Stock Exchange Board of Directors, as well as a recipient of France's Légion d'honneur, among other international awards. He is, in other words, not some corrupt desert hick. Instead of pulling out of the venture, he actually seemed *more* interested and committed once people were trying to shut us down.

In every start-up there are unexpected obstacles, but the CRTC decision was more like a brick wall. And because we'd been building momentum so rapidly, we were going full speed ahead when we slammed into it. Inside the company, people were freaking out, wondering whether they should run back to the Big Three and beg to get their old jobs back. People kept asking me whether I was panicking too, but I felt very calm. Incredulous, but calm. As I said in one WIND town hall meeting after another, "Remember: Canadians *want* us to be here. They want choice. They want lower prices." For me, this was the fence in my backyard all over again: there had to be a way to get to the other side. While Brice, Simon and I looked for it, there wasn't much point in having everyone else sit around the WIND offices wringing their hands. So we implemented a "random acts of kindness" programme: everyone would still get paid, but instead of coming in to the office, they went to work for local charities of their choice. They might as well be doing good in their communities, and feeling good about themselves. That initiative created a lot of team spirit and pride during our darkest days; very few people gave up and quit.

Our only hope of saving the company was a rarely used provision in the Telecom Act: the federal Cabinet has the ability to vary or overrule a CRTC decision. Fortunately for us, the last thing the

Harper government wanted was for its new telecom policy to be dealt a death blow right out of the gate, which is what would have happened if WIND had failed. Tony Clement, who'd taken over from Jim Prentice at Industry Canada, ordered a review of the CRTC decision. Six tense weeks later, on December 11, Cabinet overruled the decision and declared that WIND was entitled to operate. Telus immediately protested, but Clement was unfazed, telling reporters, "Consumers will vote with their feet and their pocketbooks and that's the way the market works." Globalive issued a press release declaring a new day for wireless in Canada, but by then we'd figured out that that new day would not dawn peacefully. Interestingly, although both Public Mobile and Mobilicity had higher levels of foreign ownership than WIND did, the incumbents didn't seem to care about them. Maybe they'd already foreseen that those companies weren't well-enough funded to survive and, one day, they'd be able to divide the spoils. Whatever the case, it was clear that they viewed WIND—a fledgling operation that had yet to attract a single customer—as a serious threat. We'd thought we were launching a company, but the Big Three apparently believed we'd declared war, and they were gearing up to fight to the death. Ours.

WIND finally launched in Toronto on December 16, 2009, at the height of the Christmas shopping season. Before the year was over, we had about 5,000 subscribers. We got off the ground later than planned, but we were still months ahead of Mobilicity and Public Mobile, and continued to grow in 2010, adding Calgary, Ottawa, Vancouver and Edmonton. By July, we had 100,000 paying customers.

Nevertheless, our progress was not as rapid as we'd expected, because we had to rely on the incumbents' willingness to play fair and, as the government had ordered, let us put our antennas on their cell towers. There were no mechanisms for enforcement. When, as was often the case, the Big Three didn't feel like letting us rent space on their cell towers, we had no choice but to build our own, which takes time; you need to scout locations and get approvals, because there are environmental concerns.

Suddenly, too, the market seemed to be awash in new mobile wireless brands, but in fact they were all owned by the Big Three. Telus created Koodo. Bell already had Solo and acquired the part of Virgin Mobile it didn't already own. Rogers had Fido and launched Chatr, which replicated our coverage map and used very similar branding. Chatr's advertising and marketing budget dwarfed ours, and they used that clout to claim in a nationwide campaign that they had fewer dropped calls than new wireless carriers did. In 2013, the federal government's Competition Bureau assessed that claim, determined it was false and fined Rogers $10 million, the maximum penalty, for misleading advertising. But by then, at least ten times that amount of damage had been done to our brand. (Rogers appealed the decision, which was overturned by the courts in 2014, though the Competition Bureau successfully insisted Rogers pay a $500,000 penalty for making claims without adequately testing their veracity.)

Finding retail space, especially in malls, was another challenge. One of the Big Three usually seemed to have first dibs on any space we wanted. Sometimes mall owners would tell us we needed to pay a full year or two of rent up front—a demand that, curiously enough, had never been made for any of our other retail businesses. This might be the place to mention that most of the malls in Canadian cities are owned by a handful of developers—another oligopoly— and of course Bell, Rogers and Telus had been long-time tenants.

In 2009, we hit on a solution: buying Blacks, a faltering photography chain, so that WIND could take over its leases. Blacks' retail footprint was perfect for us: the stores were the right size, in the right malls. But just when we thought we were close to a deal, Telus swooped in with a pre-emptive offer that must have been exponentially higher than ours, because we weren't even given a chance to respond. Subsequently, Blacks continued sputtering along and Telus set up little sales kiosks in the photography stores, which made about as much sense as buying Subway and wedging a phone kiosk in beside the cold cuts. Although the CEO of Telus told reporters that "Blacks' premium locations provide an established network across Canada for the distribution of Telus's wireless products," soon enough Telus began shutting down some of those 113 premium locations. In 2015, when the telco finally pulled the plug on Blacks altogether, just 59 outlets were left. Evidently, the acquisition of a photography company was a rather unwise investment—unless, that is, the real purpose was to dampen competition, in which case it would have to be rated a rather spectacular success.

All new businesses experience growing pains, but ours were particularly severe because, simultaneously, WIND was engaged in an ongoing legal battle: Telus and Public Mobile challenged Cabinet's ability to overrule the CRTC and allow us to operate. The case eventually found its way to the Federal Court of Appeals, which ruled in our favour in June 2011—a ruling Public Mobile sought the right to appeal all the way to the Supreme Court, which, a year later, refused to hear the case. Fighting a rearguard legal action is not only costly, it also takes time and energy away from your core business operation, as Telus, which eventually acquired Public Mobile, surely knew.

In less overt ways too, the oligopoly put up roadblocks that made it difficult for WIND to grow. Bell and Rogers are both vertically integrated companies that, between them, control a lot of the country's media. Coverage of WIND on their channels tended not to be particularly positive, nor was advertising particularly afford-able. Getting customers to switch was also more difficult than we'd expected, not because they didn't want to, but because the oligopoly had locked people into three-year contracts (a practice the govern-ment has since disallowed).

Then there were the ways in which the oligopoly's strength converged with the weakness of WIND, then barely nascent, to slow its growth. In the early days of building a new network, any carrier has two issues: first, the size of the area where it can provide coverage and, second, filling the holes in coverage within that area. Initially, a new network resembles Swiss cheese: you have spec-trum but not enough antennas, so even in a city or region where your coverage is generally good, there are spots where it's weak or non-existent. Since you want your customers to be able to make calls or receive texts while, say, en route to the cottage, you need roaming agreements with other telcos so that your subscribers' calls automatically switch over to those networks until they reach a spot where your own network is strong again. Without domestic roaming agreements, new companies simply can't provide decent local service, much less service across the country, until their own networks are fully built—and that takes years. Accordingly, as part of its overall policy push to introduce competition into tele-communications, the federal government mandated that the Big Three had to forge roaming agreements with newcomers, just as they had already done with each other.

Unfortunately, Ottawa neglected to impose caps on what the incumbents could charge the rest of us—and they had a field day. WIND was in no position to drive a bargain: when we launched, our technology was only compatible with Rogers', so we were at their mercy. To ensure the balance of power didn't shift, Rogers insisted that we sign an exclusive agreement so that we could not avail ourselves of other roaming opportunities that might arise in the future. That was just the beginning. The fees they charged us for access to their network were outrageous. Data charges were particularly egregious: $1,000 per gigabyte—wholesale!—though Rogers charged its own retail customers as little as $5 per gigabyte. There was no way we could absorb that cost, nor could we stomach the idea of passing it on to customers if they inadvertently strayed onto Rogers' network and checked out some videos on YouTube. The only way to protect our subscribers from extortionate data charges was to make it impossible to incur them. We made the difficult decision to constrain the accidental consumption of data by launching roaming only on Rogers' old 2G network, which was just fine for voice and text but pretty much useless for data. Since the Big Three offered 3G across their whole networks, this put us at a huge disadvantage in the marketplace, as Rogers surely intended. And then there were inbound texts. We had about two hundred roaming agreements globally, but only three parties charged us when our customers received texts: a cruise ship line, the Cuban government and Rogers. There was nothing we could do to prevent our customers from getting texts while on Rogers' network, so we had to eat the charges, to the tune of millions of dollars.

In other words, Rogers radically altered our value proposition. WIND was all about simplicity and affordability—unlimited data/voice/text with no-term contracts and no hidden fees—but because of this ludicrous domestic roaming agreement, we were forced to introduce two-zone billing. Within "home zones" delineated on maps, where WIND's network was built out (but not yet perfected), our subscribers got unlimited everything for one low fee. In "away zones," where they were roaming on Rogers' network, they could not use data and we had to pass on the ridiculously high rates we were being charged. As you might imagine, this muddied our brand's clarity and damaged our ability to compete.

Ironically, the distinctive features of WIND's brand were clearest when our customers were in the United States, where the incumbents charged a fortune for roaming and we charged $15 per month for unlimited data, text and calling, with no overages and no requirement to pay for more than one month. WIND subscribers could pay $15, go to Florida for March break and watch Netflix on their phones from dawn to dusk if they wanted. We still made a profit because American carriers charged us, and other Canadian telcos, reasonable rates. We passed those savings on to our customers. The Big Three did not.

In 2014, the CRTC finally reviewed the incumbents' domestic roaming agreements and acknowledged that WIND and other newcomers were being charged obscenely high rates, far in excess of what the Big Three charged both one another and American companies. It was a blatant attempt to prevent domestic competition, and one that hurt not just smaller telcos but also consumers, who were still paying far too much and not getting enough in the way of service. Once the government introduced caps on the prices the Big Three could charge—caps that still allowed for an impressive profit margin, since they were 3.5 times higher than the roaming rates US carriers charged us—WIND was able to slash "away zone" fees by more than 90 percent.

In the United States too, the big telcos play games, but they're afraid of the FCC and the Department of Justice. In Canada, the Big Three show no sign of fearing the CRTC or the Competition Bureau; they get away with what they can for as long as they can, knowing that any eventual penalties will be insignificant relative to the competitive advantages that can be gained in the meantime.

It's a bet worth taking, because the government often eschews penalties altogether. Again and again, the feds simply assumed that the incumbents would be polite Canadians, eager to follow the rules, and refused to get involved when we and other new telcos pointed out that in fact the Big Three were not toeing the line. For instance, the Canada Line, a rapid transit rail and subway line in Vancouver, has a shared-access system for wireless that Telus built and maintains. In late 2010, we approached Telus requesting access—not a big ask, really, since Rogers and Bell already had access—and were directed to speak to the Canada Line instead. The Canada Line told us the decision was not theirs to make. They had handed the keys to Telus, and informed us that "there will be no other wireless providers in the Canada Line tunnels unless Telus chooses to grant such access to third parties."

Uh-oh.

The runaround, with the goal of deferring or, better yet, preventing competition, was officially under way. We beat a well-worn path to Telus's door, repeatedly seeking access to their wireless system, but it took them more than a year to come up with a proposal, which, once it materialized, was so outlandish that it was difficult to believe it wasn't a joke. Despite the fact that our traffic would be relatively light—we were growing rapidly, but by early 2012 had only about 400,000 subscribers across the entire country—Telus, which had more than seven million wireless subscribers, proposed that we pay them more to access the existing system than it would have cost to build an entirely new one from scratch. In April 2012, then, we applied to the CRTC to try to force the Canada Line—the recipient of a great number of taxpayer dollars—to give us access. Four months later, the CRTC instructed WIND and Telus to go back to the sandbox, hand in hand, and make nice—a licence for yet more gamesmanship. In mid-2015, three years and well over one million dollars later (five times what it would have cost us to build our own system), WIND subscribers could finally use their phones on Vancouver's public transit system.

———

By then, Naguib was long gone. He didn't have the patience to wait for the incumbents' wrists to be slapped, and he was enraged by the government's predilection for turning a blind eye to flagrantly anti-competitive behaviour. By 2011, he had had it. His perspective was that he'd been screwed over in other jurisdictions too, but at least there it had happened quickly; in Canada, the slow burn of an incredibly protracted legal and regulatory process was more painful and also more enraging, because everyone pretended that what was happening was fair. He was planning to sell most of Orascom's telecom holdings to VimpelCom, making it the sixth-largest mobile network operator in the world, but it wasn't clear to us that WIND would be part of that package. He went back and forth, but in the end he simply didn't have any faith that the government would curb the oligopoly's excesses. On November 17, he went on the CBC to vent about how much he regretted investing in Canada. Despite the fact that WIND had driven down costs for consumers by 30 percent, he said, the government had not delivered on its promises about tower sharing and roaming access. "When we complained, nothing happens. You know there's no will here to introduce competition into this closed market," he said, and likened Canada to China.

When I heard those words come out of his mouth, my first thought was—well, unprintable. I knew the powers that be in Ottawa would not take kindly to being compared to those in Beijing.

Naguib was just getting going. Why, he continued, were the incumbents unable to succeed outside Canada? "Why aren't they everywhere if they are so good? Why can they just exist here? The answer is very simple: because here, they are protected. They can be inefficient, their core structure can be expensive, as long as the consumer is paying [the] bill they are fine . . . They are pampered, see . . . How can you create innovation, how can you interact with the other new applications of the new technologies, if you close yourself up like that?" He concluded by blaming the incumbents for "trying to pressure the politicians against the consumers, which we are trying to help—and not because we are good guys, but because we want to make money."

With Naguib poised to sell off most of his telecom holdings, I realized I'd made a major error in my deal with Orascom: Globalive didn't have a right of first refusal to try to buy WIND. In Naguib's view, the asset's value had been dramatically depressed by the broken promises on tower sharing and roaming. He was prepared to write off most of his investment—more than a billion dollars by that point (which goes a long way to explaining why he lashed out at the government on CBC)—and sell his stake for far less than it was worth. If I'd had the foresight to envision this scenario and ask for a right of first refusal, Globalive could have owned the asset outright. Instead, VimpelCom, which is based in the Netherlands but controlled by some extraordinarily wealthy Russians, got it. From being a very small piece of Orascom, we became a minuscule piece of VimpelCom.

To keep growing, we needed more spectrum, and our new partners were willing to invest more money to help us get it. For a brief period in 2012, it looked as if our troubles might be behind us. Our brand affinity was through the roof and we were the fastest-growing carrier in Canada, with close to 600,000 subscribers by the year's end. However, VimpelCom wasn't really interested in a partnership with Globalive; unlike Orascom, VimpelCom wanted to own WIND outright. The federal government would not grant approval, though, so in March 2013, VimpelCom began looking for a buyer for its stake. As it happened, Verizon was already looking at international expansion opportunities, and expressed an interest in Canada. By this point, Public Mobile and Mobilicity were floundering (both eventually failed), so the Conservative government was very interested in talking to Verizon. They wanted their wireless agenda to succeed, and a US giant had the scale and operational experience to help them pull off a win.

Verizon's economic heft would have made them a formidable market force, a fact Bell, Telus and Rogers confirmed when they caught wind of the potential deal and began running national ad campaigns attacking the Harper government for destroying Canada by selling out to American companies. I'm sure the mergers and acquisitions team at Verizon didn't know what to make of this spectacle. It would be as if they'd joined hands with AT&T to spend millions of dollars running an ad campaign against Obama. Unimaginable. Aside from anything else, American consumer advocates would have attacked them for being so shamelessly anti-competitive.

There was no such push-back in Canada. As the oligopoly's share prices tanked, they wrapped themselves in the flag to try to convince consumers that Verizon's entry into the marketplace would be the end of the world. Any number of commentators opined otherwise, including Michael Geist, the aforementioned Canada Research Chair in Internet and e-commerce law at the University of Ottawa, who wrote, "The ultimate impact is likely higher churn of customers . . . reduced roaming costs, and lower pricing. That may be bad for the stock price of the incumbents (which explains why they are going to war to keep the competition out), but it will be welcome news for Canadian consumers."

Unluckily enough, while the WIND purchase was still under consideration, Vodafone unexpectedly agreed to sell its stake in Verizon's wireless operations back to Verizon. The two companies had had an ongoing dialogue on the subject for years, but had never been able to settle on a price. Suddenly, in early August 2013, Vodafone capitulated, and the CEO of Verizon sent out a global e-mail putting a stop to all other M&A action to focus on this one, very large transaction. That was the official reason they backed out of the WIND deal, but there may have been more to it. Though I doubt that Verizon was even remotely intimidated by the Canadian oligopoly—from what I heard, they, like Naguib, seemed to feel that extreme resistance was a good indicator that they'd stumbled onto a gold mine—they may well have been concerned that if Canada's regulatory pendulum shifted back to protectionism, they could be facing a significant problem. One thing I'm sure of: observing what the government had put Naguib through was not reassuring to any foreign investor.

I didn't have too much time to think about all this, though, because WIND was still building, VimpelCom was still looking for a buyer, and a few months later all hell broke loose, eight thousand kilometres away, when the Ukrainian government backed out of a treaty to form an association with the European Union, triggering a major crisis that culminated in Russia's invasion and annexation of Crimea in early 2014. While all this was unfolding, VimpelCom began broadly retrenching and selling off its holdings in the West. They wanted out of countries that, like Canada, were vehemently denouncing the Russian government's actions. The Russians at the helm of the company were already deeply distrustful of the Harper government, and WIND was a small, non-strategic asset in their portfolio. They were ready to wash their hands of it, and rather than continue to search for a foreign investor who would also be subject to government approval, they decided that declaring bankruptcy was an easier exit strategy. Easier, and also more embarrassing for the government, which had already invested so much energy in building a fourth carrier. The only way we could see to avoid bankruptcy was for the company to recapitalize, quickly.

It was an unbelievably stressful time for me and everyone else at WIND. We'd built a great company that was picking up more and more speed every week, but it was on its deathbed. Again. Entrepreneurial ventures falter for a lot of different reasons, but this was surely the most unlikely of all: when Putin invaded Crimea in March 2014, VimpelCom felt it needed to get out of WIND immediately and decided not to invest another dollar in the business. The timing could not have been worse. In April, when $150 million in loans from vendors who'd sold us equipment came due, WIND defaulted on the loans. If we had been able to defer payments for a few months, I would have had enough equity in Globalive to buy WIND myself—but we were out of time. The only way to avoid bankruptcy was to hand the company's reins over to private equity players, knowing they would sideline me immediately (they did) and sell at the first opportunity (they did). In the end, Globalive and a consortium of six other investors bought WIND and its debt from VimpelCom for $300 million. It was an unbelievable deal for an asset that Shaw would purchase for $1.6 billion just fourteen months later—a price that was, in my opinion, ridiculously low given the current value and future potential of the company.

The network we built at WIND wasn't as good as the Big Three's, but it could have been, one day. We were on track, with one million customers who cared a lot about saving $250 or more a year. I'm proud that we helped a lot of Canadians hang on to more of their disposable income. But we didn't reshape the market: within weeks of WIND's sale to Shaw, prices were up again, across the board. And as the Competition Bureau reported in 2014, the Big Three still have "market power," defined as "the ability of a firm or firms to profitably maintain prices above competitive levels (or similarly restrict non-price dimensions of competition) for a significant period of time." The Bureau estimated that a more competitive market would deliver about $1 billion in benefits to the Canadian economy. In 2017, the OECD again sounded the alarm about the costs of the lack of competition in our telecommunications sector, and called for reform in order to reduce prices for consumers and promote the ability of businesses to "access a wider set of opportunities at home and abroad, including through digital means (e.g., e-commerce and other Internet-enabled business)."

The real problem, for all of us, is that the WIND story is not unique. The Canadian economy is dominated by oligopolies; start-ups that seek to break in reach a certain size then stall. This is a severe problem in a global economy because, for the most part, the companies that make up those oligopolies are unheard of outside our borders. They aren't industry leaders; they don't connect us to global supply chains. To the rest of the world, they're irrelevant. But here at home, they are all too relevant, ensuring that consumers are gouged, innovation is severely constrained, and Canada falls further and further behind countries where competition is promoted and ambition is not a dirty word.

You know things are bad when an organization like the OECD regularly calls out Canada because the "barriers to foreign direct investment and the regulatory protection of incumbents are higher than in many other countries" and urges the government to "do more to encourage competition." I don't blame the incumbents in Canada's oligopolies for resisting competition and doing everything they can to protect their market share. The executives who run these companies are smart and talented; their job is to maximize profits and deliver generous dividends for their shareholders, and they do it well. As with any sports team, they push the rules as far as they can in order to maintain an advantage and win. Our real problem is that our referee, the government, is either blind or terrified of the biggest players. Fouls aren't called. Penalties aren't assessed. No one ever seems to be benched. One consequence is that the biggest players don't bring their A game. They don't have to. They'll win anyway.

The other consequence is that the rest of us lose when the growth of new Canadian businesses is stifled, not just because we wind up paying high prices but because, as you'll see in the next chapter, our economy is shrinking. To protect our social safety net, our inclusive values, our way of life and our children's future, we need our economy to start growing. Yesterday.

How do we fix this mess?

The first step, I think, is a fundamental realignment. I learned many things building WIND, but one of the most important is this: our dominant business culture is not reflective of Canadians' values. We value our diversity and openness to newcomers, but our business culture is inward-looking and xenophobic. We're enthusiastic early adopters on issues ranging from gay marriage to minority rights, but our business culture is staid and traditional. As a nation, we pride ourselves on a certain ruggedness and spirit of adventure, but our business culture is notoriously timid and risk-averse. Canadians are known the world over for decency, kindness and generosity, but homegrown businesspeople who fail are savaged while those who succeed, particularly in new industries or with new ideas, are rarely celebrated.

Or, to put it another way, Canadian business is fundamentally unCanadian. And that's something we definitely can and should change.

CHAPTER 2

<u>Going for Bronze</u>

For a quick overview of the challenges our country is facing, pretend, for a moment, that Canada is a company. You don't require an MBA for this exercise, because our business model is flawed in ways the average third-grader can grasp: we don't have enough customers and our bestselling products are falling out of favour because they're bad for the environment. Almost nothing we sell to the rest of the world is unique; a lot of it can be purchased elsewhere (sometimes more cheaply). Nor do we have the kind of brand identity that piques curiosity. To the outside world, "Canada" has nothing to do with business; our brand is all about maple syrup, cold weather and nice people.

To continue the analogy, Canada is a bit like a legacy business that's being run into the ground because it hasn't changed to keep up with the times. Increasingly, the economies of other developed nations are propelled by technology, but we're still heavily dependent on the tried-and-true colonial approach: shipping raw commodities off to an imperial power, in this case the United States. We don't have much say over what we charge for our top exports, because we don't set prices—global markets do. Essentially, this means we have ceded executive control of our economy to the world market. When oil prices are high, we're in the money; when they're low, we panic.

The danger of this strategy, or lack thereof, has been obscured by the fact that, so far, it's been successful. Very successful. Between 1970 and 2000, Canada's rate of real economic growth was about three percent per year, which put us right up there with other advanced economies. Three percent is one of those magic numbers economists like: hit that level of growth every year and life is good. Canada was able to do that for a long time for three reasons. First, we had the highest rate of increase in labour force participation in the G7. Compared to the US, more women—more mothers, especially; maternity benefits were better here—got jobs and started pumping up our gross domestic product (GDP). Second, exports took off in the nineties, thanks to free trade with the US and the fact that our dollar was low. More recently, the surge in commodity prices drove growth.

But all three growth engines have sputtered to a halt. Labour force participation is declining because our population is aging. Trade has levelled off and doesn't fuel economic expansion the way it once did. And the boom in oil prices? Over, at least for now. Our GDP growth is still north of two percent, buoyed—dangerously—by a housing bubble in Toronto and Vancouver and by consumer spending. But "slowth" has begun.

At the same time that Canada's growth is slowing, the rate of technological change is accelerating, radically transforming the global economy. Business models that seemed built for the ages are under threat. Experts predict that in the next ten to fifteen years, automation will wipe out as many as 7.5 million Canadian jobs—more than 40 percent. Even if robots don't replace us, Asians might—their economies are not so much emerging as exploding. We urgently need to figure out how to compete with them in terms of exports, and also how to produce goods and services they want to import.

Sometimes an inflection point—that decisive moment before a sharp upturn or downturn—is immediately obvious. The Berlin Wall falls or the iPhone is introduced, and it's clear: a new era has begun. But when everything seems to be humming along nicely, inflection points inaugurating a sharp downturn are often visible only in retrospect. When the housing bubble burst in the United States in early 2007, for instance, few experts predicted that a stock market crash would follow or that major financial institutions would fail. Even CEOs of banks that had invested heavily in sub-prime mortgages did not instantly recognize that the jig was up.

Today, although economists have been ringing warning bells for years, most Canadians seem unaware that we too are at an inflection point. On the surface, there are few obvious signs of danger. Unemployment is relatively low, as is violent crime, and per capita income is relatively high. We have great universities and colleges, as well as a relatively strong social safety net. Yes, the loonie is weak, but consumers are still spending and our biggest companies report robust profits year after year. Canada is routinely ranked one of the best places on the planet to live. Looking around, it's hard to believe that the economy is on the ropes. And it isn't.

Yet.

But if we carry on with business as usual, the signs of trouble will be unmistakable within five to ten years. Rising unemployment, declining wages, inflation, mortgage foreclosures, bankruptcies, irreparable erosion of our education and health care systems—unless we course-correct now, they are all in our near future. Long-term, the trend is even more grim, particularly once the world swears off oil and shifts towards cleaner sources of energy.

Depending on what we do next, we will look back on this period either as the time when Canada began its climb to new heights or as the era that marked the beginning of a slide to new depths.

"Across all OECD countries, it's amazing how closely three characteristics correlate with growth: investment in innovation, trade with other countries and investment in worker training. And it's also amazing how few Canadian companies do those three things," says Kevin Lynch, now vice-chair of BMO Financial Group, after a stellar career in government that included a stint as Clerk of the Privy Council. "How can we grow if we're not changing our products over time? How can we grow if we're not trading in broad global markets? And how can we grow if we're not upskilling workers and preparing for the technological changes that are disrupting the economy?"

The answer is clear: we can't. Yet most Canadians seem unaware of the danger we are in, or how we got here. The story begins, as so many Canadian stories do, south of the border.

While the rest of the world has been trading like crazy—global trade has increased fivefold in the past decade—Canada still has only one major customer: the United States, which buys three-quarters of everything we export. We import a lot from them too, but the relationship is fundamentally imbalanced. They don't really need us, and we really, really need them. Although bureaucrats in Ottawa proudly remind us that Canada is the most important foreign market for thirty-five states, all this really means is that we have tallest-building-in-Wichita status. Exports aren't nearly as important to their economy as they are to ours; ten times as many people live there, so American companies can do extremely well even if they focus primarily on their domestic market.

Canada-US Trade (Imports and Exports) as % of State/Province GDP (2015)

Sources: U.S. Census Bureau, BEA, and Industry Canada

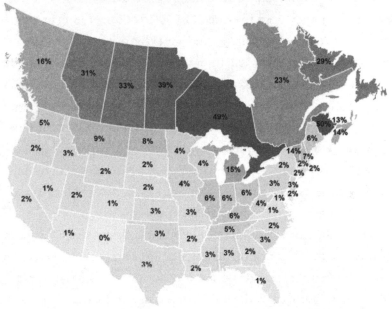

Just how little do we matter to the United States, economically speaking? Recently, Trevor Tombe, a University of Calgary economist, set out to quantify the relationship. Crunching the numbers, he found that in all but two states—Michigan and tiny Vermont—trade with Canada accounts for less (usually a *lot* less) than 10 percent of GDP. In seven Canadian provinces, however, trade with the US accounts for more (usually a *lot* more) than 23 percent of GDP. Fully one-half of GDP in Ontario and New Brunswick depends on trade with the US. If both countries stopped trading tomorrow, most Americans would not even notice, but Canadians certainly would. Our economy would be in ruins.

This mismatch in terms of dependency is not new, but we are more vulnerable than ever before for several reasons. Here's a big one: Americans no longer need our most valuable exports, at least not the way they used to. Three of Canada's four top exports are crude and refined petroleum and gas; the other is cars, manufactured in plants owned by American corporations (which, increasingly, view Mexico as a more attractive location for branch plants). But, thanks to a push for energy self-sufficiency that started in the Reagan era and the recent boom in shale gas production, the US now has plenty of petro products. While Barack Obama was president, domestic oil production more than doubled. In fact, *we* now buy a lot of it from *them*: two of Canada's top four imports are crude and refined petroleum.

The good news is supposed to be that codependency has been baked into the American economy, not just ours, because our value chains are so integrated. Before a new car rolls off the line, for instance, its parts cross the border seven or eight times. Therefore, the thinking goes, our biggest trading partner will always need us.

But Canada is not at the high-earning end of most of those value chains. We tend to do the lower-glory, lower-value stuff, according to a series of meticulously researched reports by the Council of Canadian Academies (CCA) and papers by its founding president, Peter Nicholson (who is, among other things, a computer scientist and economist who served as a key policy adviser to both Paul Martin and the secretary-general of the OECD). Canada's contributions to North American value chains are primarily "upstream": resource extraction, light processing, and the kind of follow-the-orders-from-headquarters activities that go on in branch plants. The US focuses "downstream," on the higher-value work involved in dreaming up and producing sophisticated goods and services. When the value chain is situated within a single US multinational, such as a chemical or automotive producer, as is frequently the case, the parent company "sets the overall strategy including the business model, the approach to marketing, product development (and thus decisions regarding R & D), organizational design, management practices, and the global allocation of the corporation's resources," explains Nicholson.

In short, this is not a partnership of equals. It's more like the US is the chef, making magic in the kitchen, and our role is that of busboy—important to the functioning of the overall operation, sure, but indispensable? No. "Junior partner" is the genteel designation Nicholson uses to describe our position in the relationship, but the point is the same: since we contribute much less value and have much less power, we can easily be replaced, as Mexican autoworkers already know.

Perhaps the most harmful consequence of perennially playing the underling with no chance of promotion is the least tangible one: we think like underlings. Not all Canadians, all the time, of course; to every sweeping argument there are notable exceptions. But the chronic lack of ambition and confidence that characterizes our business sector is prima facie evidence of a national inferiority complex vis-à-vis the United States.

Other relatively small countries that don't have ready access to the enormous US market conduct themselves like scrappy upstarts, not timid junior partners. They've taken on the world because they had to. Sweden has IKEA, Ericsson, H&M, Electrolux, Skype and Spotify. The Netherlands built Heineken, Shell, ING, Unilever. Switzerland is home to Nestlé, UBS, Lindt, Rolex, Credit Suisse. Canada has . . . a long history, in just about every sector, of passing up international expansion opportunities. As author Andrea Mandel-Campbell explained in *Why Mexicans Don't Drink Molson*, time and again, Canadian CEOs have dithered, hamstrung by self-doubt and an excess of caution. They've acted too late or bet too small. She traced the origins of this risk aversion to cultural attributes—an insular, parochial mindset—as well as our long-standing history of protectionism. John A. Macdonald's introduction of the National Policy in 1878 ensured that generations of Canadian manufacturers were protected from competition by the high tariffs imposed on imported American goods, but once the tariffs were removed, the anxiety underlying them—we're not really good enough to compete internationally—lingered. Canada's problem is less that we are small than that we think small.

Few would dispute the notion that American cultural attributes—individualism, for instance—have shaped that nation's business ethos. But some very smart people dismiss the idea that the complacency and timidity of our business sector can be traced to cultural characteristics. "I think we use the cultural argument too often—that somehow high achievement is not in our DNA or not a Canadian value. Give me a break," says Kevin Lynch. In his view, the problem is "not that we are less entrepreneurial but that there are more constraints on entrepreneurial behaviour and fewer incentives to innovate." John Ruffolo, the CEO of OMERS Ventures, a $500-million fund that has galvanized Canada's tech sector, agrees. "I don't think culture factors in, to be honest. I see all these amazing Canadians in Silicon Valley. To me, the culture argument is a cop-out."

Few people understand the Canadian economy as well as Lynch and Ruffolo, and I've learned more from conversations with them than I picked up from any course I took in university. I also agree with them that the incentives to innovation are weak, and that's a problem. But so is our junior-partner culture. As an entrepreneur, I have a very different perspective on the relationship between culture and behaviour. Human beings are not robots whose actions are driven solely by incentives and rational assessments of risk and reward. As I've learned first-hand, you can have all the right incentives to encourage high performance—bonuses, opportunities for rapid advancement, awesome perks and benefits—but if your corporate culture is complacent or abusive, most people will not perform nearly as well as they would in a competitive yet encouraging, high-energy environment where they feel valued. Just one backstabber can poison an entire workplace, which is why bad apples have to be rooted out immediately. Yes, you can have a toxic culture and still post phenomenal results—look at Uber—but the costs, while difficult to quantify until the lawsuits start and the tell-all memoirs hit bookstores, are very real. Culture shapes how people feel about themselves and view their own prospects, and is a crucial determinant of their loyalty, their effectiveness as ambassadors for a brand and, ultimately, their ability to fulfill their potential. When deciding whether or not to invest in a start-up, one of the key metrics I look at is the founders' ability to campaign for and create a positive culture, because ultimately, it will determine whether they succeed in attracting, retaining and motivating a great team.

A country's business culture has an equally profound influence on entrepreneurial aspirations and achievement. Surely one reason so many ambitious Canadian entrepreneurs wind up in Silicon Valley is that they feel more at home there, culturally, which is why so few of them return after they've made their millions. And surely the junior-partner syndrome has something to do with the fact that there are so few iconic Canadian multinationals. Consider the power of history and culture to shape how women and minorities perceive themselves and also how they conceive of their own capacity for achievement. Why wouldn't a dearth of positive role models and a legacy of playing second banana similarly shape many Canadians' perceptions of their own possibilities in the business world?

Certainly, Canada's underling mentality has long influenced our investment patterns. In 1972, by way of explaining why Canadian investors and financial institutions preferred to sink money into established American corporations rather than back new Canadian businesses, Kenneth M. Glazier wrote that "Canadians traditionally have been conservative, exhibiting an inferiority complex about their own destiny as a nation and about the potential of their country . . . Thus, with Canadians investing in the 'sure' companies of the United States, Canada has for generations suffered not only from a labor drain and a brain drain to the United States, but also from a considerably larger capital drain."

This capital drain is still going strong. By 2016, our direct investment in the US was $474.4 billion, with big positions in finance, insurance and manufacturing. US direct investment in Canada was less impressive: $392.1 billion—a truly stunning imbalance when you consider the disparity between the two countries in terms of both population and wealth.

Of course, there are many individual Canadians who are immune to junior-partner syndrome, but they tend to position themselves as exceptions who prove the rule. "We have a neighbour who's so influential, such a behemoth, it's no wonder that sometimes we cower in its shadow," says Joe Mimran, founder of Club Monaco and Joe Fresh, whose own presence, while supremely calm and amiable, is leonine. It's impossible to imagine him cowering in anyone's shadow. "Well, I'm an immigrant," he says, smiling broadly, as though that explains everything. It may: he grew up with the cultural perspective of an outsider. "When my family first moved to Toronto from Casablanca, we lived in a small apartment over a laundromat. My father had two jobs and my mom was tireless. She'd get home from the garment factory, she was a dressmaker, and sew all night. They wanted me to have a good education, close to the synagogue, so when I was in seventh grade I walked an hour to school and all my friends were very wealthy. That built a real desire to be financially successful."

By the time he was twenty-five, Mimran had become a chartered accountant in order to have the business know-how to run a fashion company. He wanted to do what other successful fashion retailers did, namely, import brands from the US. He went to New York to strike a deal with Oscar de la Renta, but changed his mind, he says, when he was flying home. "It dawned on me that I didn't want to import a brand. I wanted to create my own." He came up with what was, at the time, a man-bites-dog plan: he'd build a brand so special even Americans would want it. "The idea that you could create a concept with enough commercial potential that it could travel beyond Canada—people thought it was impossible." They also thought it was stupid. Why swing for the fences when you could bunt? Just bring in a well-established American brand and fire up the cash register.

Mimran saw the risk–reward ratio differently. "To me it seemed so obvious that if you built [demand for] a line for someone else, it could be taken away from you. I've since seen that happen again and again." Besides, he didn't just want to make money. He wanted to make his mark.

Unlike most of his peers, Mimran never thought of himself as a junior partner but as a potential conqueror. "Maybe it's an immigrant thing, but I had a very strong belief in myself and an adventurer's spirit." Along with his brother, Saul, and designer Alfred Sung, he launched the Alfred Sung label in 1980. One year later, Saks Fifth Avenue, Neiman Marcus and the rest of the high-end American retailers carried the line. In 1985, Mimran did it again, launching Club Monaco on Queen Street West in Toronto. "My rallying cry was, 'We're going to become a world-recognized brand.' People were like, 'Really?' The Canadian psyche makes it difficult to think in international terms. Because so much of what we consume is American, there's this idea that they couldn't be interested in anything we'd have to offer."

By the time Ralph Lauren bought Club Monaco from Mimran in 1999, there were more than a hundred stores, all over the world. Since then, however, only a few Canadian fashion brands have followed Mimran's example and gone global. "La Senza, Roots, Lululemon, Aritzia—I wouldn't classify a handful as a roaring success," he says drily. In his view, the limiting factor is not talent, which Canadian designers have plenty of, but a culture of complacency. "In a lot of countries, when you're not successful, you're *really* not successful and your quality of life suffers. Here, you can be successful even if you're not successful. We're so comfortable as a nation, so protected, so blessed."

For the nation to remain comfortable, paradoxically, the dominant business culture will need a major infusion of ambition, confidence and boldness. We have to start clawing our way up the value chain, not just in North America but overseas. We need to diversify our economy, building a lot more companies like Club Monaco, while beating the bushes for more customers in foreign markets.

Tech companies could lead this charge. Information communications technology is an internationally recognized area of strength for Canadian universities, and our ICT graduates are among the best in the world. Some of the most significant developments in computer science, including the birth of machine learning—computers "learn" to recognize patterns in big data and make highly accurate predictions—occurred on our campuses. Technology developed in the Pratt Building at the University of Toronto is now deployed in systems used by Google, Microsoft and Amazon. Waze, for instance, uses machine learning and real-time data to predict traffic jams and help us navigate away from them.

Nevertheless, in the tech world too, the gravitational pull of our national inferiority complex is evident. Personally, I never felt it, maybe because throughout my career I've looked for opportunities to provide what the incumbents do not, which has made me very aware of their weaknesses as well as their strengths. If I'd felt lesser-than, I wouldn't have had the nerve to venture onto their playing field in the first place. But there's plenty of evidence of junior-partner thinking in our tech incubators and accelerators, where Canadians with the skills to take on the world often conduct themselves tentatively and apologetically.

"I still remember a headline in *The Economist* from years ago: 'CANADA, GO FOR THE BRONZE!' It so perfectly summed up the problem, which is a lack of confidence. We have this belief that we'll never be number one, and it's embedded in a lot of the pitches I hear from Canadian entrepreneurs," says Angela Strange, an expat Canadian partner at Andreessen Horowitz, one of Silicon Valley's premier venture capital (VC) firms. You'd be hard pressed to find a more committed Canada-booster: she co-chairs the C100, a non-profit that shepherds Canadian entrepreneurs into the Valley's inner sanctums, and, for a dollar a year, serves on the Canadian finance minister's fourteen-person Advisory Council on Economic Growth.

At Andreessen, she takes a lot of meetings with young founders looking for venture capital to grow their businesses, and often finds herself rooting more loudly for Canadians than they root for themselves. "Just the other day, two entrepreneurs came in, one a Canadian and the other an American, with very similar types of businesses. Both pitches were just amazing," recalls Strange, whose manner is equal parts warm effervescence and cool logic. "The American guy said, 'We're doing X, then Y, then we're taking over China!' The Canadian company was actually ahead of the American one, but they said, 'In 2016, we're going to be at $2 million in revenue.' This was in September. I said, 'Wait a sec. Haven't you already *done* $1.95 million?' They said, 'Well, yeah, but we don't want to overpromise.' I see this kind of thing with Canadians all the time. They think they're being modest and realistic, but what they're doing is shooting themselves in the foot. When you're pitching to raise money, VCs come up with a valuation based on what they think your sales are going to be. Modesty doesn't help you!"

But living next door to the world's biggest braggart, Canadians learn early that American-style self-promotion is obnoxious. We value decorum and, like good junior partners, wait to be noticed (and get inordinately excited when a Canadian actor, singer or athlete attracts Americans' attention and receives their seal of approval, as though it's worth more than ours). We haven't come up with an effective Canadian way to sell ourselves, so, at least in the business arena, we often sell ourselves short.

An abundance of modesty can be mistaken for a lack of vision, ambition or competence, or all of the above. "There's still a widely held perception in the Valley that Canadian entrepreneurs who stay in Canada don't have global ambition, that they're going to build their companies up to X million dollars—which isn't an exciting investment opportunity if you have a billion-dollar fund—then sell," Strange explains. "And we perpetuate that stigma because although as a nation we have a really good product—great technical talent and some very strong start-ups—we are *terrible* at sales and marketing. Not just in the private sector, but everywhere: the government, throughout our entire culture."

When people succeed in business, it's as though we've taken a vow not to celebrate them, lest the praise go to their heads. Ask a kid you know to name an entrepreneur and she'll probably reel off Walt Disney, Oprah Winfrey, Bill Gates—no Canadians. "If you don't see examples all around you of companies that have become number one in the world, it's hard to believe you can build one," says Strange. "We need to publicize success stories, so that Canadians have role models and get comfortable with saying, 'I'm doing great things,' and selling their companies to the world by saying, 'We're going to be big.'" Until we learn to do that, she concludes, many

Canadian entrepreneurs will be trapped in a vicious cycle: unable to walk the walk because they don't talk the talk.

To compound the problem, Canadian founders frequently do conform to Valley stereotypes and sell their companies too early. Since 2000, only one percent of Canadian exits (versus ten percent of American exits) have had a valuation of $500 million or more. Too often, start-ups here are structured to encourage early exits, points out Jeffrey Grammer, a partner at Rho Ventures in Montreal. Like Strange, he's a fast-talking expat, though from the other side of the border. His Boston accent intact, Grammer has been a VC in Canada for the past ten years, though he still flies home every weekend. "The typical Canadian story," he explains, "is two founders who get started with money from family and friends and some angel investors. When they look for capital, a VC tells them, 'You've got a great idea, here's $3 million, create a 20 percent option pool'" to attract talented people who can help the company grow. The founders balk, not wanting to give up that much equity, perhaps because they don't really believe their company could become a global superstar.

"It's the opposite story in Silicon Valley, where founders are trying to move their companies along faster and are happy to give options to people who know how to build," Grammer continues. "Both companies have unique intellectual property, but the one in the Valley will grow much faster because it's got the right team, and will therefore be able to raise even more venture capital. If someone offers to buy them early for $25 million, it's not enough for everyone to get rich, so they'll say, 'No way,' and keep building. The Canadian founders look at a $10-million offer and say, 'We still own about 90 percent, so that's $4.5 million each. Let's sell!' I'm empathetic, because they've worked hard and the money is life-changing, obviously. But that's not how you build long-term sustaining companies. It can't be a fiefdom with a king who holds all the equity and a bunch of subjects who have none. Everybody needs to own the thing and push to get as big as possible."

It's in Canada's self-interest for that to happen, too. Bigger companies will help nudge our GDP in the right direction. In order to get back up to three percent GDP growth, we will soon need to start adding about $20 billion to the economy every year—roughly the equivalent of adding a BlackBerry (at its peak) annually.

That's a tall order, and we are under serious time pressure to fulfill it, because once all the boomers retire, our GDP growth will slow even more. The problem isn't just that they won't be in the labour force, helping to create more goods and services and generally pumping up the economy, but that retirees aren't big spenders, generally. They consume less, and tend to move money out of the stock market and into fixed-income investments—all of which makes perfect sense for seniors but will have a negative impact on Canada's already sluggish growth. At the same time, life expectancy continues to climb, which means that boomers will be increasingly reliant on our social safety net, and for a very long time. That net is already hugely expensive to maintain. The responsibility for keeping it from fraying or breaking altogether will rest with a progressively smaller number of Canadians. To prevent disaster, then, we need the economy to grow much faster. Starting now.

Growth happens for two reasons: either you add more workers or the ones you already have become more productive. Although we should be bringing in as many skilled immigrants as we can, even massively increased immigration won't compensate fully for the decline in labour force participation that will come as boomers retire. We also need to boost labour productivity: workers need to start generating more GDP per hour. The idea isn't to work longer but to work smarter, so you reduce input but increase output.

Unfortunately, we have an abysmal track record on productivity growth, falling further and further behind our global peers every year. Looking at the top 21 developed nations in the OECD, Canada is number 15 in terms of productivity growth, trailing even countries like France, where people work fewer hours on fewer days than we do.

To put our problem into perspective, Americans are also concerned about their productivity growth rate—which is now nearly *double* ours. In 1984, our relative labour productivity was more than 90 percent that of Americans, but since then the gap has widened to a chasm. Twenty years ago, a US worker generated about US$5.50 more GDP per hour than a worker in Canada. Today, it's about US$11 more. And workers in China, India and emerging markets are nipping at our Achilles heel.

If we keep going this way, in fifty years Canada will have the lowest rate of GDP growth of any developed nation. What this means is that our kids' prospects and quality of life will be dramatically worse than ours were—if they choose to stay here.

Labour productivity isn't a sexy subject, but it's crucial that every Canadian understand why we're falling short, because productivity is the key determinant of our standard of living. The problem is not that we're dumb or lazy. In fact, our workforce is highly skilled and remarkably well-educated. What we are not very good at is finding new ways to do things more efficiently, or coming up with whole new things altogether, and then commercializing our discoveries—in Canada. Many Canadians commercialize their inventions and innovative ideas all right, but they do it in the United States, thereby radically limiting the positive impact on our own economy. Here at home, Canadian businesses tend to stick with the same old, same old, rather than seeking the new.

A lot of factors contribute to productivity, but the bottom line is that innovation is the key driver. Innovation doesn't require mind-blowing, world-changing technological advances such as the steam engine or smartphone (though those are always welcome). *Any* new or improved product or process that creates value qualifies as innovation. Streamlining a manufacturing process so that you crank out more widgets in less time counts as innovation. So does dreaming up a new sales and marketing approach. So does figuring out a new way to organize your workforce. Whether by creating a whole new market or tweaking an established product or process to make it more efficient, innovation ramps up productivity.

That's why the Trudeau government is talking non-stop about innovation and the need for more of it—the same tired refrain that prime ministers have been repeating since 1916, when the push to promote technological innovation by industry began in earnest. "Almost every decade since the 1920s has witnessed renewed attempts by successive governments to achieve it, but on the whole they have all failed," was the grim conclusion of the 1970 Senate Special Committee on Science Policy. Two years later, the Science Council of Canada blasted entrepreneurial "prudence"— hesitant-junior-partner syndrome—and Canadian investors' risk aversion for our underachievement in innovation.

The feds have been throwing money at the problem for decades now and, along the way, created one of the most pro-business tax regimes in the world. But despite an annual infusion of almost $23 billion of taxpayers' money via 147 innovation-related programmes and tax expenditures, every single year Canada either declines or fails to improve on nearly every measure of innovation, falling further and further behind OECD peers (many of which, such as the Scandinavian countries, are much smaller than we are). We're in fifteenth place on the annual Global Innovation

Index, according to the World Intellectual Property Office. The Conference Board of Canada gave us a C on its last innovation report card.

Why, when we're so smart and well-educated, can't we innovate? The question has launched a thousand op-eds, and bureaucrats and academics have inspected the puzzle from all angles. Canadian businesses are laggards in terms of research and development spending: Canada is twenty-fourth on the OECD's Business Expenditure on Research and Development (BERD) index. Ten years ago, Canadian companies spent 1.5 percent of GDP on research and development, but today, after a sharp reduction in the manufacturing sector's share of the economy, they're spending only 0.9 percent. American companies are spending more than twice as much, and Israeli businesses spend more than four times as much, which helps explain why both countries are ahead of Canada on the Innovation Index. It's worth pointing out, too, that foreign-controlled multinationals are responsible for almost 40 percent of all BERD spending in Canada (and also account for a whopping 50 percent of all our merchandise exports).

Possible reasons for our low BERD rate include "business complacency, the low educational attainment of Canadian managers, the dearth of management experience and business acumen, and the aversion to risk in Canadian businesses," according to a startlingly frank 2017 report by the OECD. Evidently, Canadian executives don't invest in R & D because they are not very good at their jobs. Kevin Lynch's assessment is more diplomatic. He attributes the lack of investment to a more general trend, which he calls "short-term-ism. The press worries about this morning, the politicians worry about today, the markets worry at most about the quarter." Canadian businesses are no exception, he says. They don't think long-term, "and there's nothing more long term than R & D."

Corporate Profits in Canada and the United States, 1988–2014

*Sources: Statistics Canada, CANSIM tables 284-0038 and 187-0001 (Canada),
Federal Reserve Bank of St. Louis, 2016 (United States)*

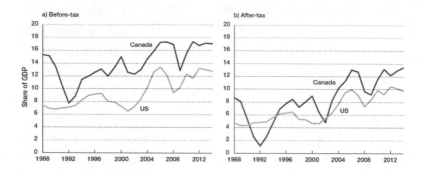

The private sector's record on investment in machinery and equipment (M & E) is particularly underwhelming. Giving workers the latest technologies spurs labour productivity, but Canadian companies' investment in ICT—telecommunications equipment, software and computers—is going down, not up. In 2008, Canadian businesses invested 68 percent of what their US counterparts did in ICT per worker; by 2014, they'd cut back further, to 56 percent. Small businesses are especially reluctant to invest in ICT, which is a real problem given that 98 percent of all businesses in Canada are small. The government has eliminated tariffs on M & E imports and repeatedly lowered the general corporate income tax rate in an attempt to stimulate investment, with no luck. Large and medium-sized Canadian corporations certainly have the money. Even when the loonie is low, their corporate profits are usually substantially higher than their American counterparts'.

But instead of investing in future growth, the Canadian mantra is all about the short term: Don't worry, keep shareholders happy. Pay out big dividends.

Not all Canadian businesses take this approach. Those exposed to significant international competition, such as the aerospace industry and auto parts manufacturers, *do* invest in innovation. They have to, to stay in business. But even Canada's eighty-seven biggest corporate R & D spenders are relatively cautious: in 2015, as their revenues rose more than seven percent, R & D expenditures declined by almost two percent.

And they're outliers. Only 30 percent of Canadian firms consider any form of innovation to be extremely or very important, according to a recent survey, and just 15 percent would assume significant financial risk to pursue it. Why? *Because they don't have to.* Trying to surpass rivals and attract more customers isn't something you knock yourself out to do when there's not much rivalry. Six companies dominate the Canadian banking industry. Four companies dominate the Internet service provider market. Three companies dominate English-language television broadcasting, the supermarket industry and wireless telecommunications. A duopoly dominates the airline industry. And so on.

When there's market concentration and the costs of entry are high—as they are in every industry on that list—incumbents don't have to worry that an upstart might pop up out of nowhere and try to take them down. Nor do they have to scramble to keep customers happy, because people have nowhere else to go. Canadian consumers tend to stick with the devil they know when the devils all seem interchangeable. The trick for an incumbent in an oligopoly is to move just fast enough to keep up with the pack, but not so fast that the bottom line is imperilled. A leisurely walk rather than a frantic sprint to cross the finish line first, in other words. Go for the bronze. There's absolutely no incentive to take big R & D bets that might not pan out. In fact, there's a big disincentive: if you spend a lot of money cooking up innovations that everyone else immediately imitates, you won't increase your market share much but you'll be stuck with a hefty bill. It's no big mystery, really, that Canadian companies don't innovate: it would be irrational.

The United States has its own oligopolies but, with very few exceptions, prices are lower and service is better there. Size matters: larger markets support more competition and companies that invest in R & D are more likely than those in smaller markets to recoup their expenses. Therefore, even where there's market concentration in the US, companies compete more vigorously for market share, and they certainly spend a lot more on R & D than their Canadian counterparts do, in part because they are making more complicated, higher-end goods but also because they are more vulnerable to disruption. When upstarts knock old stalwarts off their comfortable perches, the US government is more likely to let that happen; and US consumers are much more likely to demand action be taken to shut down anti-competitive behaviour that drives up the price of goods and services. The US has other advantages too: easier access to much deeper pools of capital, and the existence of well-developed clusters of research and industry, like the one outside Boston, where everyone in pharmaceuticals is running around trying to create the next big blockbuster drug. And then there's culture: Americans worship competition and lionize winners, and, yes, sometimes that's pretty ugly. But it goes a long way to explaining why the US doesn't have an innovation problem and we do.

When cutthroat competition is the norm, not taking a risk can be the biggest risk of all. A company that doesn't invest in innovation can be obliterated by one that does. When the uncertainty about what competitors are up to is coupled with the fear of losing traction, innovation is a necessity, not a frill.

But that's not the universe most big Canadian businesses inhabit. In their world, a well-managed company isn't one that moves the needle and delights consumers. It's one that keeps shareholders happy by focusing relentlessly on keeping costs down, yet avoids pissing off customers so much that they leave. By these standards, a lot of Canadian companies are extremely well run and the people in charge of them are doing exactly what they're supposed to do. They don't blow a lot of money on R & D or M & E. Once it's economical to do so, they adopt advances pioneered and proven in the US. Even those companies that aren't branch plants of American multinationals tend to conduct themselves as if they were, acting like followers rather than leaders.

If you don't really have to compete, you don't really have to innovate.

I think a very big part of the solution to Canada's century-long innovation drought is this simple: promote competition, and innovation—the kind that improves labour productivity and shows up in our GDP—will follow. Cozy oligopolies won't change until they're forced to, and why would they? They've got a good thing going. The only way to change their behaviour is to change the conditions that currently reward it. Do that, and I am certain that the telco incumbents, at least, would open the floodgates to R & D spending. If they faced greater competition, they'd have to, to try to protect their market share.

Continuing to focus on inputs, such as government tax credits and BERD ratios, "puts the cart before the horse. A firm must first decide that a commitment to innovation and the investments required makes business sense," according to one of the incredibly important CCA reports that only seem to have been read by a handful of policy wonks. Unless and until competition is introduced to the sectors and industries dominated by oligopolies, we will continue to waste vast amounts of taxpayer dollars on programmes that have no hope of transforming our economy because the *sine qua non* for innovation—competition—does not exist.

Eventually, competition will be foisted upon even the most protected Canadian sectors, because of technological advances, a shift in our relationship with the US, incursions into Canada by players in emerging markets, or world events we can't predict. Will our companies be ready and able to rise to the challenge? Or will a history of protected complacency have rendered them fatally weak? What is the likelihood they will be able to compete abroad if they haven't first learned to compete at home? Slim, would be my guess, but I don't think we should wait to find out. Instead of more grand talk about innovation and more spending on programmes that have failed to yield results, the government should focus on creating a more competitive, and therefore more innovation-friendly, climate right now. I'm not talking about overnight, unfettered deregulation. If the government simply aggressively enforced its own pro-competition policies—and, through its procurement activities, started giving innovative and potentially disruptive companies a chance—that would be an excellent start.

Had aggressive enforcement of existing policies and laws occurred back in 2010, I think I'd still own WIND and it would be providing a meaningful alternative for Canadian consumers. After the company was sold, I felt bitter, for the first time in my life. The government had said it wanted more competition, I tried to provide it, and their toothless approach to enforcement wound up biting me, everyone else at WIND and, especially, Canadian consumers, who are still being gouged. The Big Three got off scot-free. What the . . . ? I started spending a lot of time in the US, even toying with the idea of moving there permanently. It seemed like a better place to build my next business, whatever that might be. I couldn't imagine starting another company in Canada. Too difficult. Too heartbreaking.

But the longer I stayed away, the more I missed home and the more I felt that walking away was a cop-out. I love this country. Corny, but true. And Canada is at a critical moment, an inflection point where all of us have a responsibility to try to bend the arc of history in the right direction, so that our children, and their children, enjoy the same quality of life and equality of opportunity that we have had. That will not happen if, collectively, we keep going for bronze.

Some good news, finally: we have the talent to win global contests and create lasting prosperity. Through my work in incubators and accelerators geared to helping entrepreneurs, I've met Canadians who are as intelligent, innovative and highly skilled as anyone in the world. What they need, and what we do not yet have, is a business community that is truly open for business.

Creating one will require a deep cultural shift, not just on Bay Street but in every corner of Canadian society. We need to embrace competition and view it as an incentive to improve and achieve, not an existential threat. The challenges we are facing are serious and they are daunting. To meet them, we need to pull together and demand more and better from our businesses, our government, our educational institutions and, most of all, ourselves. We need to aim for gold and believe we can achieve it.

CHAPTER 3

The Gazelle Shortage

How do we kick-start innovation and productivity? The answer is obvious: by diversifying away from our dependence on natural resources and building new kinds of companies—bigger, bolder ones that can compete internationally and win.

That's exactly what the federal government has been trying to get people to do for years now, by promoting entrepreneurship via a tantalizing smorgasbord of federal and provincial grants, loans and tax incentives for start-ups—one of the richest sets of subsidies in the OECD. A new entrepreneur with a decent accountant can write down a lot of business costs and write some off altogether, while paying a very low tax rate overall. There's some hands-on help on offer too. Currently, more than 140 organizations, most of them heavily subsidized by the government, provide assistance to fledgling companies: not only incubators and accelerators, which tend to focus on tech-related ventures, but also national non-profits such as Startup Canada, which provides networking and education for entrepreneurs of all stripes, and Futurpreneur, which offers hands-on mentoring as well as a range of other supports, including financing, for young business owners.

On paper, it seems to be working. Canada is now the second-easiest place in the world to start a company, reports the World Bank, meaning that we trail New Zealand. And Canadians are even more gung-ho about the idea of starting businesses than Americans are, according to the Global Entrepreneurship Monitor (GEM), which has been gathering data from seventy countries for almost two decades. Sixty-five percent of us believe entrepreneurship is a good career choice, and almost as many believe there are good opportunities to start businesses here. Evidently, a lot of Canadians are acting on those beliefs. Nearly 17 percent of working-age Canadians, versus about 13 percent of Americans, either are currently engaged in setting up a company or are already owner-managers of a "baby business" that's generating revenue and is less than three and a half years old.

But despite all this entrepreneurial activity, the productivity gap is not closing. And Canada's lousy record on innovation isn't improving.

That's because most Canadian start-ups never amount to much. Very few enter the world with a bang: their average size at inception has been shrinking. And, as with new businesses the world over, the failure rate is high; one-half don't make it past the five-year mark. Most of those that do survive don't grow into thriving, bustling enterprises. The majority of Canadian companies that start out small stay small, experiencing zero or negative employment growth. Of the 1,170,000 businesses in Canada, 98 percent have fewer than a hundred employees—*many* fewer, in most cases. More than three-quarters employ ten or fewer people, and more than half are micro-enterprises, with no more than four employees.*

This is not to say that small businesses are irrelevant; they contribute roughly 30 percent of each province's GDP, and employ 70 percent of Canadians who work in the private sector. But just a handful of those small companies are actually highly productive and *growing*, creating new jobs and more wealth.

Only about two of every hundred businesses in Canada are so-called gazelles, meaning they leap far ahead of the pack, not just once but again and again. The federal government defines gazelles as companies that have been around for at least four or five years, have at least ten employees, and have had, for three or more years, an annualized growth rate of 20 percent or better.** This sets the bar quite low in terms of size and scale for a four- or five-year-old enterprise, but very few companies are clearing that bar. Most are not high-tech start-ups, as you might assume. High-growth firms (HGFs) come in all shapes and sizes, and they are found in all regions of the country and all sectors of the economy, though there are more in construction and manufacturing and fewer in retail trade and food services.

---

* On the surface, the picture doesn't look all that different in the United States. There, too, about 98 percent of all businesses are small, and more than half of them are really small; as in Canada, only 0.3 percent of all companies employ more than 500 people. However, those large US companies are *really* large and employ almost 52 percent of Americans. Another 14 percent work for medium-sized enterprises, with 100 to 500 employees. This is almost exactly the reverse of the situation here. In short, most Americans work for companies that are both far larger and more productive.

** Measured in terms of revenue growth or job creation. Most Canadian gazelles are quite a bit better at revenue growth: in 2013, 1.6 percent of companies qualified as gazelles on that basis, versus 0.6 percent of companies that met gazelle criteria because they drove job creation.

However, almost all HGFs are similar in two ways: they tend to be export oriented and to invest far more heavily in R & D than most Canadian companies do. Exporting and innovation go hand in hand. Companies that are exposed to new markets are also exposed to new technologies and global best practices in their industries—and, crucially, to competition, the stiff kind that forces them to up their game. Competing internationally creates a virtuous circle, begetting innovation, which begets higher revenues and turbo-charges job creation. Between 1993 and 2002, the 5.5 percent of Canadian companies that were in continuous operation and exported anything, anywhere, created 47 percent of the country's jobs—and three-quarters of those jobs were created by a very small pack of gazelles hell-bent on winning international races.

Our economy needs more gazelles—or even moose, which aren't so nimble but at least can lumber along at a reasonable clip when they're determined to make progress. A lot of Canadian entrepreneurs, however, more closely resemble sloths. It's hard to blame them, because, as we've seen, plodding along slowly has worked beautifully up to this point. Competition has been minimal, aggregate corporate profits have been higher than in the United States, and it's been easy and cheap to be late adopters of innovations pioneered in the US—the incentives for growth and change haven't been strong. But what's worked in the past is not going to cut it in the future, because the rules of the game have changed. Yet the sloth-like behaviour continues.

"The first, and arguably most significant, obstacle to growth is the apparent dearth of business owners with an appetite for strong development in the first place," according to a 2013 report by the Centre for Digital Entrepreneurship and Economic Performance (DEEP), a think tank in Waterloo.

On closer inspection, the entrepreneurial zeal detected by GEM has a distinctly small-time flavour. Even in the early, rose-coloured-glasses phase of launching a start-up, few Canadians are dreaming big. Only one-fifth aspire to provide twenty or more jobs five years down the road; two-thirds are not planning to have even six employees by then. As for exporting, 17 percent of early-stage business owners have no plans whatsoever to sell their products or services abroad; 55 percent aim to generate just 1 to 25 percent of their revenue that way.

Think about that for a moment. Almost three-quarters of our newest entrepreneurs, the ones the government is incentivizing left, right and centre to build businesses and revitalize our economy, do not intend to do much, if any, exporting. That's the same as saying that they have no intention of competing in the global economy. Not every entrepreneur has to yearn to be the next Roy Thomson or Ted Rogers, of course. But the days when Canadian businesses could be highly profitable without exporting and attempting to innovate are drawing to an end. If governmental policies are meant to be paving the way for the next BlackBerry and Uber, but in fact what's being stimulated is a glut of mom-and-pop operations, we urgently need to question whether our tax dollars are being spent wisely—and we need to figure out why HGFs aren't springing up all over the place, and what needs to change in order to make that happen. Artisanal enterprises are not going to save the Canadian economy, and they are no match for global behemoths.

Ambition, as it turns out, really matters when it comes to the creation of high-growth firms, so it's a significant problem that our new entrepreneurs seem to have so little of it. Ambition is a key determinant of performance, according to a comprehensive survey conducted by the Business Development Bank of Canada (BDC) in 2015. The point of the exercise was to determine how HGFs differ from garden-variety businesses, and the BDC reported,

"Though growth and size are important criteria in defining high-impact firms, the mindset of the executive team is a critical factor for competitiveness. Without the right mindset, the other criteria become far less predictive." Makes sense, right? If your main business goal is to get by and avoid bankruptcy, chances are excellent that your company won't be as big or as profitable as it would be if you'd set out to become a leading exporter to China. So, what's the right mindset? A highly ambitious, achievement-oriented one that spurs an entrepreneur to "unrelentingly pursue innovation and higher growth by investing and taking appropriate risks." In the BDC survey, the most ambitious, risk-tolerant Canadian entrepreneurs had 10 percent greater revenue growth and 9 percent more international sales than moderately ambitious ones. Risk tolerance was key: highly ambitious entrepreneurs with a lower appetite for risk didn't do as well.

In a glass-half-full way, this is great news: Canada's gazelle shortage isn't related to a shortage of business talent. We have an attitude problem, related to our traditional, junior-partner business culture and its resistance to competition.

The problem may not be so much a lack of entrepreneurial ambition as uneasiness with the whole concept of entrepreneurial ambition. While it's socially acceptable to admit to an ambition to cure cancer or win the Stanley Cup, saying you want to build a billion-dollar business just sounds so . . . tacky. Overweening. American. As Angela Strange, the VC at Andreessen Horowitz pointed out, even a lot of the Canadians who show up in Silicon Valley looking for money aren't comfortable selling themselves and telling the world that they want to build big, bold companies. We need to create a culture where it's okay to do that, because billion-dollar businesses don't just happen. They start with unapologetic ambition.

To make entrepreneurial ambition socially acceptable—desirable, even—we could start by cleansing the word *ambition* of its brassy overtones and reframing it in positive terms that are aligned with Canadian cultural values. For instance, the ambition to export, which we should be encouraging and rewarding, could not be more Canadian. Canada is as far from xenophobic as it's possible for a country to be. More than 20 percent of us were born somewhere else, which should give us a massive advantage in terms of understanding, and being able to make inroads in, foreign markets, as we desperately need to do.

What's truly unCanadian is our lack of ambition when it comes to trade, and the fact that we can't seem to see beyond our own borders. Only 12 percent of small businesses, and 28 percent of medium-sized ones (meaning, with 100 to 500 employees), ship stuff out of the country. Despite the spike in revenues that comes with exporting, more than one-quarter of non-exporters see no benefit in trying to branch out, according to another study by the BDC. Unsurprisingly, then, export activity is heading in the wrong direction: as a percentage of GDP, exports dropped from 46 percent in 2000 to 30 percent in 2012. This was not some unfortunate worldwide trend. Almost all of the other countries in the OECD increased their exports as a percentage of GDP between 2005 and 2013; only one country, Israel, experienced a decline worse than Canada's.

We should be encouraging new entrepreneurs to be a whole lot more ambitious, not so they can ape Americans but so they can be successful in a distinctly Canadian way: by reaching out to the outside world and sharing the best of what our country has to offer.

Many entrepreneurs are proud that their businesses are small and independent, and some of their customers probably are too. A fair number of us love to hate big-box retailers.

But the smaller the company, the less productive it is; big firms can take advantage of economies of scale, and they have much greater resources to put towards R & D, new technology and all the other kinds of things that help companies become more efficient. The small firm disadvantage is especially pronounced in Canada. While American companies with fewer than 500 employees are 67 percent as productive as those with more than 500 employees, in Canada smaller companies are only 47 percent as productive as big ones. Forty-seven percent! It's not the story we like to tell, but the hard truth is that "the small size of companies in Canada, while often celebrated, is actually a drag on productivity and the wider economy," as was noted in the DEEP report.

Nevertheless, Ottawa continues to wheel out ever more enticing incentives to encourage yet more people to start yet more new businesses. Unfortunately, because just about every new business starts out small, what's being incentivized may only be the creation of more small businesses that are "a drag on productivity and the wider economy."

Why aren't more of these start-ups becoming HGFs and sparking an economic miracle? Because, explains Case Western University economist Scott Shane, that's not what most start-ups actually do. It's "a dangerous myth" that start-ups are some kind of "a magic bullet that will transform depressed economic regions, generate innovation, create jobs, and conduct all sorts of other economic wizardry." Very few start-ups actually spur any economic growth—they can't, because they're not more productive than existing companies, Shane argues in a paper debunking start-ups myths that won a global award for entrepreneurship research in 2009. Unless new businesses are disruptive—think smartphones, which have all but wiped out digital cameras and camcorders— they are usually less productive than older firms, because, typically, a company's productivity *increases* with age and, as we've seen, size.

Nor does the average start-up create a ton of jobs. Longitudinal research in the United States, Sweden and Germany shows that most new businesses shed employees as time goes on, Shane reports, so that "as a whole, new firms have net job *destruction* after their first year." That may not be so terrible, either, because the jobs they do create are more likely to be part-time and, overall, new firms pay less and provide worse benefits than established firms. Then there's the job security issue: many start-ups simply don't last very long. When Shane ran the US numbers, he discovered that "43 people have to try to start companies so that we can have 9 jobs a decade from now"—not exactly, he observed tartly, a "spectacular yield."

In other words, the typical new business has absolutely nothing in common with legendary start-ups such as Facebook or Google, and the main reason is that the typical entrepreneur is nothing like Mark Zuckerberg, Larry Page or Sergey Brin. Shane explains that start-ups tend to be home-based businesses run by people with pretty modest goals: making a living and having some degree of autonomy. They're not looking to set the world on fire, and they don't. Some of them simply aren't very good business people. Often, they strike out on their own because their job options aren't so hot. People who really understand how to run a business are more likely to have good jobs already, ones they don't want to leave. The average first-time entrepreneur, then, may be brave and passionate but is not particularly talented when it comes to business, as viewers of *Dragon's Den* are already aware.

"The typical entrepreneur is very bad at picking industries," Shane observes, "choosing the ones that are easiest to enter, not the ones that are best for start-up." Therefore, most of the businesses they build will remain sub-scale or fail outright. In itself, failure is not tragic, but along the way, many entrepreneurs (and the family and friends who've invested in their businesses) lose their shirts, and that *is* tragic. That's why whipping up entrepreneurial passion and subsidizing the creation of any and all new businesses, the way the Canadian government does, is bad public policy. You wind up incentivizing a lot of "typical" entrepreneurs, whose businesses are likely to tank.

"All entrepreneurs are not created equal," is how Shane sums up the situation, advising governments to "stop subsidizing the formation of the typical start-up and focus on the subset of businesses with growth potential. Getting economic growth and jobs creation from entrepreneurs is not a numbers game. It is about encouraging high-quality, high-growth companies to be founded."

But Ottawa is still playing a numbers game, focusing on quantity rather than quality. The government's main incentive for entrepreneurship is an indirect subsidy: the small business tax deduction (SBD), which was recently lowered to 10.5 percent on the first $500,000 of active business income. That's great news for small business owners, but not such great news for the rest of us unless those small businesses are creating a lot of jobs, because the SBD costs the federal Treasury more than $3 billion a year. That kind of outlay would probably be worthwhile if the SBD helped businesses grow and become more productive, but that's not what it does. In fact, growth is penalized. If your business starts generating a ton of revenue, well, sorry—you don't get the deduction anymore. It might as well be called the "stay small" business deduction.

A massive tax deduction that stimulates entrepreneurial activity but not economic growth is a triple whammy: it encourages Shane's "typical" not-so-good entrepreneurs to enter the ring, it doesn't provide the boost "atypical" entrepreneurs need for their businesses to grow, *and* it costs the rest of us a ton of money. The government has to recoup all that forgone revenue somehow, either by cutting spending or by raising taxes somewhere else. Citing a major review of taxation in the UK that concluded "there was no economic case for a reduced small business corporate tax rate," the OECD recently suggested that Ottawa review the SBD, with an eye to putting the kibosh on it and offering assistance that's targeted to promote growth.

But Ottawa likes tax deductions and tax credits: they're egalitarian! Canada is the most decentralized country in the OECD in terms of public spending, with provincial, territorial and local governments managing almost 80 percent of the total spend, and one result is that the feds live in fear of being accused of favouritism. Hence the appeal of "come one, come all" indirect subsidies: no one can claim to have been snubbed. The entrepreneur in Calgary whose main goal is kicking back at the cottage for the summer gets exactly the same amount of tax relief as the entrepreneur in Regina whose main goal is building a kick-ass company that employs a lot of people and creates a lot of wealth. It's as though the government believes that ambition is irrelevant, and maybe even a little obnoxious.

Instead of gazelles, all this fairness is breeding a large herd of marginal businesses. "Canada lags behind most international peers in its capacity to nurture firms with high-growth potential," according to the DEEP report. "The UK, New Zealand, the United States and Spain, for example, have all been more successful in generating a larger share of high-growth firms that go on to compete internationally and make significant contributions to both national growth and job creation."

If so many of Canada's small businesses are sluggish, how do they manage to stay afloat? Well, the DEEP authors explain, they survive because there are not enough disruptive upstarts and strong-armed rivals battling for market share: "the degree of creative destruction and competitive pressure in many sectors is insufficient to either weed out poorly run companies, or reward superior enterprise performance." The result is a myriad of "stagnant firms" and oligopolies, featuring fat and happy "incumbents that inhibit progress."

In other words, Canada is a great place to start a mediocre business because, thanks to a lack of competition, it will probably survive longer here.

If that is true, though, this should also be a good place to start a growth-oriented business, because nothing much would be standing in the way. And Canada does have "atypical" entrepreneurs who want to build big, bold companies, ambitious women and men who are immune to the junior-partner complex and possess the entrepreneurial ability to realize their goals.

But rather than smoothing the path for their new businesses to grow, the government often erects roadblocks or, as with WIND, fails to clear away or even acknowledge the existence of obstacles to competition. The problem isn't just with Ottawa. Interprovincial trade barriers make it much more difficult to build businesses that are truly national in scope. The requirement to register and report businesses separately in each province does not promote growth in any area except accounting and legal fees that are onerous for new businesses. Despite recent attempts to reduce internal trade barriers, they're still estimated to reduce Canadian productivity by between three and seven percent; meeting different regulatory standards and getting different certifications and inspections for every province wastes a lot of time. And of course consumers pay, too, because interprovincial trade barriers drive up the cost of goods and services, to the tune of $7,500 per Canadian household. Every year.

Regulatory hassles, combined with protection of incumbents—which, per the OECD, "is high by international standards and arises primarily from an above-average use of antitrust exemptions"—do not make Canada an easy place to build a high-growth firm. Some ambitious entrepreneurs give it a go and quickly decide to get going, right across the border. Even though total corporate tax costs in Canada are the lowest in the G7, almost 50 percent lower than in the United States, and R & D tax incentives are insanely generous. Even though there's a highly educated talent pool here, and employees are a lot more loyal than they are in Silicon Valley, where poaching talent is a sport. Even though our cities are safe, our education and health care systems are strong, our political system is stable, and our quality of life is extraordinarily high. Even though, in many cases, they would prefer to stay.

Understanding why some of our best business people give up on Canada is crucial if we're going to hang on to the next generation of growth-minded entrepreneurs and attract talented immigrants with a similar mindset—and reel in more foreign direct investment (FDI) too. Such investment is vitally important to Canada's future, because it helps fund new businesses (WIND would have been dead in the water without foreign investors) and revitalize mature ones, raising productivity, competitiveness and living standards. Foreign investment also strengthens trading ties with other countries and helps build new export markets. Every country in the world, including the US, is scrambling to get more of it, but once again, we are bringing up the rear: on average, FDI has been increasing by seven percent a year in OECD countries, but by just two percent a year in Canada. Foreign investors are turned off by Canada's regulatory environment; we rank thirty-third out of forty countries on the OECD's index of restrictiveness in terms of foreign direct investment.

The regulatory environment is also a turnoff for growth-oriented entrepreneurs like Lorne Abony, who, in 1998, quit his job practising securities law at a top Bay Street law firm in order to start an online pet supply business with Andrea Reisman, who'd built up the beverage division at Cott from $3 million to $100 million and was helping her mother, Heather, get Indigo Books up and running. Those were the heady days of the dot-com bubble, and Abony and Reisman aimed to build a massive e-commerce business.

"We really wanted to run this business from Toronto, and take advantage of the fact that we were right next door to the largest economy in the history of humanity," says Abony. The clock was ticking: American competitors in the space were already securing financing and getting their companies off the ground. But in Canada, the pair hit one obstacle after another. "We discovered that we couldn't produce dog food, even if it was solely for export, without putting French labelling on the bag. That was a non-starter for US retailers. That guy in Texas isn't buying a bag of dog food that says '*pour chien.*' We also had to use metric measurements, but Americans were buying dog food in twenty- and forty-pound increments," he recalls. "We still thought we could wrestle with all that, until we realized we'd have to set up a depot in Buffalo, because Canada Customs couldn't give us any comfort in terms of how long our shipments would be held at the border. Then we thought, 'Oh, wait, we could just pick up and move to San Francisco and all these problems would disappear!' And it was no contest."

Moving provided the solution to another problem too: they'd only been able to raise "a tiny amount of money" in Toronto. In San Francisco, however, the pair landed meetings with top-drawer venture capital firms and, within a few months, secured US$9 million for their company, Petopia.com. Over the next two years, they raised another US$100 million to scale up, before selling the company to Petco. By that time, the dot-com bubble had burst and the sale was the kind that generates sighs of relief rather than headlines. But in the meantime, Petopia had created two hundred full-time jobs and paid a whack of corporate tax—in the United States, not Canada. Another loss: Reisman never came back, but she kept building companies, co-founding ThisLife, a cloud-based photo and video organization platform, which Shutterfly acquired in 2013. More jobs and corporate tax for Americans.

Abony did return to Toronto, where he co-founded FUN technologies, an online gaming company, in 2002. The following year, FUN completed an IPO on the London Stock Exchange, raising more than $11 million, and in 2004, when the company listed on the Toronto Stock Exchange, Abony became the youngest CEO on the TSX (though, at thirty-five, he was a little long in the tooth by Silicon Valley standards). Helped by eight strategic acquisitions, FUN experienced almost exponential growth. By 2006, the company had 35 million registered customers and a new owner: Liberty Media, run by American billionaire John Malone.

It was Abony's first big exit, though he followed up quickly with another, more personal one. He moved to the States permanently. He still loves Canada, he says, over lunch at a Toronto hotel, because "you can't make new 'old friends.'" Though Abony leads the life of a gazillionaire, he is unassuming and genuinely curious about other people, with the common touch of a guy who grew up in subsidized housing in Toronto. Warming to the subject of Canada's virtues, he continues, "People are nice here—I know everyone says that, but it's really true. You don't have the sleazeball factor of Miami or California, and people are generally smart. I also have family here, and I just feel at home." Then the nostalgic moment ends and he snaps into matter-of-fact mode to explain why he has no intention of leaving Austin, Texas, and returning to Canada: "The government does everything possible to make it difficult to do business, without seeming to recognize that Canadians can just move across the border." Relocation is simple if you have a good idea and the ability to raise money and build a company around it.

Even Donald Trump welcomes such immigrants with open arms. In fact, in 2006, Trump did something he's never done before or since: he wrote a letter of support for a US green card application—Abony's—pointing out that FUN had been one of the fastest-growing companies in the history of the TSX and, at the time it was acquired, employed more than 475 people in seven offices around the world. "To sell a public company to Liberty and Malone for $484 million is a very complicated and sophisticated undertaking and one that could only be carried out by a person with extraordinary business skills," Trump wrote, predicting that Abony "will make a very positive contribution to the US economy."

This was no Trumpian exaggeration. Abony, who received what's known as a "person of exceptional ability" green card in the US, went on to turn a sleepy little company with fewer than ten employees into the world's largest integrated provider of in-store background music, video, digital signage and scent, with more than 500,000 commercial locations globally. Whether you're at KFC, Gucci or TD Bank, chances are excellent that your retail customer experience was designed and provided by Mood Media, which is headquartered in Austin, generates hundreds of millions of dollars in revenue each year and employs more than two thousand people around the world.

That's a lot of revenue and a lot of jobs, which is why the US government will do backflips to attract and hold on to entrepreneurs like Lorne Abony. The Canadian government, however, doesn't seem to bat an eyelash when they leave. "I don't need a red carpet," Abony says, "but it's not like anyone has ever said, 'Gee, you're Canadian and you'd probably love to live at home. What could we do to make that happen?'

"We absolutely could have headquartered Mood in Canada and created a lot of jobs and paid a lot of corporate tax here," he continues, then adds a giant caveat: the Canadian government would have had to demonstrate some flexibility. Given the government's position on dog-food labelling, Abony thought the chances of that were nil, so he didn't even bother to investigate. The problem, he says, was that in Canada "music is a culturally protected industry, so if we'd headquartered here, a certain percentage of the content would have had to be Canadian." That would have been a non-starter with the giant American retailers that hire Mood to create their in-store ambience and marketing.

"Let's say Abercrombie & Fitch wants playlists for all their stores in the US. Mood will put them together, handling all the rights and royalties and so on," explains Abony, who left the company in 2013 to start another venture. "Of course, what's procured for a store in Tennessee may be different than what's procured for Brooklyn. But guess what? We'd have had to call the folks in Nashville and say, 'Notwithstanding that you like country music, we're going to jam Canadian content down your throat.' We're lucky because we have global stars, Celine Dions and Avril Lavignes, but still . . . What if the store wanted an all-Christmas repertoire, or all Michael Jackson? We'd have had to say, 'Sorry, we can't.' Try doing business like that. You won't get very far."

Another disincentive: Canada's securities regulations, which Abony understands well, since they were his specialty as a lawyer. "You have to file your financials in French and English or you can't distribute securities in Quebec, which takes time and is more expensive—and that expense is an issue for a lot of start-ups," he says, ticking the negatives off on his fingers. "Then you have to file with ten securities regulators, which just unnaturally elongates the process. Let's say the regulator in Manitoba has five things on his desk that week—he can put your file at the bottom of the stack, or ask inane questions that slow everything down. And you've got that problem times ten provinces." Speed is important, because "if you file a prospectus in a bull market then have to wait three months to get ten separate regulators to sign off, you run the risk of being in a bear market. You need the capital markets to be efficient, especially if you're trying to attract foreign investment. If a big American investor is putting money in, you can't call them and say, 'Sorry, folks, we're still waiting on Saskatchewan'—they don't need it." They have plenty of other places where investing is easier. The US, for instance, which has a single national securities regulator.

Despite emotional ties to Canada, then, he had excellent reasons to leave. "It's not one thing," Abony continues. "You don't say, 'But for the provincial securities regulatory regime, I would have remained in Canada.' It's the totality of all the difficulties, one of which is that *profit* is a dirty word in Canada. Starting a business is hard enough, and no one here seems to want to make it simple. I think it reflects a kind of two-facedness: we think we're liberal, but really, in practice, we're not very liberal at all."

We've been wringing our hands about brain drain for years, but generally we've been lamenting the loss of doctors and top academics. With good reason: there's a ripple effect when a top performer in any field leaves the country. If a leading scientist packs up and moves from McGill to Stanford, the best graduate students in the same discipline will follow. But when a growth-oriented entrepreneur leaves, there's not so much a ripple effect as a riptide, because potential wealth and jobs are sucked right out of the country. To make matters worse, really good entrepreneurs have an unusually high "multiplier effect," as the finance minister's Advisory Council on Economic Growth recently pointed out, "meaning they create more indirect jobs across all income groups, such as lawyers, doctors, retail workers, etc."

There are other, less obvious, costs too. Up-and-comers lose role models and, crucially, potential sources of angel investment and strategic guidance every time someone like Lorne Abony decamps. Now CEO of FastForward Innovations, an investment firm focused on early-stage tech ventures, he's actively scouting for start-ups that need capital, but he has only two investments in

Canada, "a disproportionately low number given that I grew up here and am still connected here," he says. But he doesn't want to invest in ventures that are likely to stall when they're still sub-scale, and that's been his experience with Canadian companies. So he remains focused on American businesses, including two he recently helped to found: Abony is executive chairman of Vemo Education, which provides alternatives to traditional student financing options, and Schoold, a mobile app that uses machine learning and social media analytics to help students find the right colleges and universities.

Canada, he concludes, before he says goodbye and heads up to his hotel room, is a wonderful place to visit but a terrible place to try to build a big, new business. He's not alone in that opinion: according to the World Bank, Canada ranks twenty-second in the world in terms of ease of doing business, trailing countries such as Macedonia, Latvia and Lithuania.

Ambitious entrepreneurs who aim to create HGFs don't just need a regulatory environment that's conducive to growth. They also need infusions of capital. A lot of capital, in order to scale.

Good news: angel investment is much easier to find here than it was ten or even five years ago, and entrepreneurs with a good idea and a strong team usually don't have trouble getting seed financing—$250,000 to $1 million—to start a company. The problem is the next step, when early-stage companies need money to grow: the average early-stage deal in the US is 53 percent larger than it is here. The bigger a Canadian company gets, the less growth capital is available, which helps explain why so many promising small companies stall as they approach medium size, a crucial point in their development. In a nutshell, finding big chunks of money for ambitious new ventures is really difficult, particularly for first-time entrepreneurs who are trying to commercialize new, potentially disruptive technologies.

Although the government incentivizes entrepreneurship, it does not incentivize investment in new ventures. Let's say you want to invest in your daughter's start-up. Go right ahead! But you won't get any kind of tax break for it, the way you did when you contributed to her RESP, unless you live in British Columbia—which has more small businesses per capita than any other province, offers a 30 percent venture capital tax credit and, not coincidentally, outperforms all other provinces in terms of VC investment per capita.

"When I write an angel investment cheque, I always kiss the cheque, because this may be the last time I see that money," says Allan Lau, co-founder of Wattpad, an online network where writers can share work with readers around the world, and an active angel in the Toronto tech scene. "In most other types of investment, your principal is protected, but with early-stage investments the risk profile is much, much higher. I think it would be only fair for the tax system to reward that type of risk taking, whether through a credit or perhaps a special exemption on capital gains." Tax credits for Canadians who are brave enough to take a leap of faith and back new Canadian businesses are a no-brainer, not least because, if they existed, many angels would writer larger cheques.

All of that said, entrepreneurs who are trying to raise millions of dollars can't rely solely on family, friends and angels. They need help from institutional investors, but many of those prefer to put their money into older, more established businesses. American businesses, that is, which seem like safer bets to the Canadian institutions that control mountains of cash—the banks, the pension plans, the insurance companies. They're conservative, by definition: their shareholders, accustomed to fat dividends, would squawk if they took on much more risk. And our venture capital firms are anemic, controlling funds that are a fraction of the size of those in

Silicon Valley and New York. There isn't a VC in Canada who can write a cheque for $100 million for an early-stage venture.

The Canadian government, on the other hand, is a major player, spending as much on innovation and start-ups every year as several of the biggest VC firms in the Valley combined: billions of dollars, via a bewildering mishmash of federal and provincial grants, programmes and tax breaks. The Jenkins panel, whose mandate was to review federal support to business R & D, reported in 2011 that many of these programmes are too small to have much impact; others might be useful—but entrepreneurs aren't even aware they exist. "What we found was a funding system that is unnecessarily complicated and confusing to navigate," explained Tom Jenkins, the panel's chair as well as the chair of the board of OpenText, Canada's largest software company, when the panel released its findings. "There are also significant gaps that hinder the ability of our businesses to grow and that keep Canada from taking full advantage of this country's innovations."

This is an exquisitely diplomatic summary of the crazily dysfunctional "system" the panel's report describes: more than sixty unconnected innovation programmes spread over seventeen different government departments with no common evaluation framework for determining whether those programmes are even effective or not. "As a result, standardized performance and outcome indicators do not exist for the roughly $5 billion of business innovation programs," the panel noted in its report. In other words, every year, the government throws billions of dollars at one of Canada's most urgent problems without following up to find out what happens to all that money.

Most of those billions are going towards the Scientific and Experimental Research and Development (SR&ED) tax credit, which offsets the cost of private sector R & D projects. Each year, SR&ED credits alone amount to three to four billion dollars in forgone tax revenues, making it one of the most generous tax incentives for innovation anywhere in the world.

The programme heavily favours small businesses, which makes sense. About three-quarters of Canadian companies have ten or fewer employees, remember. Companies that size often don't have a decent coffee machine, much less a dedicated R & D team. In order to encourage businesses to undertake the kind of research projects that will help them grow and become more productive, the government lets them deduct their R & D expenditures from their business income for tax purposes, and also provides them with an investment tax credit that can be used to reduce the amount of income tax they have to pay. But as with the small business deduction, the programme overtly rewards failure to scale. Growth is not rewarded. Staying small is. Small companies get a much larger refundable tax credit than big companies do: 35 percent versus 15 percent on qualified expenditures—wages of employees and subcontractors conducting R & D, as well as materials, equipment and machinery—up to a maximum threshold of three million dollars. Expenditures have to meet three main criteria: they must be related to a scientific or technological advancement; the project must be truly experimental, so that it's unclear whether it will succeed or not; skilled personnel who know what they're doing must be involved.

Overall, small businesses love SR&ED (though they complain about the tiresome, confusing application process). It's a godsend for start-ups that aren't generating revenue yet. Here's why: Let's say you've raised a $300,000 seed round for a tech start-up, and you're spending like crazy on engineers to help develop and refine your product, but you don't have any paying customers yet. On the plus side, you won't have to pay taxes, because you're operating at a loss—and you'll still get a big cash refund from the government to cover a large percentage of what you paid the engineers. What's not to like about that arrangement? You get money even if your product is a bust and your company folds.

But there's a lot that's wrong with the programme from the taxpayers' perspective, as the many, many experts who have studied it over the years have pointed out. Some argue that the public benefit SR&ED delivers—the incremental investment stimulated by the subsidy—is exceeded by its costs. Administering the programme, which employs many hundreds of people, isn't cheap, and additional tax revenues have to be raised to finance it. Then there's the ease of submitting bogus claims: more than twenty thousand businesses claim SR&ED credits, and there aren't enough auditors in the land to sniff out all the phony projects. Another serious deficiency is that SR&ED credits can't be used to offset the cost of marketing expenditures, which is really dumb when you think about it, because figuring out whether you've got product–market fit is essential to commercialization. Coming up with new and improved stuff and then discovering no one actually wants to buy it isn't innovation— it's a waste of time and money. And there's something else: Canada's biggest and most profitable corporations are pocketing millions of dollars' worth of refunds a year (and, as explained earlier, many of them *still* aren't investing a whole lot in R & D).

Full disclosure: some of Globalive's businesses have benefited from SR&ED credits, to the tune of millions of dollars of cash back. But they didn't undertake R & D because the government provides a tax credit for it. They undertook R & D because they wanted to compete and win market share. Essentially, the federal government (and the province, which tops up SR&ED) rewarded our businesses for doing exactly what they would have done anyway. Many of those claims were 100 percent legitimate and linked directly to the pursuit of scientific and technological advances, but the programme's criteria are broad enough, and good accountants are savvy enough, that borderline, iffy expenditures can be dressed up in R & D jargon in order to qualify for refunds—and, over the years, Globalive's businesses have probably received some of those too. If a benefit exists, and everyone else is taking advantage of it, we'd be idiots not to do the same. But that doesn't mean the tax advantage should exist. I hope my friends will forgive me for putting in writing what we all say behind closed doors: SR&ED is a massive boondoggle for big businesses, which don't need and shouldn't get "free money" handouts from the government.

Without question, SR&ED has been hugely helpful to smaller companies that could not otherwise afford to undertake research and development. But helping those companies does not require an obscenely bloated programme that in more than thirty years of operation has not reversed Canada's dismal record on innovation or made the country a whit more competitive internationally. If anything, SR&ED may have made big companies less competitive: you don't have to push as hard when you know you've got millions of dollars of "free money" coming at the end of the year. And that's no exaggeration: some of Canada's biggest companies are receiving seven- and eight-figure cheques from the government, thanks to SR&ED.

Possibly the most remarkable feature of SR&ED is that a programme whose ultimate purpose is to stimulate research that will make Canada's companies more competitive is itself structured so as to *prevent* competition. As with the small business deduction, instead of concentrating resources where they are most likely to result in wins for our entire economy, the government's approach is "come one, come all." The result is that our flagship "innovation" programme hands out the equivalent of diamond-encrusted participation ribbons to any company that bellies up to the trough and claims it took a crack at innovating. These are tax credits for *trying*—for attempting to do something new, not for actually doing it. What's being incentivized is undertaking research, which Canadians are already very good at, not commercializing it, which Canadians are bad at—and commercialization is the essence of innovation. Companies can't move the needle on productivity, job creation or wealth creation until they figure out a way to make money off research.

Nevertheless, you qualify for SR&ED even if, year after year, you have nothing new to show for your efforts except that year's application forms—forms that have become so complicated, by the way, that there's a booming business in filling them out. SR&ED consultants pocket as much as one-third of the billions of taxpayers' dollars that are going into the programme. No doubt many of those consultants are upstanding individuals who, like specialized accountants, help firms get tax credits for the legitimate R & D they've undertaken. But some are in the business of hammering square pegs into round holes using the blunt instrument of jargon, whereby "finally broke down and bought a new cash register" becomes "undertook a risky investment in a stunning technological advance that's projected to revolutionize sales." In recent years the government has clamped down, investigating and denying more claims and trying to curb the abuses for which SR&ED had become notorious. Ottawa is well aware of the programme's imperfections, but it seems to have sacred-cow status, because many recipients—including big companies with robust corporate profits—insist they couldn't possibly live without it. Therefore, the programme is forever being tweaked, but its overall emphasis remains the same.

Determining funding based on a company's innovation output, measured in terms of increased productivity, revenue or job creation, would be difficult if not impossible, especially in the case of new firms. As SR&ED recognizes, achieving those outputs can take years and many false starts. But government programmes themselves should absolutely be assessed on the basis of outputs. Surely, after three decades, we have enough information to decide whether this one is working. Most of the studies and reports the government has commissioned (and spent millions of dollars on) are in accord: SR&ED is doing a less than stellar job of stimulating innovation, and the government should rebalance its approach by simplifying SR&ED, spending less on these kinds of indirect measures, and channelling a lot more towards direct cash infusions and grants for new businesses with high-growth potential. That's what the OECD has called for too—repeatedly—with a myriad of policy wonks and pundits supplying backup vocals.

SR&ED aside, the government's approach to innovation spending is not meritocratic, and it should be. Rather, regional and sectoral fairness has been fetishized: a little here for a programme in Manitoba, a little there for Prince Edward Island, a pat on the head for manufacturers, a pat on the head for software developers. Everyone gets something, but no one gets enough to make a gazelle-like difference—and funding is not tied to outcomes. There isn't even much interest in *measuring* outcomes, as the Jenkins panel noted, to see what kind of bang we're getting for all those bucks.

But outcomes are crucial. They will determine our future prosperity and what kind of country Canada becomes. The outcomes of businesses on the receiving end of all this government assistance are uneven, but not because business is some completely random crapshoot where it's impossible to predict who will win. The reason is that the ability to build powerhouse companies that rev up the economy is actually pretty rare.

Unfortunately, the Canadian government does not have a mechanism to double down on entrepreneurs who seem to have the right stuff. And too often, Canadian investors don't have enough money, or simply aren't willing, to bet on them.

———

"We've all been to those family get-togethers where someone says, 'Aunt Sue, your cookies are unbelievable, you should sell them.' And everyone else chimes in, 'They're so much better than anything at Loblaws. Do it, Aunt Sue, start a cookie company!'" says Lorne Abony. "But it doesn't matter if her cookies are the best in the world, because she's up against Nabisco, which is paying a fortune for shelf space in grocery stores. Pricing power, distribution, manufacturing costs—all of it is skewed to the benefit of the scaled player, who can also buy eyeballs on Amazon and use Twitter and Facebook to push sales. Unless Aunt Sue can attract a lot of capital, scale up and buy her own shelf space, her cookies will never see the light of day in Loblaws."

Still, doesn't it make sense to encourage Aunt Sue to get out there and *try* to create some more jobs and wealth by starting her own company? Maybe she's the next Mrs. Fields.

Abony, who has the year-round tan and open, confident manner of a tennis pro (he's a United States Tennis Association doubles champion in the men's over-forty division), raises an eyebrow, then answers with a question of his own. "But what are her chances of attracting capital if Uncle Dave in Boston is also making great cookies?"

Zero, in his opinion, even if her product is way better. Most Canadian investors are too cautious to place big bets on homegrown entrepreneurs (unless their businesses involve plundering natural resources). And American investors would rather bet on Uncle Dave, he says, because "they don't take Canada seriously."

Abony, who has raised more than a billion dollars for his various ventures, concludes, "There's this romantic notion that Canada is open for business, because there are so many small companies. But it's just empty rhetoric, because no one is helping those small businesses form financial capital. And without capital, they will always be small."

Attracting sufficient capital is an especially big problem for entrepreneurs whose ideas have the disruptive potential to upend whole industries. Abe Heifets, CEO of Atomwise, is one of them. An American who did his undergraduate work in bioengineering and computer science at Cornell, he came north for his doctorate. The computer science department at the University of Toronto is widely considered one of the best in the world; machine learning (ML) was invented there.

Heifets explains the power of machine learning by way of a very American analogy: baseball. "Say you own a team and you're trying to figure out whether you should hire this player or trade that one. With machine learning, you feed in hundreds or thousands of players' stats—batting averages, runs, whatever you want—and then you'll get a prediction of how many runs a particular player will score next season, and that information will help you make the decision."

ML also makes it possible to rifle through reams of biological data and drug molecules and make accurate predictions about which medicines hold the most promise. That's what Atomwise does, by developing algorithms to predict which molecules could combat specific diseases. Like any good CEO, Heifets has his pitch down to an art, patiently explaining this extraordinarily complex process in layman's terms.

"You can think of the proteins in your body as machines on an assembly line, in that every machine takes in a very specific input, transforms it in a particular way, then passes it on to the next machine. Disease occurs when one of those machines malfunctions," he says. "Let's say the machine—the protein—that governs cell growth and division gets switched on but it never switches off, so that cell keeps growing and dividing, growing and dividing, and becomes a tumour. Cancer. If you were standing in a factory and you saw a machine on the assembly line going haywire like that, you'd throw a monkey wrench into it so it got busy chomping on the wrench instead. That's how a lot of medicine works today: you come up with a monkey wrench to throw at the protein and turn it off when it's going haywire."

But a new medicine shouldn't interfere with other proteins that are working just fine. It should zero in on the problem protein and leave the others alone. A molecule that's both potent and selective is the proverbial needle in the haystack and, traditionally, researchers have only been able to find them by picking through the haystack manually, laboriously testing one molecule after another in the lab.

Physical experimentation is expensive and enormously time-consuming; for every successful discovery, there are many more wild goose chases and dead ends. "Boeing doesn't build a thousand different kinds of airplane wing and then test them to see which ones crash," observes Heifets. "They use a computer to simulate how they'll fly, and only when the computer indicates that wing 212 will be quiet and keep the plane up do they actually build it and test it in a wind tunnel. They build a few wings, not a thousand."

Atomwise aims to do the same thing with drug discovery: using computer models of proteins and drug molecules, the company simulates interactions to predict which molecules merit further exploration in lab tests. Computation is exponentially faster than physical experimentation; while it might take researchers five months to test 2,500 molecules, Atomwise can test one million in a single day. Physical experimentation still needs to occur, but, says Heifets, "We can say, 'Don't even bother with those molecules, they're not going to be effective—try testing these other ones instead.' And that means that the pipeline to a useful drug, which is on average about fifteen years right now, will be shorter."

When Heifets and his Canadian co-founders, Alexander Levy and Dr. Izhar Wallach, realized in 2012 that they could commercialize the predictive technology they were creating, they started looking for financial backing in Canada. "It was quite difficult," Heifets says mildly. Impossible, actually: not one VC was willing to invest in a company that proposed to use artificial intelligence (AI) to predict which medicines would be effective. "One investor said, 'People tried to do this twenty years ago. What's different now?'" Heifets resisted the urge to say, "Gee, let me pull out my cellphone and google that." He figured that if he had to point out that technology had advanced some in the last twenty years, this was probably not the right investor for his venture.

But other Canadian VCs were equally skeptical. "I understand skepticism," Heifets concedes, "because we're building something that any number of people have said cannot be built. But no one thought a computer could beat a human chess player or Go player, either. And when Captain Kirk talked to his computer and the computer talked back, that was considered science fiction too, something that would never actually happen. Every new techno-logical advance 'can't possibly be done' until it's actually done, and then the story becomes, 'It was obvious and inevitable that this advance was going to happen.'"

For several years, Atomwise limped along, subsisting on research grants. Luckily, the company also got free office space and "really fantastic support," Heifets says, from the Impact Centre, a University of Toronto incubator for science-oriented ventures. But without capital, the company could not grow. "You can't bootstrap when what you're doing requires massive computing power," he says. "This isn't the kind of research you can do on a laptop—you'd have to have started before the pyramids were built." And to develop its technol-ogy, the company needed to hire more computational biologists and machine-learning experts, but there was no money to pay them. "You can't say to someone, 'Come work for us, and in four months we'll know whether we're getting another grant and if we can pay you.'"

Then, a breakthrough: Atomwise applied to and was accepted by Y Combinator, the premier Silicon Valley accelerator for early-stage start-ups. By the time the three-month programme ended in June 2015, Atomwise had raised almost US$6.3 million from some of the heaviest hitters in the Valley. Heifets even had to say no to some VCs who wanted in on the seed round, which felt "surreal. Turning down million-dollar cheques is something grad school didn't prepare me for."

The company hadn't been looking to move to the Bay Area, but now had to choose: return to Toronto, where they had no investors, or stay? The decision wasn't difficult.

In Canada, Atomwise was a dubious proposition unworthy of funding. In California, Atomwise is on the leading edge of a field that holds the promise of revolutionizing drug discovery.

Why were Canadian VCs unwilling to bet on the company? Heifets has a theory: "It's very hard to tell whether a company will succeed, so it's always a good idea to wait another week, and then another, until there's proof that something will work. There's not a lot of competition in Canada because there aren't many VCs, so you don't have to worry that someone else will snap up a deal. You can afford to wait and see—the deal will still be there next week. When there's no competition, the appetite for risk is lower."

But entrepreneurs who need capital can't wait and see. They have to go look for money, and they're more likely to find it in Silicon Valley, Heifets thinks, because "competition creates a sense of urgency. There's fear of missing out. If you wait another week, someone else might close the deal." Competition fundamentally changes the perception of the risk. In Canada, the risk is that you back a company that fails; in the US, the risk is that you fail to back a company that succeeds and makes your competitor wealthy. It's obvious which country is more hospitable to first-time entre-preneurs with big, bold, disruptive ideas. "The attitude is just very different," says Heifets. "In the US, one of my first meetings was with an investor who said, 'You know, twenty years ago I funded two companies that were doing something like what you're trying to do.' But unlike the Canadian investor, he viewed the fact that people had already tried to do this as a plus. He said, 'Maybe now is the right time to try again.'" That investor was Timothy Draper, founder of Draper Fisher Jurvetson, a top-tier VC firm.

Would Atomwise have stayed in Canada had funding been available? Heifets doesn't hesitate. "Definitely. I don't think we would have even questioned it. The universities are fantastic and have great people in the niches we need. There's a depth of Canadian expertise in machine learning because Canada funded this research when nobody else would. And no one in their right mind would choose to start a family in San Francisco—it's just too expensive. Toronto is a much nicer place to live if you've got kids."

Still, he doesn't sound as though he plans to return any time soon. He's focused on creating a high-growth company, and the Bay Area is an easier place to do that, a place where it's perfectly normal to say something like, "We are working to create the future, and of course we'd like the company to be worth a billion dollars someday." But Heifets sounds perfectly Canadian, American passport notwithstanding, when he adds, "If we fail to do that and still find some cures, or even advance the fundamental science, I'll be happy." He sounds pretty happy already when he talks about the company's recent work on multiple sclerosis. "So we found this molecule and identified computationally that it had more than eight million compounds, and told the researchers, 'Test these fifty.' Of those, nine hit their target, and the researchers selected one to put into mice. On our website we have pictures of a mouse that looks dead from the severity of its MS symptoms and a mouse that was injected with the compound we helped to find, and it looks totally healthy. Getting results like that feels great."

Atomwise is working on more than a dozen different disease areas now, ranging from cancer to rare genetic disorders, and if it succeeds in helping to isolate even one cure, it will be a truly revolutionary business—a testament to the excellence of the top-notch education its founders received at a publicly funded Canadian university, which also provided great, publicly funded incubation to help the company get up and running. But though it was born in Canada, Atomwise is already thoroughly American. Essentially, we gift-wrapped some talented entrepreneurs in tax dollars and shipped them down to the Valley to create jobs and wealth for Americans.

When Canadians start disruptive companies that have the potential to shake up whole industries, they need American-sized funding. Canadian VCs, even those who embrace risk, can't provide it; their funds are too small. But the Canadian government could—if, instead of spreading incentives around evenly, like so much peanut butter, it doubled down on companies with the greatest potential to win.

That's what we do with elite athletes: the Own the Podium (OTP) programme allocates funding to train and prepare Olympians and Paralympians based on their chances of winning medals. The ones with the best odds get the lion's share of the cash, and everyone else gets very little. This "targeted excellence" approach is not at all egalitarian, as the programme's critics have noted. Some worry that athletes in sports that don't get much funding will never have the opportunity to rise to the top; others are concerned that the next generation of athletes is being short-changed and underdeveloped. Still others argue that the emphasis on winning will reduce average Canadians' willingness to participate in sports. Thomas Hall, who took bronze in the sprint canoe event at the 2008 Olympic Games, goes further: he believes that

OTP's approach is "antithetical to Canadian values," which, in his view, are all about inclusion, not excellence. The OTP programme, Hall wrote in 2016, is unfair because "not all athletes, and not all sports, are benefiting. OTP is a short-term funding strategy that gives low priority to any sport, or athlete, unlikely to yield a dividend of gold, silver, or bronze on the country's 'investment.'"

Most Canadians aren't losing sleep over this, though. They don't want to go back to the old days, when funding was more "fair." They want more medals. And OTP delivers them. Pre-OTP, Canada hosted the Olympics twice without our athletes winning a single gold medal. At the Vancouver Games in 2010, the first test of the six-year-old programme, Canada led the world's gold medal count: fourteen, a record for any country at a single Winter Games. Afterwards, according to pollsters, 95 percent of Canadians were happy with the country's performance. No wonder: Canada had set a wildly ambitious goal—to dominate competitions between the best athletes on the planet, despite having a smaller pool of talent to draw from than many other countries—and achieved it.

What if we took the same approach with entrepreneurs?

Entrepreneurs are not athletes, of course. But that's exactly why we should care a whole lot more about their performance. In business, the difference between winning and losing is measured not in hundredths of a second but in thousands of jobs, hundreds of millions of dollars in corporate tax revenue, and, in some cases, the life and death of cities and even whole industries. What's at stake is not national pride but sustainable prosperity—and a mind-blowing number of taxpayer dollars, on the order of a hundred times greater than the $70 million that OTP helps parcel out annually. As it stands, we are spending a fortune to *not* own the podium, even before you factor in the potential losses in terms of wealth and jobs when Canadian companies are starved of resources and therefore unable to grow. (We have some idea of the magnitude of those losses because most really ambitious entrepreneurs don't throw in the towel—like Heifets, they leave and set up shop elsewhere.)

Bizarrely, though, there is a reluctance to acknowledge that just as not every athlete is a Jennifer Heil or Penny Oleksiak, not every founder is a Joe Mimran or Lorne Abony. The idea of the government "picking winners" alarms a lot of people. Most fret that bureaucrats will botch the job and back the wrong horses. Others have a more self-interested reason to oppose the idea: if the criteria for disbursing "free money" changed, they might no longer receive handouts.

And what about fairness? Is it really fair for one company or entrepreneur to get more funding than another? Maybe not. But scrupulous fairness has become ridiculously unfair to taxpayers, who have a right to expect a decent return on their investment in the form of Canadian gazelles and global leaders. "Governments may be bad at picking winners, but overgenerous tax credits allow any loser to pick the taxpayers' pockets," observes David Naylor, the former president of the University of Toronto who served on the Jenkins panel.

An egalitarian approach to funding works about as well with entrepreneurs as it did with athletes, which is to say, not very. Victories are achieved despite governmental policies, not because of them. High-growth tech companies such as Shopify and Hootsuite aren't winning on the world stage because they got SR&ED credits (though surely they did). They're winning because they're more innovative and productive and they're not afraid to go toe to toe with the best companies in the world. They're winning because they actually compete.

And that is what's fundamentally wrong with the government's approach to innovation: if you want to stimulate more of it, you have to stimulate competition, which requires more than "free money" but almost certainly costs a lot less in the long term. First, you need a funding process that is itself competitive, and where stronger applicants with better chances of growth get more money. Second, you need really strong domestic competition policies that are enforced, swiftly and vigorously, so that incumbents cannot squash the little guys—or shoot the gazelles, like WIND, which couldn't even count on the federal government to enforce its own policies on tower sharing and roaming. Third, you need to encourage foreign direct investment, particularly in sectors that are dominated by oligopolies and where consumers are being gouged. Just think what would happen if consumers had more choice because, say, a new carrier with substantial foreign backing were allowed to fly domestic Canadian routes, or foreign telcos could set up shop here (the latter won't happen any time soon, though, because international operators certainly took notice when WIND's foreign investors were ridden out of the country on a rail). Some Canadian companies might fail. But the rest would start experimenting and innovating like mad to try to hang on to or gain market share. And then they might start exporting their goods and services too, vigorously attempting to become international powers rather than big, slow fish in a small pond.

Small businesses need what Olympic athletes need—the best and most advanced training, as well as funding that targets and rewards excellence—in order to have a decent shot of winning on the world stage. But we don't need to create a Ministry of Winning, staffed by bureaucrats with no private sector experience. Own the Podium didn't pluck a few mandarins from behind their desks in Ottawa and pack them off to the slopes to hand-pick the most promising giant slalom skiers. It's a non-profit organization that operates at arm's length from the government, though it receives public funding (and private funding too). It's run by high-performance sports advisers and data analysts, not government bureaucrats who've never thrown a javelin. OTP replaced a patchwork-quilt approach to funding elite sports with one that "prioritizes and determines investment strategies for National Sport Organizations" with a laser-sharp focus on excellence and outcomes.

The government doesn't have to pick winners in business. It can create an OTP-like organization to do that, one that streamlines and centralizes funding, eliminates waste and cronyism, and ruthlessly adjudicates excellence. As it happens, designing such an organization would not require endless studies or costly commissions and consultations. The blueprint already exists. It's neatly laid out in the fifth chapter of the Jenkins panel report.

The panel's key recommendation: consolidate the sprawling mess of innovation programmes into a single, streamlined Industrial Research and Innovation Council (IRIC)—and for God's sake, don't let the government run it directly. Make it an arm's-length funding and delivery agency, like the ones that work so well in the UK, Australia and New Zealand. IRIC would depoliticize innovation by having smart business and technical people provide clear direction on where funds might usefully flow—and call bullshit on phony projects that waste taxpayers' dollars. Among other things, IRIC would devise and implement a federal business innovation talent strategy, eliminate waste and overlaps, establish a single application portal for funding, introduce vouchers that qualifying businesses could use to defray the costs of commercialization services from approved providers—and track outcomes like crazy. But as with so many other eminently sensible reports crafted by teams of experts who did their research, the Jenkins panel's recommendations are still gathering dust on a shelf in Ottawa. Yes, a few recommendations were implemented, piecemeal, and the Trudeau government has more recently taken some steps to review and consolidate R & D programs. But no arm's-length agency like IRIC, with its focus on accountability, exists.

An organization like IRIC could also administer a growth trust like the one proposed by Dan Debow, a ferociously smart tech entrepreneur and extremely active angel investor who's more or less the patron saint of an extraordinary number of Canadian start-ups. Debow is the kind of guy who teaches law in his spare time and doesn't suffer fools gladly, but his idea is really simple: the government should provide matching loans to private companies that manage to attract venture capital from accredited investors, whether the VCs are Canadian or American. Let's say a Canadian VC invests $500,000 in a start-up; after performing due diligence on the VC, the government would also invest $500,000—to be repaid when the company is sold, goes public or just feels like getting rid of its debts. Just one catch: if the company moves its headquarters out of Canada, it has to repay the loan. Immediately.

That thumbnail sketch doesn't do justice to the scope of Debow's proposal, but it should give you some idea of its merits. In his plan, the government doesn't pick winners, the market does—and the government piles on, so the companies can grow faster. Although winners are notoriously difficult to identify ahead of time, Scott Shane points out that "one dimension on which they can be identified is their source of financing": venture-backed companies tend to be winners. Currently, 43 percent of all public companies in the US that were founded after 1979 received venture backing; these include household names such as Google, Amazon and Starbucks. Venture-backed companies employ millions of people, they invest billions more than other companies in R & D, and their market capitalization is sky-high.

If our government provided matching funds—not so hard to finance if you take SR&ED credits away from really big Canadian companies that don't need them in the first place—it would almost certainly embolden Canadian VCs to take more risks, and attract more American investors, too, because their money would go twice as far in Canada. Innovative Canadian companies would be better capitalized, more likely to grow—and more likely to remain on this side of the border. There would, no doubt, be problems with this system too, but it's hard to imagine they could be worse than the problem we have right now: we're spending a fortune and have very little to show for it.

There's a good reason other countries don't rely so heavily on indirect measures to spark R & D. On their own, indirect measures don't work—and they are especially unlikely to yield the hoped-for results in a country like Canada, where, historically, companies have not needed to innovate in order to be profitable. To overcome the inertia that has resulted from a lack of domestic competition, we need to stir in some strategic government procurement that favours home-grown innovative companies. And to squash the junior-partner mentality, whereby it's fine to let the US do all the heavy lifting in terms of innovation, we need to light a fire under a new generation of risk-taking entrepreneurs, using a lot more direct investment in companies and risk-sharing with VCs. Whether the answer is IRIC or matching funding or some other mechanism, we need to find a way to provide more direct funding to those entrepreneurs with the best shot of owning the podium, and we need to do it right away.

A note to naysayers who believe that dismantling the existing, fragmented system for public funding of R & D and creating a new, more focused, OTP-like entity cannot be done, or at least cannot be done quickly: the Own the Podium programme was created in response to a 2004 report whose set of bracing recommendations was implemented more or less immediately. Even though the report called for radical strategic change. Even though existing stakeholders—the national sports federations—were required to cede some power and a lot of control to a brand new organization. Even though people who were used to receiving funding were summarily informed that they wouldn't be getting much of it anymore. Even though the federal government was required to double its investment in sport. Even though some people thought the whole idea of giving more talented people more funding was darned unfair.

The gears of government can shift very quickly when there's sufficient political will and the cause is considered important. Remember how quickly the government said no when our largest trading partner was trying to convince us to lock arms and march into Iraq? Look how quickly the government decided to admit forty thousand Syrian refugees, a move that is forecast to cost at least one billion dollars.

It's hard to imagine any cause more important for our country's future than winning economically. In order to protect the environment, preserve the social safety net, and promote education, immigration, health, human rights and everything else we believe in, we need to help good, small companies become great, growing ones. That means scrapping incentives that aren't working and doubling down on the programmes and institutions that deliver results—which we should be tracking and quantifying, by measuring not just inputs but actual outcomes in terms of jobs and revenue.

Public policies that encourage entrepreneurial activity simply for the sake of it, as though entrepreneurship rather than economic growth is the goal, aren't good for Canada.

If we want to increase the competitiveness of our businesses, it makes no sense to focus on a funding approach where no one even has to compete to receive funding, and no one cares whether recipients win or lose. Nor does it make sense to lavish R & D handouts on big businesses, which become addicted to them, when small businesses are the ones that really need help. We should be trying to identify those with the highest potential for growth, and then giving them the kind of targeted, direct assistance that Own the Podium provides to athletes.

It's probably easier to determine which entrepreneurs have the greatest likelihood of success than it is to figure out which athletes are most likely to win medals. You can look at their experience and their business plans, and what industries they're going into and whether those industries are already crowded, and whether they've actively attempted real R & D, and whether they're interested in exporting and have a plan as to how to go about it, and whether they have leadership and managerial ability, and, very importantly, whether they've managed to attract investment from anyone other than friends and family. You can also require them to compete for funding, vouchers and/or assistance, then track their outcomes in terms of growth and productivity, and adjust accordingly.

As Canada proved at the Vancouver Games, size is no barrier to excellence. Small countries can field winning teams. The same is true in business: Canada can field a team of new businesses that are productive, growth oriented and internationally competitive—but not by handing out the world's most expensive participation ribbons to every entrepreneur who wants one. That approach does not serve our collective long-term interests. We are competing in a global contest with incredibly high stakes, and ultimately, we are all on the same team: Team Canada. We need to give our strongest and fastest competitors the means and the right incentives to go for gold—not just so they can win, but so all of us can.

CHAPTER 4

The Aspiration Gap

O il, timber and potash are not Canada's most important natural resources. Talent is.

Canadian kids are really smart, right up there with Asian kids, according to the comprehensive exams the OECD administers to fifteen-year-olds in seventy-two countries. Canada's teens rank 2nd in the world in reading, 7th in science and 10th in math— miles ahead of Americans, who place 24th, 25th and 35th, respectively. Also important: poor kids here do much better on these tests than poor kids just about anywhere else in the world, posting results closer to those of rich kids. Our school system is obviously very good.

So are our post-secondary institutions, though they have slipped somewhat—the University of Toronto, the top Canadian institution in the most recent *Times Higher Education* world rankings, was number seventeen in 2010 but has fallen to twenty-second place; of the others, only the University of British Columbia and

McGill are still ranked in the top 100. But Canadian universities are still among the very best in the world in some broad domains of research: information and communications technology (ICT), physics and astronomy, health and related life sciences, and natural resources. Canadian polytechnics, which are industry-facing colleges focused on advanced technical and technological education, also punch far above their weight, with impressive outputs in terms of applied research. Every year, students and faculty crank out hundreds of prototypes and conduct thousands of R & D projects for small and medium-sized businesses.

So why don't more smart Canadian kids with good educations grow up to become entrepreneurs who build innovative companies that propel the country forward?

Because they don't have enough role models or networking opportunities, says Reza Satchu, a serial entrepreneur and founding partner of Alignvest Capital Management. "Kids at Harvard and Yale aren't necessarily any smarter than kids at Queen's or McGill, but they have a big advantage: they're exposed to superstars, and that gives them an expanded sense of their own possibilities. American kids don't just aspire to write a book. They aspire to win the Pulitzer Prize. In their classes, they've actually met Pulitzer Prize winners, so the goal seems achievable. It might seem like a small difference, but it's huge. It changes everything about how you view the world."

To try to close that aspiration gap, Satchu co-founded Next 36 in 2010, along with economist Ajay Agrawal, social entrepreneur Claudia Hepburn and Tim Hodgson, formerly the CEO of Goldman Sachs Canada and a special adviser to the Bank of Canada. The idea behind the programme is that if you identify thirty-six entrepreneurial undergrads, surround them with superstar mentors and academics, shower them with resources and then demand that they perform, they will build great tech companies. Each year, the non-profit charity, funded by the likes of Galen Weston, Jimmy Pattison and Paul Desmarais Sr., brings students to Toronto for a summer of intensive training by heavy hitters on Bay Street and hoodie-wearing tech founders alike. While this is going on, and for six months beforehand, the undergrads compete in teams to build companies. It's a phenomenally ambitious programme, and Globalive has been a corporate sponsor since its inception.

As with Own the Podium, N36 is all about going for gold. It's unCanadian, in other words, Satchu says, unapologetically. "Our selection process is not very politically correct. The goal isn't to pick kids who are a 3 and try to get them to 6. We pick winners, kids we think will get to 7 or 8 regardless, and then we try to get them to 10, because you need to be a 10 to build the next Facebook or Instagram. That's what Canada is missing: people at the far right end of the tail who can build companies that create massive amounts of value. Those businesses then lift the boats for everyone. They create a job for the person who's a 3 that will lift him to a 6 or 7. One reason we don't have those companies is that so many of these kids who are 7s and 8s in their third and fourth year of university leave. We can't chain them to Canada, but at Next 36 we go through a rigorous process to identify them and set them on their way and help them realize they can stay and build great companies right here."

N36, then, is not a ticket for a free ride. The recipients of all this largesse are meant to feel a sense of obligation, and be sufficiently dazzled by the star power of mentors and donors that they choose to stay in Canada and pay it forward. They are also expected to work their tails off. Despite the swanky receptions and opportunities to rub elbows with the country's business elite, this is a nationalistic boot camp, designed to toughen kids up so they're ready to play for Canada in the big leagues.

Satchu sets the tone in his entrepreneurship class, where he plays drill sergeant with the flair of a showman, tossing out latecomers and zeroing in on students' weaknesses. The kids who dread public speaking will be called on to present, again and again; the showboats will be humbled. "There's no point babying them," he says with a shrug. "In the real world, entrepreneurs aren't coddled. They have to address their weaknesses and correct them." When he's harsh, in other words, it's for the students' own good. And they seem to love him for it: when Satchu taught the same course in the same way at the University of Toronto—he volunteered to do so, and accepted no pay—it had a 100 percent retake rate, meaning that all his students said they'd happily sign up to take the class all over again.

For many students, the demanding and competitive nature of Next 36 is a whole new experience. "The emphasis in the Canadian school system is on making students feel happy and safe, and the trade-off is that you don't push them or encourage them to push themselves and build confidence," says co-founder Ajay Agrawal, a professor at the University of Toronto who is the programme's academic director. In a lot of Canadian schools, kids learn that pretty good is good enough—preferable, even, to a winner-takes-it-all competition, because no one has to lose. Agrawal argues, "Competition doesn't need to alienate people. It can help you realize, 'To compete, I've got to get better at math.'" And, he continues, competition stokes ambition. "You see that clearly in the way top students think about their prospects. If you ask top engineering students in Toronto what their ambition is, they'll say something like, 'I'm going to lead the AI group at Google.' The same students at MIT will say, 'I'm going to start the next Google.'"

According to co-founder Claudia Hepburn, the CEO of Immigrant Access Fund Canada, which, like N36, focuses on developing human capital, "A big part of our mission was to show young Canadians that they could and should dream big, that competing is about making a choice to step up and set your sights high. We wanted them to define themselves as people who aspire to solve significant problems, build things, and compete with the best and brightest." The first step, she continues, was "to change the way young Canadians thought about themselves, then surround them with a peer group that also identified themselves as innovators, and surround that group with the supports to try to grow."

Canadian kids need all this scaffolding because they are discouraged, both explicitly and implicitly, from taking risks. "There's a whole culture built around fear of failure in Canada, and it prevents people from even trying to do something ambitious because they're so worried it won't work out," explains Satchu. "It starts in elementary school and is in full flower by high school. A great example is the difference in the university admissions process between Canada and the US. There, marks are only one factor universities consider. They also look at what you care about, what you've achieved in your extracurriculars, your leadership and philanthropic activities, how well you tell your story in the application essay, how engaging you are when they interview you, how you did on the SAT, what your references say about you. American kids know that to get to Stanford or Harvard, they've got to think outside the box and do *big* things, take risks, so they stand out. Here, that's totally discouraged, because the only thing Canadian universities care about is your high school marks. It doesn't matter what kind of person you are, or what your potential is. It's all about your average. So if you're a kid who wants to go to university, you're not going to take a course you might bomb, or pick up a bunch of extracurriculars that might stretch you. The system is structured to discourage creativity, entrepreneurship and leadership, and to penalize risk-taking really harshly."

One consequence is that Canadian kids also don't learn *how* to fail: how to pick yourself up, apply what you've learned and try again. One of the unspoken goals of N36, then, is to teach kids how to survive failure—the majority of start-ups do fail—and wear it as a badge of honour, so they're not afraid to take even bigger risks in the future.

While invention does not necessarily entail risk—the very long list of accidental discoveries includes X-rays, dynamite and vulcanized rubber—innovation always does. Commercializing inventions and ideas, and finding markets for them, is speculative. Failure is a very real possibility. To get from invention to actual value-added innovation, the kind that drives productivity and boosts GDP, requires both a willingness to risk falling flat on your face and a preternatural determination to succeed.

As every N36 graduate knows, Satchu's preferred definition of entrepreneurship is "the relentless pursuit of opportunity without regard to resources currently controlled." The motto neatly sums up his own backstory too. The relentless pursuit of opportunity is what motivated his parents to leave Mombasa, Kenya, in 1976. Prime Minister Pierre Trudeau had, at the Aga Khan's urging, opened Canada's doors to twenty thousand Ismaili immigrants. Members of the Shia branch of Islam and predominantly South Asian, Ismailis in East Africa were fleeing prejudice and persecution whipped up by Idi Amin. The Satchu family didn't have a soft landing in Toronto. At first, they camped out in a relative's basement in Scarborough. Taunted about his accent (too British), skin colour (too brown) and size (he'd skipped a grade), Reza felt he'd never fit in in Canada.

But even when he felt like a loser, the culture within his own family was all about reaching for the stars, and that made all the difference. His father impressed upon him that being an immigrant was actually an advantage: all newcomers to Canada are forced to reinvent themselves, and along the way they develop a talent for taking risks and persevering through disappointment. Having to work harder was, in his father's view, a benefit, not a burden, because it increased the likelihood of success. His mother taught him to dream big. "You're going to Harvard," she confidently informed both her kids, though neither she nor her husband had attended university. When relatives visited, she took them on tours of Toronto's posh neighbourhoods, airily announcing as they passed one sprawling mansion after another, "One day, my sons will live in houses like that." She was right on both counts—and so was her husband, who, less than a decade after arriving in Canada, had carved out a highly successful career in real estate.

Today, Satchu feels duty bound to share the lessons he learned from his parents with "more fortunate" Canadian kids who've never had to struggle—if they're hungry enough to make it into the Next 36, where first- and second-generation immigrants seem to predominate. His motivation for founding the charity is less noblesse oblige than straight payback: he owes Canada. Pierre Trudeau changed everything for his family just by opening the door to opportunity. Doing the same thing for thirty-six kids a year has put a sizable dent in his psychic debt.

In 2016, more than 1,100 undergraduates applied to Next 36 from forty-four Canadian universities and colleges, as well as top American schools such as Harvard, Cornell and Wharton. In December, the seventy-six semifinalists converged on a hotel in downtown Toronto for selection weekend, which starts with a carefully orchestrated frenzy of lectures and back-to-back interviews with business leaders such as Jeannette Wiltse, the CFO of Relay Ventures, and Ted Reeser, president of Celco Inc., a distributor of commercial food service equipment. Applicants also interview one another, scouting for potential team members, and, whether they know it or not, they are being assessed throughout the day by programme staff and mentors.

In the early evening, interviewers' scores are tabulated, informal observers' comments arc collated, and the top fifteen or so applicants automatically earn spots. The fate of the rest is decided in a window-less deliberation room where, over chicken and Caesar salad, a handful of judges debates candidates' merits, with occasional input from Next 36 staff.

Aside from anything else, it's great theatre, both because the stakes for applicants are so high and because the judges themselves are so different. While Satchu is a world-class schmoozer, warm, conspiratorial and prone to acerbic asides, Professor Agrawal is coolly cerebral, understated and imperturbable, speaking in polished paragraphs and measured tones. The judges also weigh candidates' merits differently. Janet Bannister, a low-key, keenly observant general partner at Real Ventures and the founder of Kijiji, has zero tolerance for intellectual sloppiness. Andrea Matheson, the convivial and polished former CEO of Sapphire Digital Health Solutions, puts a premium on communication skills. Thoughtful and steady, Peter Carrescia, formerly at OMERS Ventures and now an executive at Wave, which develops online software and financial services for small businesses, is concerned above all about fairness.

"It looks like there are about thirty applicants we should call back to plead their case," Carrescia said, squinting at the aggregate scores projected on a screen at the far end of the room. A collective groan: six o'clock has already come and gone. "We don't want to let someone really good slip through the cracks."

"Well, let's bring them in two by two, not one at a time," Agrawal responded, perhaps mindful of the deliberations in 2011, which ended at midnight, with at least one judge prone on a couch. "It's more efficient."

"More competitive, too," added Satchu. "If they can't compete, they don't belong in this programme."

And then the horse trading began, with Agrawal the de facto chief justice. Satchu wanted to call back a student who had an idea for a social networking app, but, after consulting her notes, Bannister crisply nixed the guy: "He has no idea of competitors in the space. He just hasn't done his homework." Later, when she pushed to call back a business student with borderline scores from other judges, Matheson lowered the boom: "So arrogant. He'd pull a whole team down." Students with high GPAs are not shoo-ins (several with distinctly unimpressive marks made the final cut). Nor are those who have started revenue-generating businesses (those with failed start-ups, who could weave a compelling narrative around what they'd learned, had just as good a chance). The judges are looking for a paradoxical mixture: applicants who are strong-minded yet coachable, confident of their own abilities and generous about their peers' strengths, and possessed of an indefinable "it" factor recognizable only to the trained eye.

When the callback list was finalized and pairs of applicants were summoned to the airless room, now uncomfortably warm and redolent of garlic, Satchu started off cordially enough. "This is your opportunity to tell us why you should be in the programme," he told one engineer. After a moment of silence, he added, "Because I saw no evidence of entrepreneurial ability." Haltingly, the engineer explained that he had all kinds of business ideas, but hadn't yet had the time to pursue any of them.

"That's an awful answer," Agrawal said pleasantly. "Maybe you should tell us what's interesting about the work you are doing now." The applicant rambled about his courses for a minute or two, visibly wilting, while the applicant standing beside him looked increasingly alarmed. When it was his turn to speak, he babbled energetically about a business he'd started on campus, until Janet Bannister smiled brightly and said, "Thank you." After the pair left the room, the judges unanimously rejected the engineer.

Professor Agrawal, however, wasn't so sure about the other guy. "Doesn't he remind you a little of Sameer?" he asked. Matheson said she could see the resemblance to one of the programme's alumni, but Satchu shook his head emphatically. "No. Sameer is charismatic, but that kid . . ." He didn't need to finish the sentence. The name had already been crossed off the list.

When Reza Satchu first met Sameer Dhar, during selection weekend in December 2013, he put a question mark beside his name. "What I worried about initially is that he's very charming, so he can coast. He can do nothing, and people will like him. I've met lots of charming kids, and they usually don't accomplish much. They're not willing to do the hard work, since everything comes so easily to them. So my concern with Sameer was, 'Will the kid actually do the work?'"

"What's special about you?" is how he'd kicked off their one-on-one interview. Some kids respond to that challenge by crumpling, but Dhar, in his final year of a bachelor of commerce degree at the University of Alberta, was unfazed. He felt he *had* done something pretty special: in high school, he'd co-founded a charity to help Edmonton families who'd fallen on hard times, giving them months' worth of necessities so they could get back on their feet. The poverty relief effort, Geomeer, was still going strong and had raised close to $1 million.

It was an answer that would have made an Ivy League admissions officer swoon, but Satchu was unmoved. "That's not exactly entrepreneurial," he said flatly.

Dhar, who is prone to fiery speeches, wisely held his tongue. He knew better than to debate the definition of entrepreneurship with Reza Satchu, who, along with his brother, sold his first company for US$925 million when he was thirty-one years old. Nor did he point out that Next 36, also a charity, was in his opinion pretty entrepreneurial. No point pissing off the head honcho. He *needed* one of those thirty-six spots. A summer internship at

Morgan Stanley had crushed his long-time dream of becoming an investment banker; he'd discovered he just wasn't that interested in making a killing. Dhar wanted to make a difference, as he had with Geomeer, but he didn't have the first clue how to go about it in a way that would enable him to make a decent living too. Next 36 seemed like a good place to figure that out, so, instead of arguing that being an effective do-gooder requires the same scrappy resourcefulness as founding a start-up, he told Satchu what he'd learned about leadership by running Geomeer.

Satchu was on the fence. The kid seemed to have the makings of a good leader, but his summer jobs, all in financial services, were cookie-cutter traditional. He'd never tried to start his own business, like a lot of other N36 applicants, and he was a little too sunnily confident for Satchu's liking. He wanted Dhar to understand that he was a long shot. Maybe that would light a fire under his ass.

Later in the evening, when Dhar was summoned to the deliberation room for a grilling, there was a flash of heat all right. He mounted an impassioned defence—of one of the other callbacks, a champion curler with a background the judges found insufficiently entrepreneurial. "The perseverance and grit that's required to get to his level in curling are exactly the qualities an entrepreneur needs!" Dhar protested. "Just because someone hasn't tried to start a tech venture doesn't mean he doesn't have the potential to be a good entrepreneur." The judges bought his argument—the last part, anyway. The curler didn't make the cut. Dhar did.

When acceptances were announced the following day, he barely had time to feel relieved, much less celebrate. Within minutes, three-person teams formed to start the work of coming up with tech-oriented business ideas to pitch the following day. Since Dhar didn't know anything about tech, he and another finance major were thrown together with someone who did. Together, they came up with a pitch for a baby monitor that could sound an alert when, say, a diaper change was in order. Wearable sensors attached to the infant's clothing would relay a signal to the monitor . . . somehow.

It's the kind of idea that sounds good when you have no first-hand experience with babies and are unaware of their talent for letting the world know when they're uncomfortable. But once selection weekend was over and the team had dispersed to their respective campuses, they began analyzing different ways to use wearable technology. Their focus quickly shifted to the other end of life, for business reasons: old people are a huge and growing market, and also an underserved one. All they had to do was figure out how to make seniors' lives better.

Dhar was in charge of market research, so, back in Edmonton, he started knocking on doors, seeking input from geriatricians and operators of seniors' homes. "It wasn't scientific. I just asked them to tell me what their pain points were. And that's how we were introduced to the idea of incontinence," says Dhar, who didn't know what the word meant the first time he heard it. Nursing home staff filled him in: 80 percent of nursing home residents can't control their urination. At night, caregivers wake incontinent residents every two hours in order to change their diapers, needed or not, because they have no way of knowing whether a slumbering resident is wet. It was the worst part of their job: unpleasant, time-consuming and often unnecessary—a big deal when a single caregiver may be responsible for twenty or more residents. Not uncommonly, nursing staff told him, they'd wake someone who was perfectly dry but who then became confused and disoriented, and might, a few minutes later, wet himself. But the resident would have to wait two uncomfortable, sleepless hours until it was his turn to be changed again. The staff could see the toll the nighttime routine took on residents, especially those suffering from dementia and Alzheimer's, who coped best when they were well rested.

124

In January 2014, the problem seemed straightforward enough to Dhar's team: nursing staff didn't have the data to determine when to change residents. The solution seemed obvious: attach a sensor to the inside of a diaper. Once moisture was detected, a transmitter would alert caregivers electronically, so they'd know a change was required. No more waking people needlessly, no more wasting staff time. The team tossed around different names for their company. Smart-ePants. Sensopeace. They wanted something that alluded both to the sensor and to their ultimate mission, which was ensuring dignity for the elderly wearer. In the end, Dhar's mother came up with the name that fit: Sensassure.

Now came the hard part: figuring out the technology, which was especially difficult since the team members who actually knew something about technology kept quitting Sensassure, to go to grad school or get a job working with someone a little less . . . *intense.* By the time Dhar had collected his diploma in Edmonton and moved to Toronto to work at the start-up full-time, in between N36 courses and seminars, he had blown through five co-founders. "I'm sure I had a part to play in that," he admits. "I felt like I cared about what we were doing more than anyone else did, and I was also way more blunt. The culture I wanted to create was based on Reza's conduct in the class setting—just being very upfront and putting all issues out there on the table. I learned from him that that's a really productive way to move the ball forward quickly—just not being afraid to challenge other people or be challenged by them."

The total-honesty approach to team management was not to everyone's taste, however, which is why the composition of the Sensassure team kept changing, and why Dhar wound up contracting out the fabrication of a cumbersome little transmitter box to a company in California. Next 36 releases up to $60,000 in funding to each start-up in stages, as certain milestones are met. Sensassure blew through $20,000 just for that little box, which Tim Ahong says he could have cobbled together in a day or two, if only he'd been on the team at that point. A third-year aerospace student at the University of Toronto, Ahong ditched his own Next 36 team in June 2014 to join Sensassure as chief technological officer, becoming the co-founder who stuck. Almost two years older than Dhar, Ahong was methodical, sardonic and unflappable—the perfect match for a high-intensity CEO. In one key respect, the two were identical: they were hell-bent on doing something meaningful. Trying to reduce the amount of time elderly people were forced to endure discomfort fit the bill a whole lot better than, say, trying to build a dating app.

Sensassure's first product iteration was a disposable peel-and-stick sensor pad that could be attached to the inside of any commercially available adult diaper, with that costly, clunky transmitter box attached to the outside, poised to send a signal to a caregiver's iPad once the sensor detected moisture inside the diaper. The get-up was less than ergonomic, as the Sensassure team knew very well. They'd all tried it out, to see whether the sensor actually worked.

"It was the initiation to Sensassure: if you're passionate enough, you'll wear a diaper and pee in it. We did it for the first time in a group, and we played the song 'Let It Go' from the movie *Frozen*," remembers Dhar. "When the chorus got to 'Let it go, let it go'—we did. I've gone to a bar in a brief, worn them to work—we all have. We had to test this thing and really understand what it felt like to wear it. Peeing in it was just an incredibly uncomfortable feeling." Their passion to make wearing a disposable brief as pleasant an experience as possible increased dramatically after these test drives.

For Dhar, this was no longer a business idea but a calling, which might make him sound insufferably high-minded, but he is that rarest of types: a cool nerd. Clean-cut, with bold black glasses and a smile that indicates familiarity with orthodontics, he is clever in a light-hearted, generous way that draws people in rather than turning them off. Nursing home administrators throw open their doors to him; crusty corporate types brighten when he asks them for money.

He won over at least one audience member when Sensassure unveiled its less-than-perfect product on Venture Day in August 2014, the big reveal of the Next 36 programme: Jeremy Dabor, a whiz-kid scientist as buttoned-down as Dhar is ebullient. A year older, Dabor had dreamed of being a doctor before realizing that sitting in a classroom at McGill didn't agree with him. After dropping out, he'd worked in San Diego and the UK on developing sequencing technology for human DNA, and then returned to Toronto to figure out what he should do next. After watching the Sensassure pitch, he knew. He went out for drinks with Dhar and Ahong and never left, becoming the company's third co-founder, chief product officer and deadpan voice of reason.

Dhar had a lot to celebrate that evening: he'd snagged the Satchu prize for best exemplifying the spirit of the programme. Awarding it, Reza couldn't resist a parting shot: "You're a risky proposition, Sameer. Fifty percent of people love you, and fifty percent think you're a used car salesman."

Everyone laughed, including Dhar. But the message wasn't lost on him. He needed to build a viable company, to prove his mentor right for giving him the prize—and to prove him wrong: more than ever, Dhar now believed that doing good could be highly entrepreneurial.

One thing that's striking about Next 36 alumni is their maturity. After all that networking and all those tough-love lectures, the graduates who exit the programme every August tend to be almost unrecognizable from the kids who stammered and blustered through interviews during selection weekend nine months earlier. But what's even more effective at smoothing out their rough edges is repeatedly bumping up against the hard limits of their own knowledge and ability, a humbling process that, for Sameer Dhar, didn't begin in earnest until the programme was over.

Even when he was casting about for a good idea and trying to figure out what a start-up should look like, he'd known that Next 36 was the pivotal and most formative experience of his life. Bay Street was out; he was an entrepreneur now (or, as he put it, a "wantrepreneur"). But, after the programme ended in August and the team was no longer surrounded by pinstriped cheerleaders singing the praises of entrepreneurship, the grimmer aspects of the road less travelled came into sharp focus.

His parents couldn't hide their disappointment and concern when he told them that he was sticking with Sensassure. Both are first-generation immigrants who've made good. His mother, a dietitian, is a manager at Alberta's provincial health authority, while his father, a mechanical engineer who earned his MBA at McGill, specializes in business transformation projects in sectors ranging from telecom to oil and gas. In India, education had been their ticket to a better life in Canada, and they had high academic expectations for both their kids. Their daughter, ten years older than Sameer, had already delivered. "She's a surgeon—a rock star in East Indian terms, because the dream is to become a doctor, engineer or lawyer. I'm the failure of the family," says Dhar, only half joking. His parents had been puzzled when, in high school, he'd served on student council and then started Geomeer: why put anything else before school work? Wholly immune to the lure of entrepreneurship, they were genuinely alarmed that their son was neither going back to school nor getting a job. What would become of him?!

Sameer Dhar began to wonder about that himself when he set out to raise seed money. The Next 36 imprimatur didn't translate into clout with angel investors; the big names in Toronto, some of whom Dhar and Ahong had met during the programme, weren't interested in what they were up to. "They were hesitant about the nursing home market in general," Dhar says. "And I had a remarkable number of people, who weren't familiar with tech investments, asking things like, 'What's your manufacturing plan?' We didn't even have a working prototype yet."

While Jeremy Dabor and Tim Ahong worked on developing one, along with Sensassure's first employee, hardware engineer Danny Porthiyas, Dhar went home to Edmonton, where at least he knew more people, so it was easier to network. When his first investor, John Ferguson, the former chairman of Suncor Energy, agreed to kick in $50,000, Dhar thought he had it made. He didn't. It took four months to raise $250,000 more, primarily in Alberta. "I knew my stuff cold, but it was really tough. I didn't have a well-established relationship base, so I had to meet with seventy-five people, at least. At the seed stage, investors are betting on the team, basically, and whether they believe their idea has market potential. We were 21- and 22-year-olds with one degree between us and no track record."

After closing the seed round in November 2014, Dhar discovered they also had no viable business. The results of an initial, tiny pilot project in an Edmonton long-term care home had been promising: the Sensassure system had reduced the amount of time residents spent in wet briefs and saved staff time. But it turned out that no one really wanted to *pay* for these kinds of improvements.

"It was a can of worms we should have opened right at the beginning: who will actually buy this thing we're making?" admits Dhar. The team hadn't really understood the funding system for long-term care in Canada, which, he says, "is not conducive to innovation. If you're an operator, there's a copay system where the government pays a significant portion and the amount the resident pays is capped by government, so your top line is completely capped. Therefore, you're working on very thin margins to begin with, and the only thing you want to pay for when it comes to innovation is direct cost savings, like having to buy fewer diapers or do less laundry. Quality-of-care types of outcomes, like the residents being more comfortable and the caregivers spending less time changing diapers, don't have an immediate impact on your bottom line, so there's no incentive to invest in them."

There was another disincentive to pursuing innovation: the lack of competition in long-term care in Canada. "There's 100 percent occupancy across the country—a net shortage of nursing home beds, actually. So everybody can talk about improving quality of care, but they don't really need to do it because there's no competition."

In December, an older and wiser potential investor gave him some advice: just pay back the $300,000 and fold the company. "'You don't want to walk around with a diaper on your head in embarrassment,' were his exact words," recalls Dhar. As it happened, it was his twenty-second birthday. He spent the day wondering whether the guy was right. But how could he tell his investors, the ones he'd pitched so confidently just weeks before, that the diaper idea was a dud? It wasn't a decision he could make on his own; his co-founders had as much on the line as he did, maybe even more. Tim Ahong had decided to stay with the start-up full-time instead of completing his final year of university, a move that hadn't delighted his parents. Jeremy Dabor, who was highly employable because of his scientific know-how and work experience, was eking out an existence on the meagre salary he took from Sensassure. To save money, the two of them were crammed into a small apartment with eight other roommates, while Dhar crashed on his sister's couch.

If Dhar and Ahong hadn't been through Next 36, they might have cut their losses at this point. But they'd learned that entrepreneurs don't retreat; they double down, pivoting and looking for new markets and product improvements until they've exhausted all options. They had been taught to view crises as opportunities, and many of the programme's mentors had described their own moments of despair as rites of passage that led to big break-throughs. So the Sensassure team decided to keep going. The worst that could happen was that they'd fail, a fate that no longer terrified them—though they did feel ill when they thought about spending their investors' hard-earned money and having nothing to show for it in the end. But failing was definitely preferable to chickening out—a course of action they knew would be far more disappointing to the people at Next 36 who'd invested so many resources in them.

So they researched whether infants might not be a better market after all, speaking to more than seventy parents of new-borns and doing a deep dive on the economics of the baby-diaper market. Or what about people with disabilities who were confined to wheelchairs? More heavy-duty research. Looking into the adult-diaper market in other countries, they cold called US long-term care operators. A glimmer of encouragement: Americans seemed a lot more excited about their idea than Canadians had been. The team figured they had to go on a road trip to find out why. Maybe it would turn out to have been a waste of time, but no one would be able to say they'd left a stone unturned.

Piling into a rented Dodge Caravan in February 2015, the three co-founders set out to meet with nursing home operators and home care agencies in nine states. They didn't have a working product; they'd already concluded that their peel-and-stick dis-posable sensor wasn't cost-effective, and nurses in the pilot project had told them that positioning the strip and the transmitter added too much time to diaper changes. So, instead, they'd created a non-functional prototype for show-and-tell purposes: a blue

SmartPatch, a reusable sensor about the size and shape of an insole, which could, in theory anyway, be attached to the exterior of any existing incontinence product. In their meetings with American long-term care operators, they explained that the sensor would determine from the outside whether a diaper was wet inside, then wirelessly relay the information to caregivers. The ask: "If we created something like this, would you pay for it?"

Maybe. Probably. Yes! American seniors' home operators were interested in improving incontinence management—and in getting a leg up on the competition. "Occupancy in long-term care in the US is about 85 percent, so each bed they can fill is important to them and there's a greater incentive to be forward-thinking," explains Dhar. And there, public funding was shifting away from fee-for-service and towards quality-of-care outcomes, creating another incentive for innovation. The litigation environment in the US also motivates operators to prove they are not just complying with regulations but seeking to outperform them.

The response was enthusiastic enough that the trio felt energized rather than exhausted by their seven-thousand-kilometre odyssey. At the end of their last meeting, with an operator in Columbia, Maryland, Dhar finally popped the question: "We'd really like to co-develop this product with you—would you let us live here for a while so we really understand your needs?"

And so it was that, three months later, Sameer Dhar, Jeremy Dabor and Tim Ahong became possibly the first individuals on the planet who were genuinely thrilled to move into a nursing home. "Cool! Let's do it," Dhar said on May 4, 2015, bounding up to the door of Lorien Harmony Hall, a Maryland assisted living community. Glancing approvingly around the expansive lobby, appointed with faux vintage street lamps and a fleet of pale-blue sofas, he remarked that the accommodations represented a significant upgrade from his sister's couch. The place was deserted and deathly quiet—9 p.m. had come and gone—so he and Dabor lowered their voices to a less exuberant register while walking down the hall to their new quarters. Each unit had a mini-kitchen, a freshly painted living room, a small bathroom and a neatly made single bed in the compact bedroom. Sweet!

Dhar's parents, back in Edmonton, were flabbergasted by the move. *This* was the best he could do with a finance degree? His friends couldn't decide if it was more hilarious that a 22-year-old was living in an old people's home or that he'd become obsessed with incontinence.

"It's not a sexy problem," Dhar concedes. "But it's a prevalent one, and when you can't take care of yourself in that way, it just strikes at your most basic sense of self-worth. Living in a nursing home, you see that people of all ages and levels of functioning want dignity. Some of the residents are fighters and therefore pains in the ass for the staff, but it's really because they're just desperately trying to preserve what little dignity they have left. And then there are people who've just succumbed to the situation and given up, and you can see how lonely and helpless they feel."

The Sensassure team no longer thought of incontinent seniors in the abstract, as potential customers. They were neighbours. And friends.

The move finally extinguished any lingering doubts Reza Satchu might have had about whether the kid was actually willing to do the work. "When Sameer told me he was going to go live in a nursing home to see if his product really worked, I was impressed," he says with something close to paternal pride. "It was a ballsy move, and a smart one, because even if Sensassure ultimately failed, he was doing exactly what we want kids to do. He was upping the ante, thinking big and going for broke."

The Next 36 founders had discovered it was not so easy to convert Canadian kids to Mark Zuckerberg's gospel of moving fast and breaking things. Some alumni had only ever mastered the first part: moving fast as soon as things started breaking—right out the door to "safe" jobs in investment banking and consulting. One unintended consequence of the programme's marquee status, Claudia Hepburn points out, is that it had started to attract some people "who just wanted to put 'the Next 36' on their resumé" and hobnob with the rich and powerful mentors. They didn't value "what the programme aimed to teach, or the community we were hoping to build," and, in any event, had no intention of taking the road less travelled.

But while there are climbers in every N36 cohort, there are also, always, alumni such as Sameer Dhar and Tim Ahong, who drink the Kool-Aid and exit the programme determined to go all out to try to make their ventures successful. Perhaps a few would have started their own businesses even if they hadn't gone through the programme, but not very many, and definitely not so soon. Between student loans, family pressure, needing to make money and generalized am-I-really-smart-enough-to-do-this anxiety, there are a lot of good reasons to choose a safer path—reasons that are particularly compelling if you haven't met a lot of entrepreneurs you can relate to and haven't had the benefit of a crash course in building a start-up. Pre–Next 36, the wunderkinds who created awesome tech ventures existed only in Silicon Valley (or they were the only ones most Canadians heard about, anyway). NEXT Canada—the umbrella organization not only for N36 but for a newer programme specifically geared to helping founders of existing start-ups and also, as of 2017, an incubation programme for AI ventures—has made a very big difference. So far, alumni have founded more than eighty ventures, raised more than $250 million in funding and created more than 750 jobs—convincing validation of the thesis that role models really matter.

The Sensassure team did not, however, have any role models when it came to product development. But Satchu had told them that good entrepreneurs proceed with imperfect information and no guarantee of success, a dictum they decided could be expanded to cover the development and testing of their incontinence-management solution. They'd figure out how to do it as they went along. That's not to say they were cavalier about research. In fact, they tended to over-compensate for their lack of experience with an approach so labour-intensive and time-consuming that it bordered on overkill.

Before moving to Maryland, the team spent time at Telfer Place, a retirement home in Paris, Ontario, that's operated by Revera, one of North America's largest providers of accommodation and care for seniors. Tim Hodgson, the N36 co-founder, had offered an introduction to Revera's board chair, one contact led to another, and the team had been allowed to shadow nursing staff at Telfer Place to better understand their jobs and residents' needs. This was not a hands-off exercise. They were there round the clock, asking questions and taking notes. They collected and weighed soiled diapers to get a handle on what Dhar calls "voiding patterns in the community," and then cut the things open to understand how urine was distributed throughout the briefs. Their enthusiasm and hunger to learn won over the nursing staff, who became allies and advisers.

Simultaneously, the team undertook as much benchtop testing of their reusable sensor as possible in Toronto. But to find out whether it would work in the real world, they planned to test it in Maryland, at Encore, another of Lorien's assisted living facilities, about fifteen minutes away from their home base at Harmony Hall. Although they were saving a lot of money by living there rent-free, the Sensassure team was still spending—they'd had to buy a used car and a lot of equipment, and everyone except Dhar was drawing a small salary—and they needed to spend more to hire a few engineers on contract. Grants from the Canadian government's Industrial

Research Assistance Program (IRAP) helped, but still ... they were burning through $10,000 to $15,000 a month, and had nothing to show for it yet. "We were really learning how to develop a product while we were at the home," says Dhar. "It was a shit show."

They created a daily video blog to report on their progress, in case their families, investors or friends back at Telfer Place, who were now shipping them care packages and notes of encouragement, wanted to see what they were doing. In the videos, Dabor appears slightly mortified to perform for the camera, Ahong is alternately matter-of-fact and wry, and Dhar is, except for the sanitized language, in his element. "Hey guys, it's day 11 at a nursing home. It's about 9:30 p.m. Eastern," he opened cheerfully on May 14. "We've had a pretty good and productive day, let's go see what Tim and Jeremy are up to!" Allotted three residential units in the assisted living wing at Harmony Hall, the team had decided to turn one into a makeshift engineering lab where they could assemble and solder prototypes. There, Ahong and Dabor were hunkered down over a table strewn with bottles of glue, scissors, pliers, tissues, tape and laptops, modifying the circuitry of the same kind of sensors used in EKG monitors, then attempting to embed them between two thin sheets of grey, rubbery material that would be attached to the exterior of a diaper. It was fussy work, the kind that requires a steady hand and infinite patience, but the mood was upbeat: soon, very soon, they'd begin testing this prototype on residents.

The next day, they discovered that the SmartPatch they'd spent twelve hours constructing didn't work. Soon, the vlog became a catalogue of even bigger setbacks and roadblocks. Everything took longer and was far more difficult than they'd expected. Final approval from Lorien's internal review board to proceed with the trial didn't arrive until day 64, so in the meantime they'd commenced testing on the only diapered guinea pigs available: themselves.

There were ongoing issues with the SmartPatch's battery. They had connectivity problems: the Bluetooth chip in the SmartPatch needed to communicate with Encore's wifi network via a Bluetooth bridge. But at least, as of day 53, there were more hands on deck: Danny Porthiyas, Sensassure's hardware engineer, came to Maryland along with Tim Lynn, another Edmontonian with a finance background, who was researching Medicaid reimbursement protocol and helping figure out the business plan and anything else that needed doing.

When the first reusable SmartPatch prototype was finally ready to be tested on someone other than a team member, on day 71, it was a grey, bulky thing shaped like a barbell and bulging with wires. Long-term, the plan was to attach the patch to the outside of a brief with Velcro, but the prototype was, at 229 grams, too heavy. To circumvent the design challenge, the team was manually gluing four ECG electrodes to the outside of every diaper that would be used in the trial, so the patch could be clipped on. The more diapers they glued, the faster the process became—Porthiyas could whip one up in two minutes—but then the glue had to dry. Gluing diapers became the thing you did whenever there was a spare minute, which was not very often, given the endless technical glitches and the difficulty of designing the pilot study and figuring out how they'd collect and crunch data.

Even though they were surrounded by incontinent seniors, finding ones who were appropriate for the pilot study was not easy. The SmartPatch was not invasive, but there were privacy and liability issues, so Sensassure needed trial participants who were capable of giving consent—people who were cognitively aware but still didn't know when they'd urinated. "There were some residents who met the criteria and were open to the idea but changed their minds once they saw the device—it was that hideous. Some of the families, too, were like, 'Holy crap, you're not putting that thing on my loved one!'" Dhar remembers. "We felt embarrassed, but at the same time, we couldn't invest $100,000 in industrial design until we knew the patch was going to work."

In the end, four residents at the Encore facility agreed to give the sensor patch a try, and when any of them was wearing the device, two team members had to be there, on the floor, at all times. Once, between solving a technological problem and shadowing residents, Jeremy Dabor worked for forty hours straight. The team took to creating their daily video blogs at 1 and 2 a.m., bleary-eyed, punchy and, more often than not, struggling with some new problem or setback. "It was ridiculous how sleep-deprived we were, but we couldn't figure out another way to do these tests," says Dhar. "Things were breaking all the time, so we needed people awake to fix them at the last minute." And for the field tests to be valid, they had to be conducted right away: as soon as a soiled brief was removed from a resident, it was weighed, to check the accuracy of the data relayed by the sensor, and then opened up, so the team could figure out whether different patterns of urine distribution reduced the sensor's accuracy. Sometimes, of course, there was more than urine, but the nursing staff at Telfer Place had, in one of their care packages, sent toothpaste and a helpful hint: dab this in your surgical mask to combat unpleasant odours. It worked. Pretty soon, though, all squeamishness evaporated, as it will after one deals with hundreds of dirty diapers.

While all this was going on, there were meetings to update Lorien staff and comb through the data, and an ongoing quest to detect a market for Sensassure's product, if they could ever perfect it. No one took time off. Eighteen-hour days were the norm. Throughout, Dhar made a point of remaining upbeat, at least on the outside; the tone he set helped inoculate the team against stress, so that struggling mightily and failing frequently became a bonding experience rather than a soul-destroying one.

But by September 2015, amidst ongoing technological issues, there was still a very basic unanswered question: how wet is so wet that a diaper should be changed? "No one had ever asked that question before. The diaper manufacturers have perpetuated this myth that adult diapers have a litre capacity," Dhar explains today, his voice tinged with outrage. "Well, they arrived at this number by basically dunking a diaper into a tub of water then taking it out and, when it stopped dripping, weighing it. But that doesn't tell you about comfort at all, and that's what really should matter. A diaper filled with a litre of liquid is incredibly uncomfortable and can lead to all kinds of skin problems. At the same time, caregivers don't want to change a diaper if there are just a few drops of liquid in it and the resident is not uncomfortable." Coming up with an algorithm to detect the threshold where wetness became uncomfortable was extraordinarily challenging, even for a programmer as talented as Ahong.

For the team, a run to the supermarket or hardware store became a welcome diversion from the laborious and frustrating aspects of the work. But when they walked back into the home and were hit by the institutional aesthetic again, none of them was ever overcome by a desire to march right back out. If anything, the nursing home ambiance motivated them to work harder. Living there had made the team very aware of their own mortality, which heightened their sense of urgency. "I wasn't there at the exact moment when someone stopped breathing, but I vividly remember the death rattle, the wheezing, the way the nurses are repositioning people just trying to give them the last bit of care they can possibly deliver," Dhar continues. "Once, I left a resident's room and then came back a few minutes later, and that span of a few minutes was the difference between life and death. Seeing what the end of life is like just brought home to all of us that life is so fricking short. It makes you put things into perspective, and reinforced my initial hypothesis, which is that you have to make a difference in other people's lives because none of this other shit matters."

By this point, all of them had developed real friendships with the residents. Dhar felt especially close to Christine, who was in the trial at Encore. "She's the sweetest lady ever," he says, producing a photo of himself with a white-haired woman in a wheelchair who is planting a kiss on his cheek. "I spent a lot of time sitting on her bed listening to her stories about living in Germany during the war, the fear and uncertainty she experienced, then getting married to an American officer who'd been stationed there. I felt so depressed some days during our six months in that home, because so many things went wrong, but when Christine woke up in the morning and said, 'I feel dry, and I slept a lot better last night'—you can't put a price on that. That's when you realize you're making an impact, because it's miserable to be woken every two hours. She and the other residents really kept us going."

On day 170, their last in Maryland, he cried while saying good-bye to Christine, but there was little else to feel sad about. Their prototype was still ugly, but it now worked, reducing the time residents spent in wet briefs by 60 percent and cutting sleep interruptions by 86 percent. And Dhar had discovered something else in his time there, something potentially life-changing. "I was amazed by how some people were exceptionally happy, even if they were totally demented, and the nursing staff loved to be around them. And others were just totally miserable to be around," he says. "So I started asking people, 'What led you to have a happy or an unhappy life?' Across the board, the happy ones said it came down to their life partner. They'd had a good marriage. As a 22-year-old who was living in a nursing home and couldn't get a date, that really struck me. I could see with my own eyes the difference it makes at the end of life if you've married the right person, even if your spouse is no longer alive. It's night and day in terms of how you feel."

He had no time to act on that insight, however, because the team's adventures in a nursing home were not over: next, they were moving into Telfer Place, the Revera home in Paris, Ontario. Once the higher-ups at Revera had seen the Maryland data, they agreed to let the Sensassure team move in to continue refining its solution, this time working with patients who were not cognitively intact, for whom the benefits might be even greater. "For people with dementia, getting a good night's sleep is really important in terms of the progression of the disease and their ability to cope. Aggression, for instance, is connected to not getting enough sleep," says Dhar.

In February 2016, after two and a half months at Telfer Place, the team, now larger by several people, drove 4,500 kilometres to take up residence in yet another senior living facility. This one was in San Francisco, close to a hardware start-up accelerator called Highway1 where, for four months, they worked with industrial designers and branding experts to create a prototype that was both functional and more attractive.

Dhar was proud of the team's frugality and how far they'd been able to stretch $300,000. Aside from a $100,000 venture tech prize they'd won in Edmonton, which had been plowed right back into the company, Sensassure hadn't had any further infusions of capital. But now they needed a lot more money to get their product to market; eventually scaling up and expanding the company in order to reach more markets would require even more millions. Raising money, however, proved to be just as hard the second time around, despite the positive results of their (many) pilot studies, and the fact that they had an actual customer: Revera had committed to a $440,000 pre-purchase order. Looking for a strategic investor, Dhar reached out to major incontinence-product manufacturers. In March, SCA, a global hygiene and forest products company based in Sweden, offered to buy Sensassure outright.

The unexpected offer gave the team pause. Explains Dhar: "Raising capital in Canada is a daunting challenge because investors are very short-term focused, they want a return on investment right away, while American investors take a much longer view. We had commitments for $1.2 million, but we needed more, and our market is very tough because we're halfway between a hard-core medical device and a consumer product." His mentors urged him not to sell—"You've put together a great team, keep going"—but no one was offering to pony up the kind of cash Sensassure needed. "The prospect of being able to work with a company like SCA that has the sales channels in place, and unlimited resources to develop the product, made a lot of sense in terms of our initial vision, which was to make an impact. Ultimately, the team agreed that we'd make a bigger impact going with them than slugging it out trying to raise money on our own."

In September 2016, SCA bought Sensassure for eight million dollars. Sameer Dhar was twenty-three years old; he'd be off his sister's couch for good. His Canadian investors, who got back five times what they'd put in, were delighted, but by now Dhar knew that eight million dollars was, in the grand scheme of things, a pittance. "In Silicon Valley, eight million dollars is not a successful exit. Even in Toronto, that's not a big exit. But the team is happy. We're not sleeping on air mattresses in a nursing home anymore." The deal came with golden handcuffs—the team has to work for SCA until March 2018 to get the full buyout—and, predictably, they have chafed a little. Working for a multinational is less fun than running your own show.

Some people urged Dhar to leave the rest of the money on the table and just walk away. Why waste time working for someone else when he could be building another company that might be far more valuable than the rest of the buy-out? If he washed his hands of Sensassure, he'd be free to focus on the next big thing. But Dhar didn't see things that way.

"I know there's an opportunity cost and I could be building another business that might ultimately make more money," Dhar says. "But we didn't live in nursing homes to make money. We lived there to achieve our mission of making a difference. I think working with SCA is our best shot at doing that and getting this thing we've worked so hard to build out into the marketplace, where it can actually help people. I also care about the relationship we've built with SCA. I don't want to be the jerk who doesn't keep his word."

Today, Dhar is absolutely certain that doing good and doing business are not mutually exclusive activities. "In the not-for-profit world, you have to go hat in hand year after year asking for donations, but if you're creating a viable business that's making a difference, you're generating sustainable cash flows that will help you make an even greater impact." He might have come to that conclusion without Next 36, but he never would have met the people who have helped him make his vision a reality, nor would he have developed the mental fortitude and business know-how to keep thinking big when he wasn't succeeding.

In the end, having a role model, even one he didn't agree with all the time, had been life-changing. "If Reza thinks you have potential, he pushes you to be even better, to never settle, never get comfortable. That message really stuck with me, because he doesn't just say it, he lives it. As an entrepreneur, he's still building upon his previous successes and trying to do more, and the amount of time and effort he gives to Next 36 is unbelievable. He could be playing golf or making money, but he's in the classroom, leading by example." Dhar had long since figured out that, despite the fierce exterior, Satchu is a bit of a sheep in wolf's clothing: he cares just as deeply as Dhar does about making a difference.

The sale of Sensassure helped sell Dhar's parents on the idea of entrepreneurship, so they have turned to fretting about his health. Playing poker with the residents at the seniors' home in San Francisco was often a boozy affair, and he is now trying to embrace wholesome living, with uneven results.

The truth is, he misses hanging out with people who aren't his own age. "Intergenerational coexistence leads us all to have more fulfilling lives. It's sad that in Western society we throw elderly people into institutions and then forget about them. It was really shocking to me how few families visit residents, and I've been thinking a lot about how we make our society one where we coexist," he says, looking out the window of the kitchen in the cramped warren of rooms that make up the Sensassure office in Toronto. "The conventional wisdom is that people want to live at home as long as they can, but I'm not sure that someone who is frail and lonely really wants to be home alone, isolated. They want to be part of a community, so how do we create that?"

That sounds less like philosophical musing than the germ of a new venture, and Dhar confirms that he does have something in mind. "The next thing I do is going to be way bigger and—I won't say better, that's cheesy—hopefully more meaningful and built more efficiently." The only hint he'll give is this: "By the time I leave this earth, it should be uncommon for a twenty-year-old *not* to have seventy-year-old friends."

It does no disservice to Sameer Dhar to point out that he is not a uniquely gifted or fortunate individual. He doesn't come from wealth, nor did he attend a top university. He was not, by his own admission, "the kind of person who gets 99 percent on every test." He doesn't have a tech background or any rarefied credentials. He's your average above-average young Canadian who, after a nine-month programme that exposed him to new possibilities and new ways of thinking, did something extraordinary.

What would happen if entrepreneurship were taught in this hands-on, real-time way in every school in this country? What would happen if Canadian kids grew up hearing stories like the Sensassure story, and taking for granted that they too could build businesses that make a real difference? What would happen if Next 36 became Next 360 or 3600?

These are not rhetorical questions or pie-in-the-sky proposals. They are every bit as realistic as the idea that three twenty-somethings could live in nursing homes for a year and, starting from scratch, build a product that has the potential to make a measurable difference in the lives of elderly people around the world. To do that, they didn't have to invent sensors or adult diapers, or even come up with the idea of giving caregivers iPads. They just had to figure out how to put those ingredients together in a new way, and then work their asses off.

Canada is blessed with many, many bright, hard-working kids like Sameer Dhar, Tim Ahong and Jeremy Dabor. We need to figure out how to help more than thirty-six of them a year to think of their own prospects differently and aim higher. We need to show more of them that ambition is not a dirty word, and that you don't have to sell your soul or move to Silicon Valley to build something great. Let's start by telling different kinds of stories about Canadian business, ones in which "business" isn't synonymous with greed and exploitation—and oligopolies. We should celebrate entrepreneurs who build innovative companies such as Sensassure that exemplify Canadian values: decency, kindness and tolerance. And we should get behind them, in aggressively unCanadian fashion, to help them become global leaders.

CHAPTER 5

It's Not Rocket Science

People who talk about innovation often make it sound like a grand, mystical process undertaken only by brilliant scientists. In the real world, however, innovation is usually not particularly dazzling: you spot a problem, come up with a solution and persuade people to pay for it. A lot of the time, you can do that by devising a different business model, or a more efficient way to produce a product or deliver a service, or a practical new application of some brilliant scientist's invention.

Adapting other people's inventions and using them in a new way is the bread and butter of a lot of tech innovation. Sensassure found a new way to use sensors to solve an old problem. Bridgit, whose founders were in the 2013 cohort of Next 36, found a new way to use mobile phones to solve a very different problem: communication on construction sites. Lauren Lake, one of the company's co-founders, was studying civil structural engineering at Western University when she was selected for N36. As luck would have it, she was thrown into a team with another Western student, Mallorie Brodie, who was in her final year at the Ivey Business School. When the team was given twenty-four hours to come up with an app-based business idea during selection weekend, Lake immediately suggested they do something construction related. On the job sites where she'd worked for the previous three summers, clipboards, handwritten notes and broken telephone were the order of the day. Surely there was some way to use technology to make it easier to share information? Brodie thought that was a great idea and, mindful of the resistance to new technology in traditional industries, suggested a name: Bridgit. Their company would be a bridge that made it simple to cross from the old way of doing things to a new, more efficient way.

The team had twenty-three and a half hours to figure out how, exactly, to do that. "Rather than waste time trying to come up with some genius idea, we called twenty people that night—friends of the family, anyone we could think of with a connection to construction—and asked them what their pain points were," remembers Brodie. The next day, when all the teams pitched for the first time to Next 36 staff and mentors, Bridgit rolled out their idea: a digitized logbook for construction sites to keep track of everything that was going on. They knew it wasn't quite right, though. Too vague. So when they got back to campus, Brodie and Lake decided to keep going with their market research. They hadn't known each other before Next 36, but their personalities meshed. Brodie, who'd started an online art gallery in 2011, was all about the big picture and pushing to get to the next thing; Lake, an avid baker who'd started a catering business on campus, was thorough and detail oriented. "I always say that if it were just me, I'd make too many mistakes," says Brodie, "and if it were just Lauren, she wouldn't make enough mistakes."

Their first stop: the work site of the new Ivey building, where they showed up unannounced and started quizzing the construction team. What's frustrating about this site? How does money get wasted? What would you change if you could? And then they did that five hundred more times. Literally. They'd drive around and, whenever they spotted a crane, whip out their laptops and the spreadsheet they'd devised to track responses, and start asking questions. Partly they kept interviewing people because they're diligent, but partly they stuck with it because they didn't know what else to do. They had no clue how to build an app—like Sameer Dhar, they'd quickly parted ways with the original team member who had technological expertise but wasn't quite as fired up about the venture as they were. However, unlike Dhar, they never tried to recruit a replacement.

"We were panicking because all the other Next 36 teams were already building their apps," says Brodie. "But in hindsight, it was wonderful that we couldn't build yet because we were learning so much from the interviews." After each one, they quantified every piece of feedback and ranked that data, zeroing in on product–market fit. Without a technical co-founder, they were going to have to spend some of their N36 money to hire coders, and they wanted to be sure they didn't waste a penny. They decided not to proceed until they were 100 percent certain they were building something people would actually use.

By now they were aware of many problems in the industry. Which should they focus on? They went back to their most helpful sources and asked them to rank four problems from most to least painful. The one that came out on top was deficiency management. Anyone who has ever bought a newly built house knows all about "deficiencies." At the end of every construction project, myriad glitches—a ding in a cabinet, a missing electrical outlet—need to be addressed. On big projects, workers don't get paid until every last repair has been completed, and often the "punch list" includes hundreds of items. Typically, general contractors track deficiencies on, say, a condominium project by walking through units and slapping Post-its or painter's tape wherever they spot problems, manually logging issues on gigantic spreadsheets, sending hundreds of e-mails to individual subcontractors, and then yelling their heads off when they come back to inspect a few days later and things *still* aren't done. Bridgit was going to create a tracking system to automate the punch list and eliminate miscommunication.

Once they'd found their focus, Lake and Brodie went back yet again to their top sources and showed them initial design ideas as well as features of unrelated apps, such as voice-to-text and photo markup, then asked, "Do you think this feature would help you? Would you mind trying it for a day?" When summer rolled around and they moved to Toronto for N36 courses, the pair set up a business making sandwiches for the other teams in order to cover some of their living expenses, and they hired two first-year Waterloo co-op students as coders. By the time the programme ended, they had a beta product—and a paying customer. They'd decided not to let contractors trial the software for free, but they wanted to be sure it was affordable so that customers would stick with them while they hired engineers and coders to upgrade it. "Our first customer was running a forty-million-dollar construction project," Brodie remembers. "He started laughing when he heard our price, and pulled a few bills out of his pocket. 'Forty bucks a month? I'll pay you right now.'"

Today, the company charges considerably more, and its customers include hundreds of contractors with multi-million-dollar projects in cities from Seattle to Miami to Toronto. They use Bridgit's app, Closeout, to upload photos of deficiencies that are then automatically routed to the appropriate subcontractors, who submit photographic proof when the problem has been corrected. The company's website is full of glowing testimonials from clients about all the time and money they're saving, and Bridgit, based in

Kitchener, Ontario, where talent is plentiful and relatively cheap, has more than thirty employees and continues to grow. It's not just a successful start-up. The company is well on its way to becoming a gazelle.

Bridgit has received a lot of good press, in part because the company is getting traction in the United States, helped by American venture backing, and in part because, as Brodie says, "it's a story people don't hear all that often: women in construction." But no one has pointed out the other obvious angle: their business could easily have been started by any number of people working in the construction industry, all of whom were so familiar with the headaches of deficiency management that they were able to describe them in great detail to Lake and Brodie. The two women are smart, creative and enormously hard-working, and Brodie's background in business no doubt helped, as did Lake's familiarity with the construction industry. But the secret to their success was the immersive nature of their research. They were outsiders who learned to think like insiders. Their main advantage over people in the construction industry who hate dealing with deficiencies is that they believed they could do something about the problem.

Canada needs more Bridgits, companies that harness technology to automate processes in ways that drive businesses' profitability— and, importantly, do so without eliminating jobs. Bridgit isn't replacing humans with robots; it's helping humans work more efficiently, and it's making it easy for businesses to track data in order to figure out how to become even more productive.

But we also need more insiders who think like outsiders: people within industries who recognize problems and set about looking for solutions because they believe they have the capacity to be innovative. In order to innovate, though, most of them will need some help.

———

A lot of small business owners have very good ideas about ways to make their companies more productive. What they don't have is the know-how, much less the time, to conduct R & D. They don't need a tax credit to spur them on as much as they need actual hands-on assistance. Here's the good news: highly skilled help is available, and it's cheap. The bad news is that a lot of small businesses don't even know it exists. Certainly when Sameer Dhar paid a California company twenty thousand dollars to fabricate a transmitter for Sensassure's first prototype, he had no idea that a Canadian poly-technic could have whipped one up for him at a fraction of the cost.

Polytechnics are a subset of community colleges: degree-granting institutions that combine the applied approach of a college with the depth of study associated with a theory-based university programme. But their students aren't pondering abstract questions and hypothetical case studies. They're being trained as technologists, technicians and skilled tradespeople in programmes tailored to meet employers' specifications. Since the idea is to equip graduates to march out the door with a diploma and right into the workforce, the focus is on experiential, hands-on learning—and a lot of it is very high-tech. For instance, students in the biomedical engineering programme at the British Columbia Institute of Technology (BCIT) develop products for people with disabilities—an add-on that allows a conventional manual wheelchair to negotiate curbs, a vest that helps blind people navigate in crowds, a computer mouse that can be controlled by eye movements—while over in the robotics and mechatronics programme, students toil over laser spectroscopy projects.

Faculty and students also work directly with small and medium-sized businesses, trying to help them innovate by identifying and solving the problems that are stifling their growth. Thousands of problems. Between 2008 and 2016, the postsecondary institu-tions that belong to Polytechnics Canada, a national advocacy association for thirteen of the largest research-intensive institutions, partnered with more than 10,800 businesses to conduct almost 10,000 applied research projects. Unlike universities, polytechnics are not trying to generate patents or licensing fees, so they usually allow the companies they work with to retain their intellectual property (IP)—a major selling point for entrepreneurs.

Applied research projects lack the glamour surrounding big drug breakthroughs or advances in quantum computing, but they are essential to helping businesses become more profitable and productive. And that's essential to our future: while big, bold, disruptive companies are absolutely necessary to spur economic growth, we also need the small Canadian companies that are always going to be small to pick up their game and start churning out a lot more value per hour of labour than they currently do. If the relative productivity gap between small and large businesses in Canada were at American levels—67 percent, rather than the current 47 percent—it would go a very long way to closing our productivity gap with the US. This is where polytechnics can really help, and it's a win-win: small and medium-sized businesses get R & D services that help them become more productive, and students get the kinds of real-world experience that will make them more productive employees. For example, students in the business operations programme at BCIT recently spent four months at an autobody franchise near the Burnaby campus, looking for ways the business could save money. Meanwhile, back in the classroom, they were being trained to identify and rectify inefficiencies. By the end of the exercise, they'd come up with recommendations that are projected to increase revenue by more than $600,000 next year at that single location. The autobody chain has thirty-nine other shops in the province.

Entrepreneurs can also get help from polytechnics with the nitty-gritty aspects of product development, such as creating prototypes and conducting beta testing—the kinds of things that a lot of people with great ideas simply don't know how to do. In Calgary, for instance, Stephen Neal approached the Southern Alberta Institute of Technology (SAIT) when he needed help with the aquatic barrier system he and his brother had developed to contain oil spills. Imagine a large floating fence made of a thick filter that looks a bit like a flexible version of the box spring your mattress sits on; you unspool the fence so it encircles and contains an oil spill until skimming equipment arrives. Containment booms to trap and hold spills have been around for a long time—in fact, the Neals' own product is an update of one their father patented in the 1970s. But the XBOOM, as they call it, offers several advantages over existing systems: although compact and much easier and faster to deploy, it stands up to wind and waves much better, it traps and retains a higher percentage of oil (as well as water-borne debris such as silt and algae), and it can be reused, over and over. Or so the Neals believed. To bring their idea to market, they needed third-party verification and scientific studies of the XBOOM's effectiveness—which is where SAIT came in. Students and researchers in the environmental technologies programme conducted tests which demonstrated that the Neals' fabric trapped more than 94 percent of hydrocarbons while still allowing water to flow through—validation they needed in order to file for patents, and which also helped the brothers' Canadian Floating Fence Corporation land a UN contract to clean up the Niger Delta and a Mexican government contract for remediation of tailings ponds.

Stephen Neal knew that a polytechnic could help him get his product to market because he's a SAIT graduate himself, with a degree in Aircraft Maintenance Engineering. But most small business owners have no clue this kind of skilled, hands-on help is available. One reason for that is that the thought leaders, academic experts and government bureaucrats who are driving Canada's innovation agenda often speak of innovation as though it is a higher-order activity that occurs exclusively in universities. In Canadian companies that actually perform in-house R & D, however, most of that work is not done by people with doctorates. Only about 18 percent of R & D employees have PhDs. Fifty-two percent are technicians and technologists—college and polytechnic graduates, typically.

Nevertheless, the combination of snobbery about universities and ignorance about polytechnics' and colleges' role in the innovation ecosystem is reflected in the way the federal government allocates the $3.1 billion it spends on higher-education R & D each year. More than 98 percent of that money is earmarked for university research projects. Only $53 million is set aside for applied research projects conducted by more than 130 colleges and polytechnics. Aside from anything else, this creates a core imbalance, whereby university faculty are paid to conduct research—as they should be—but college faculty are not. Though they should be.

"In Ottawa, they're all talking about moon shots and breakthrough science, and all of that is important, sure," says Nobina Robinson, the CEO of Polytechnics Canada. "But you also need people who know how to build, service and maintain that rocket and get it up to the moon. Innovation is not some elite game that can only be played in a university lab by a PhD. It's a team sport." The goal, remember, is a win in terms of sales, not Nobel Prizes.

"There's a grubby side to innovation, the part that has to happen in order to figure out how to get your idea out into the marketplace, and that's enabled by technicians and technologists like our graduates," she continues. "Innovation is *not* research. It's *not* invention. It's commercializing new products and processes and creating value. But when you look at the billions of dollars the government is spending, it's mostly targeting PhDs and post-docs—people who want to research for a living. That's not the same as people who want to innovate for a living. And you need both. Look at Germany, where only 23 percent of the population goes to academic programmes at university, and everyone else gets professional, technical or vocational training. When the Germans allocate R & D spending to higher education, it's not all going to the academic researchers. They recognize that you need all the different players, working together. And guess what? Germany is very far ahead of Canada in terms of productivity and innovation."

Robinson, one of the six experts who served on the 2011 Jenkins panel on federal funding for business innovation, says that one of the biggest practical problems the panel identified has yet to be addressed: a lot of harried small business owners still have no idea which supports are even available to them. Most entrepreneurs who find their way to polytechnics do so "by chance," she says. "And that's the other half of my frustration with the federal government: why are you not navigating companies to us? The government's job as an enabler of R & D should be to match companies' needs with existing resources, and they don't do nearly enough of that." Robinson is something of a firebrand, and you'd think her combination of high energy, sharp intellect and personal authority would scare the living daylights out of the average bureaucrat. No chance, she says. She doesn't think anyone in Ottawa has even listened to her central message: to become more innovative, small and medium businesses need exactly the kind of help that polytechnics excel at providing—and could provide more of, if they were better funded.

Colleges in general and polytechnics in particular are afterthoughts in the government's innovation agenda. Businesses can claim SR&ED tax credits for collaborating with universities on basic research or experimental development, but applied research and commercialization help from polytechnics doesn't qualify for credits because it's not experimental enough—it's too close to market. In other words, it's too much like actual innovation. "SR&ED is *not* an innovation tax credit," Robinson says flatly.

"I really hate it when people blame industry for not investing enough in R & D and say that's why Canada isn't innovating. Why don't people ask, 'Is the system actually doing what businesses need, when they need it?' From where I sit, the answer is no, not often enough."

In part to address this concern, Technology Access Centres (TACs), whose explicit purpose is to help smaller companies become more productive and innovative, were introduced in 2010. Today, there are thirty TACs across the country, affiliated not just with polytechnics but also with colleges and CEGEPs, offering industry-facing help in fields ranging from aerospace to metallurgy to beekeeping. However, there's no new funding to support their research. They have to jostle for a piece of that paltry $53 million earmarked for college research projects.

At the Food Innovation and Research Studio (FIRSt), a TAC at George Brown College in Toronto, students and faculty work directly with entrepreneurs to help them get new products—vegan pasta sauce, gluten-free flour alternatives and just about anything else you might put in your mouth—into stores. This help isn't free—government funding doesn't cover all of a TAC's costs—but it's affordable, and entrepreneurs can get grants and tax credits to help offset the costs. "We are not not-for-profit," says Tricia Ryan, director of food and beverage research at FIRSt. "But the goal is to break even." In other words, the goal is to give as many small businesses as possible as much help as possible

Located in a gleaming modern building in downtown Toronto that also houses an upscale restaurant run by students and state-of-the-art wine labs, FIRSt has a full-time staff of eight and, at any given time, twenty to thirty students working with George Brown culinary scientists, chefs and marketing faculty to perform R & D for small businesses. This is innovation in action, and it is often a little "grubby," as Nobina Robinson put it.

"One of our clients has a small juice business, so she's buying fruit, cold-pressing it and then delivering it. She's spending every minute on her business, but she has a real problem because every day she winds up with pails full of wet, heavy fruit pulp," Tricia Ryan explains. "It costs six dollars a litre to get rid of the stuff—a big cost that eats into her profits and also her time. Another issue is that her business is environmentally conscious, so she doesn't want to just dump the pulp. She wants to find a way to use it somehow, so she came to us to help figure out how to do that. We investigated a number of different options, and then we found a tech company in BC that has a really unique dehydrator. She could use it to dehydrate all her pulp, turn it into large chunks and then make it into flour—or something else, we're still working with her on that."

A lot of the entrepreneurs who come to FIRSt are passionately committed to their businesses and completely worn out by them too. They don't have time to find solutions to the problems they're facing—problems that reduce a company's productivity and inhibit its growth.

Sometimes, too, they need help figuring out whether and how to grow, which is a significant challenge even for large, established businesses with the resources to investigate new markets and test new product lines. Small businesses with just a few employees simply can't do that without Big Brother–type organizations like TACs to help them figure out whether the risk of expansion is even worthwhile.

"One of our clients has a completely all-natural mouthwash that's already on the market. It was originally developed for children, but now they want to come up with a version they can market to adults. The challenge is that their product has a bit of a different mouth feel, so you don't get the same degree of refreshment you'd experience with something like Scope," explains Ryan, who has the cool precision and unruffled air of a woman accustomed to putting out fires all day. "We put together a sensory flavour profile, did some market research, did some consumer research, and then experimented with tweaking their formula to change the sensory delivery. It's not so easy as adding a little alcohol or reducing the sweetness, because they already have Natural Health Product approval from Health Canada, so there are aspects of the formula that cannot be changed. And of course, everything has to be organic."

Walking briskly through FIRSt's cavernous industrial kitchen, where a chef is puzzling over a client's kale chips—"I'm not sure about these sweet ones," he says, "what do you think?"—Ryan rattles off a list of current projects. "We're working with Entomo Farms, helping them develop insects into food. They're pioneers and big thinkers, they will probably be world leaders in that area. Then, every Monday, students are in here helping develop recipes for a seniors' home for people who have trouble swallowing. We've figured out how to make something that looks like a burger but is easy to swallow. And for our kale chip client we're doing some sensory research, because she's had some shelf-life problems. We reviewed her facility and found it was very humid, so we're helping her develop packaging that's less permeable. Another client has a chocolate butterscotch syrup that's caramelizing in the bottle, so we helped figure out that technical challenge."

Those are the kinds of problems that can kill a small business that can't afford to hire consultants from McKinsey. Low-cost access to culinary scientists and chefs—and small armies of eager, skilled students who will work for free—is a godsend. Connecting with someone like Tricia Ryan, who has more than twenty-five years' experience guiding project launches and designing media campaigns for the likes of Kraft, Unilever and Nestlé, could be life-changing. A superstar in the world of marketing and branding, she helped propel Riceworks into a top-ten, $50-million Canadian snack food in under two years, and persuaded fifteen thousand dentists to endorse Wrigley gum. "I started in marketing, then went client side, then agency side, then did PR, and ended up in consulting, with a number of consumer packaged goods clients," she recalls. "It was a fun business, but then I decided to go get my MBA in food and spirits in London and Bordeaux. At FIRSt, I have the opportunity to put all of that together, optimizing products for clients, and conducting quantitative and sensory testing, and then helping them get their babies out into the world."

Polytechnics and Tech Access Centres could and should be a key piece of the solution to help small businesses become more productive. Aside from expert faculty and skilled students, they have cutting-edge equipment and facilities that small business owners could not possibly afford on their own. If innovation is the goal, it makes no sense that a major chunk of our post-secondary education system, one specifically dedicated to technology and commercialization, is treated as a bit player.

If Canadians are embracing innovation, they're not telling pollsters. Twenty-nine percent more Americans have a strongly positive attitude towards innovation than Canadians, according to a 2016 survey. Here's what's really scary about that disparity: the thousand people who were surveyed all had at least a college degree and were employed in the knowledge economy. In other words, innovation is supposed to be their line of work! And yet, on every measure—willingness to take risks, willingness to persevere when something is really difficult, self-professed drive to innovate— Canadian respondents were significantly less enthusiastic than Americans were. The divergence was especially pronounced among respondents over the age of forty-four, which is very troubling when you consider that about half of all small and medium-sized business owners in this country are over the age of fifty. The authors of the study, which was conducted by the Impact Centre at the University of Toronto, were disturbed by their findings because just as ambition is a key determinant of achievement, "attitudes to innovation are one of the precursors to a successful innovation economy."

Maybe all the high-flown blather about innovation has intimidated, or bored, or just confused the hell out of Canadians. Perhaps the reason people are not so keen on the concept is that they believe, mistakenly, that innovation is synonymous with rocket science. Demystification is crucial to persuading Canadians they have the capacity to be innovative. All they need is a new or newish idea that will result in some modest improvement or efficiency gain, and the willingness to roll up their sleeves and do the grubby work to implement that idea. WIND's business model—offering unlimited texting and calling, simple bills with no hidden costs—was along those lines: not earth-shatteringly novel, but innovative enough to attract a lot of paying customers. Like the "good-enough mother," the "innovative-enough business" gets the job done, which is to say, it creates jobs and wealth. In fact, a mildly innovative approach that ramps up productivity by a few percentage points is preferable to a wildly innovative approach that achieves the same gain, says Ajay Agrawal, the economist and Next 36 co-founder. "My view is that innovation is costly," he explains. "So if you can get the same amount of output with less innovation, you should do less. It's not innovation that we want more of. It's productivity."

"Mildly innovative" is an attainable goal even for entrepreneurs who aren't brimming with ambition. Joelle Faulkner is not in that group, though her company is mildly, not wildly, innovative. In fact, she's highly ambitious and could probably even pull off rocket science if she wanted to, given that she's a Rhodes Scholar and a Fulbright Scholar with law degrees from Stanford and Oxford and a degree in chemical engineering from Western. But her line of work isn't particularly intellectual, nor is it disruptive: she helps small family businesses become more productive and profitable. Nevertheless, her dazzling academic credentials go a long way towards explaining how a 28-year-old managed to persuade high net worth individuals and institutional investors to put money into a fund that today, five years on, has grown to $150 million.

Area One Farms (AOF), which Faulkner and her brother Benji founded in 2013, is innovative-enough in a let's-just-do-this-a-little-more-sensibly way that's perfectly suited to their industry: agriculture. It's a kind of Own the Podium for farmers. AOF picks winners—family farmers who are in the top five percent of producers—then partners with them to help them buy more land, and also provides capital and R & D support to improve that land and increase crop yields. Because it's an equity partnership, the farmers don't pay rent, fees or interest; in ten years, they can buy out Area One's share of the partnership. In the meantime, AOF provides steady, patient capital that won't be yanked away if there's a bad crop one year. Growth, in other words, entails no risk of losing the farm.

"The idea is pretty simple: the farmers always have to do better with us than they would on their own," says Faulkner, who is that rare very, very smart person who does not use her intelligence to make others feel dumb. Although relentlessly upbeat and cheerful, she is no Pollyanna, nor is AOF a charity or a not-for-profit. It's a business whose ten employees are very interested in making money, as are its investors, who expect a healthy rate of return, especially since their money is locked up in the fund for ten years.

The Faulkners' model depends on driving up each farm's profitability and productivity, and the first step is identifying top farmers who want to expand their operations. "Typically, they have three or more kids who want to farm, so they need a lot more land, which means they need outside capital," Faulkner explains. Often the farmers already have their eye on an overgrown plot that, to an outsider's eye, doesn't look at all promising. "Most farmers in Canada are fourth and fifth generation, so they have really deep knowledge of their local areas. They'll say, 'We should buy that piece of overgrown land—it doesn't look like much now, but when the Smiths lived there, they always got a good crop.' You can do soil tests, of course, but there's no substitute for that kind of institutional memory. The other thing is that 95 percent of farmland sells privately, so if you're not living in that community, you won't even know it's available—which is why, luckily for us, other funds usually have a very hard time buying good farmland."

Once the land has been purchased, the farmers clear it, drain it and improve it to make it more productive. Being able to access capital to do all that, without taking on debt, is a key reason to partner with AOF. Banks will provide loans to buy land, but usually they won't loan money for land improvement, which is expensive and time-consuming—it takes four years, generally, from purchase to first harvest.

From the get-go, farmers have loved the AOF model, and no wonder: it allows them to grow their businesses with much less risk, and after ten years they wind up with four to seven times more farmland than they could acquire on their own by renting or taking out a bank loan. Investors, at least initially, were a little less keen, because farmers earn 100 percent of the income and appreciation generated by their own investment—and they also earn income and appreciation generated by AOF's investment. Generosity is

Faulkner's secret sauce, the key, she believes, to attracting the very best farmers and creating an incentive for them to maximize profits, year after year. But to potential investors, who were well aware that earning appreciation in such a capital-intensive industry is rare, the strategy seemed ridiculously benevolent: why give the farmer such a big piece of a pie that might not even materialize?

Although she is clearly very good at it, fundraising, Faulkner says, was difficult. "In our society, we give a lot of the capital return to the capital provider. With this model, if the value of the farm only appreciates by a dollar after ten years, the farmer still gets a percentage of that dollar, which I think is only right because, after all, they're managing the farm we're investing in. But that was a real stumbling block for a lot of investors. People didn't tell me I was crazy, but they did tell me they'd invest if I changed the deal and gave the farmer less."

Faulkner wouldn't budge. She'd created the kind of nice, Canadian model she wished had been available ten years earlier, when land near her parents' dairy farm in London, Ontario, came up for sale. The Faulkners wanted to buy, but at the time, they were building new barns and couldn't afford another big capital expenditure—and they didn't want to take on the risk of assuming more debt. So they passed, forgoing an opportunity for growth. That story is now part of her pitch to investors, along with the fact that the profitability of AOF's farmer partners is already up about 20 percent. They are clearing and improving their new land for about one-half to two-thirds the normal cost; the combination of talent and strong financial motivation, plus patient capital, seems to have a salutary effect on productivity. And without loans to repay, they can afford to wait until prices peak to sell their grain crops—lentils, soybeans, wheat, chickpeas—rather than unloading them immediately for cash flow.

Despite the fact that her family has been farming for

seventy-five years, Faulkner never imagined she'd be CEO of a company with ninety thousand acres under cultivation in Ontario, Manitoba, Saskatchewan and Alberta. She didn't think she'd go into the family business, period. She wasn't cut out for it, as she discovered when she went to work on the farm after finishing high school. Benji, two years older, was already running the place and she was excited to be working with him. On the first day, she fed the calves then asked him, bright-eyed, what to do next.

"Go feed the calves," her brother said.

"No, no, I already did that!" she said, expecting to be congratulated for being a star employee.

He was unimpressed. "You eat more than once a day, don't you?" She nodded. "Well, go feed the calves."

Her first day was also her last. "I realized very quickly that this was just not going to work for me. You milk the cows three times a day, you feed them two or three times a day—dairy farming is really, really repetitive." And also, she was so good at going to school that the degrees just kept piling up. She still wanted to work with her brother, but thought maybe she'd design a medical device—she had become a bio-design fellow at Stanford—and he could help her build the company. All the education she was getting, she was sure, would be useless in agriculture.

She reconsidered after a worldwide food shortage in 2012. Investors were buying up Canadian farmland, betting that it would, over time, become increasingly valuable. Their reasoning made sense to Faulkner. As demand for food surges worldwide and arable farmland declines, Canada will have some very big advantages: a lot of land and, crucially, a lot of rainwater. Moreover, meteorological experts predict that global warming will devastate large swaths of farmland in the southern United States—while lengthening the growing season in parts of Canada and making it possible to grow different, more valuable, crops here.

Farmland seemed like a good bet, then, but leasing it to tenant farmers, as other investors did, didn't suit the sensibilities of a farmer's daughter. Her idea was that to achieve premium returns, it would be smarter to add value by converting uncultivated land to productive farmland, then improve operations by using the most innovative farming techniques. AOF is working on the last part of that equation now, conducting R & D on one of its partners' farms, with the aim of helping its network of farmers achieve another 20 percent profitability gain.

Testing out researchers' theories about farming is necessary, Faulkner says, in order to persuade farmers to adopt new practices. "If there's a newly engineered seed, the company throws a ton of money behind it and the farmer knows what to expect and why this innovation is worth trying or not," she explains. "But getting a farmer to adopt a new practice is much more difficult if the only information they have is that it worked on a one-acre plot at a university. To be willing to implement a new practice at scale, you need to know not just how much extra the crop grew, but what the machinery cost, how much longer the process took, whether you need more labour, and how you need to change the way you do things in order to fit in this new practice. The research doesn't tell you any of that. We're testing ten different new practices that look great on paper, on between ten and twenty acres each, so we can tell our partners which ones really work, and how."

AOF is, in other words, working on the practical, meat-and-potatoes phase of innovation: commercialization of new ideas. "We're trying to implement regenerative farming research—ways you can farm that will actually improve your soil quality and increase your yield—and we're testing a new mechanical weeding process using this kind of Edward Scissorhands machine that pushes the crops down with combs then cuts the weeds. Next year we'll test the practices that really work this year, only on a hundred acres rather than ten, then we'll write up our findings so that our operators know exactly how to implement." And, in quintessentially generous, Canadian fashion, Faulkner intends to share the findings with farmers everywhere.

So will Area One Farms be applying for SR&ED credits to offset the cost of all this research and development? Faulkner pauses, surprised. "You know what? That never even occurred to me."

Changing things for the better, and making a profit doing it, doesn't require blinding, eureka insights or rarefied academic training. Craig Campbell didn't finish high school, yet he built a high-growth firm that, when he sold it in 2013, had nearly three thousand employees in Canada and the United States. His mildly innovative idea was to bundle security services—cameras, alarms, guards—so as to provide a single point of contact for major corporations.

Security is something that vanished from Campbell's own life when he was seventeen years old. He'd had a standard-issue, middle-class upbringing in Toronto. Then his father died, which was terrible enough, but it turned out that he'd been keeping a secret: his automobile wholesaling business had been declining for quite a while. Campbell's mother had a job as a receptionist, but no savings. The family was out of money. Campbell decided he'd quit school and go work with his older brother Brent in their father's business, in order to help support their mom and little brother. Brent, who was eight years older, put his foot down. "Dad would never want this for you. It's a terrible business."

But he didn't nix the leaving school part, so Campbell dropped out and became a security guard at the Eaton Centre in Toronto. Truthfully, he didn't miss high school at all. Getting a set of handcuffs, a bulletproof vest and an opportunity to keep the peace in a mall filled with roaming packs of girls was pretty much the best job he could possibly imagine. He decided that the minute he turned twenty-one and could apply, he was going to become a police officer.

He was a natural at that kind of work, the gentle-giant type who could defuse a gang fight and persuade the homeless people dozing on the mall's benches to move along, without hauling off and kicking them, the way some guards did. By the time Campbell turned twenty, he'd moved up to managing security and surveillance at a casino in Port Perry. Since he was the hard-working, highly competent type who gets noticed and gets other offers, before long he was back in Toronto, doing something entirely new: selling security cameras. No salary, but he'd be paid a 10 percent commission. Despite the $500,000 sales quota, he figured he had to take the risk. What if he knocked himself out and sold even more, and made $60,000 or even $70,000 in commissions? That would really help turn things around for himself and his family. If he missed the mark, well, back to Plan A: he'd become a cop. As it turned out, Campbell was pretty good at sales. High-level people such as the directors of security at big banks and corporations liked his easy, self-deprecating manner and the fact that he's the kind of guy who tosses and turns at night when he thinks he might have let someone down. That first year, he chalked up $2.8 million in camera sales.

When he went to collect his commissions, however, his boss decided he didn't feel like paying some whippersnapper $280,000. He forked over less than half that amount, announcing that there was a new sales quota of two million dollars, and a new commission rate: three percent. Campbell tried appealing to the guy's sense of fairness and honour. No luck. Campbell weighed his options. He was old enough to apply to the police force now, but even though he'd been ripped off, he'd just made a lot more than he'd ever make as a cop. Plus, two other security companies wanted to hire him. He was trying to decide between them when the head of security at TD Bank, who'd become something of a mentor, said, "You're smart and ambitious. Why not start your own company?" Campbell thought about it: that was what his dad would have done. A day later he had a business card, had given himself a title—VP of sales, which made his company sound like it was more than just one guy with a cellphone—and had three clients, including Brinks and another armoured car company, which followed him because they'd liked dealing with him in his old job. He was twenty-two years old.

At first, CBC International—Campbell's initials—just sold security cameras; he'd design and order the surveillance systems then hire subcontractors to install them. But in January 1999, a teller was shot and killed during a bank robbery in Brampton and suddenly everyone in Toronto wanted security guards, including his mentor at TD Bank. Two hundred and forty of them, stat. Campbell, who'd been dabbling in providing guards to movie sets and bars, had four. Fine, his mentor told him, send them over. They turned out to be better than anybody else's guards—fit, alert, conscientious, just like Campbell. They didn't stare vacantly out the window or flop down in a chair and read the paper. TD wanted more guards just like them, so Campbell started running around town, in and out of gyms, looking for recruits.

His big idea, the mildly innovative one, came to him one weekend, fully formed. The security business was fragmented; many clients had one contract for guards, another for surveillance systems and so on, with different suppliers in every city. What if Campbell provided one-stop shopping—cameras, alarms, guards, employee background checks, the whole shebang—and national contracts? He wasn't sure yet how, exactly, he'd expand to other cities, but he knew it was a good idea. And his guards would be a cut above: they'd be paid more than other security guards and they'd be trained by retired police officers, who'd perform random, unannounced spot checks at bank branches to be sure no one was sleeping on the job. Bundling services and adding ex-cops to the mix didn't strike Campbell as innovation. "It just felt like, 'What do banks really need? That's what we'll provide.'"

He immediately set about forming partnerships with existing security providers in Vancouver and Montreal, and brought retired police officers on board to help with hiring. By the end of 1999, his company, now called Total Security Management (TSM), was TD Bank's national security provider. And within a year, he had some new national clients: CIBC, BMO and Scotiabank. Campbell had created not just a gazelle but a carnivorous one, and it was snatching contracts right out of the jaws of multinational competitors, for the least innovative reason imaginable: those corporations were big and impersonal and all about cost reduction, and TSM was all about Craig Campbell's word being his bond. He pledged to his customers that in every postal code in the country he'd take full responsibility for his company's performance, and if something did happen to go wrong, he would make it right. Personally. It's the kind of thing you can do when you're twenty-four years old and don't need a lot of sleep and really believe that what you're doing is important.

Whereas other people viewed the big companies that hired TSM as impersonal monoliths, he saw their cracks and vulnerabilities, and felt protective of them. "People are always coming up with new ways to trick, lie to, steal from and manipulate businesses," he marvels. Increasingly, he could relate to his big corporate clients, because his own company was getting pretty big. In 2005, BMO asked Campbell to expand to the United States in order to provide security for its BMO Harris operations in Chicago. The business was different there—"guards are armed, and a huge number of them are veterans"—but TSM adapted and expanded opportunistically when customers did, eventually operating in eight American cities.

In 2013, Campbell decided to expand further, and when a rival Canadian company came up for sale, he bid on it. "We put out what we thought was a good number, but we didn't even make the second round of bids," he says. Campbell, of all people, could recognize an alarm bell when it sounded. His competitors, he realized, were sitting on a lot of cash and had big private equity partners. He had to decide whether to stay and fight them or get out while the going was good. After hiring an adviser to perform a strategic review, he decided to run a limited auction. One hundred days after the adviser walked in the door, Campbell closed on an all-cash deal.

"All my wealth was in the business," he says matter-of-factly, to explain why he sold the company that had been his life's work. He'd generated a fifteen-year compound annual growth rate of almost 29 percent and built Canada's largest privately held security company, providing services for hundreds of companies. But if TSM couldn't continue to grow, Campbell risked sliding backwards and losing a lot of the capital he'd worked so hard to generate. Nevertheless, it was hard to let go of his company, so when, in the dying days of the deal, it turned out that the buyer wasn't structured to acquire the US arm of TSM, Campbell was more than happy to hang on to it. Today, Resilience Capital, the investment holding company he created after the sale, controls the American remnant of TSM and invests in security-related, mostly mildly innovative companies with high-growth potential. Campbell figures he should stick with what he knows. So far, it's worked out pretty well for him.

Creating an innovation nation starts with a very clear understanding of what innovation is. It's not, fundamentally, about science or technology. It's about people. People who recognize a problem or an opportunity and do something about it.

That's why we can't write off attitudes, ambition and culture as squishy, soft and irrelevant diversions that take us away from the hard work of economic growth. They are the heart of the matter. Attitudes towards innovation determine whether people feel capable of undertaking it, ambition determines how high they aim, and culture determines whether they receive the support and practical help they need to succeed.

Encouraging Canadians to be more innovative, then, whether they work in construction or on a farm or as a security guard, isn't simply a matter of changing economic incentives and governmental policy. It's also a matter of changing people's perceptions about their own capabilities. Demystifying innovation is an excellent place to start.

"Innovation is best understood as a mindset. It involves the fundamentally human quest for better ways to do and create things that are valued by others. It can be disruptive or incremental and sweeps in every imaginable good or service. And it is at once tangible and far more pervasive than any gadget-du-jour," as David Naylor has written. What's remarkable about this down-to-earth definition is that Naylor himself is a highbrow par excellence: the former president of the University of Toronto, he not only served on the 2011 Jenkins panel but also chaired the government's 2015 panel on Healthcare Innovation as well as its 2017 Fundamental Science Review. But he's exasperated by the notion that scientists and engineers have a monopoly on innovation, and observes that "the greatest threat to Canadian innovation" may be the "political and media obsession" with it. Innovation is being made to sound like such an esoteric, high-tech pursuit that the average person may feel incapable of it, and conclude that it's someone else's responsibility.

From kindergarten on, kids should be learning that mild innovation is opportunistic, pragmatic and a little bit grubby—and well within the reach of the average Canadian. But all of us do need to reach for it. Yes, the addition of a few wildly successful tech companies would be great for Canada, but it wouldn't be enough to accelerate economic growth to the point where sustainable prosperity would be assured and the rest of us could kick back and relax. That will never be an option, because innovation is not the sole responsibility of any one group or elite. It's a team sport. And to win, more Canadians need to play.

CHAPTER 6

Sometimes It *Is* Rocket Science

I f you really want to feel optimistic about our country's prospects, visit a Canadian university and sit in on a lecture or two. Not every professor is spellbinding, of course, but overall, the quality of the faculty is extremely high. And they're not just good at opening the minds of undergraduates. They're also great researchers: across all academic disciplines, when measured by output as well as quality of research, Canada is solidly in the top ten in the world, though well behind the United States and China. In several broad domains of research—ICT, physics and astronomy, clinical medicine—we are ranked in the top five in the world, according to a recent survey of top academics in forty countries.

Outside academic circles, though, our universities have not been marketed very effectively. Everyone "knows" the Ivy League is great, though most people have no clue why; one of the most important reasons is definitely their branding. No such effort has been made with Canadian universities. The average Canadian has a vague sense of pride about our academic institutions (and a certain smugness about their affordability relative to American universities). But few people are aware of the fact that we have cutting-edge programmes in fields such as quantum information processing and machine learning, which will be extremely important in the knowledge economy.

"People think of Canada as a safe place, or a beautiful place, or a place with a lot of natural resources, not as an innovation nation. But there's so much research going on across the country, and nobody even knows about it," says Molly Shoichet, a University of Toronto professor and world-renowned expert in tissue engineering and regenerative medicine who's created a social media campaign, Research2Reality, to publicize some of the work being done on campuses around the country. "Taxpayers fund my lab and other labs," she reasons, "but why would they continue to support us if they don't even know what we're doing with the money?" Good question.

Here's another one: why does research matter, beyond giving us bragging rights? The answer is that although innovation can and does happen anywhere, the research that occurs on university campuses sometimes leads to the kind of wildly innovative breakthroughs that just don't happen anywhere else. Insulin, stem cells, canola, machine learning—Canadian academic research has changed the world.

Because basic research is geared towards discovery, not commercialization, academics have the freedom to ask big, open-ended questions like, "How do cells grow and what controls them?" and "Can a computer 'think' like a human being?" Though making money is not the intent, such research can wind up creating a broad foundation for the growth of new businesses and sometimes even whole industries. The seeds of some of the most disruptive developments in artificial intelligence, for instance—the ones that will generate billions of dollars for some companies while automating others right out of existence—first sprouted on our campuses. Three of the world's most influential pioneers in AI have taught or still teach at Canadian universities: Geoffrey Hinton at the University of Toronto, Yoshua Bengio at the Université de Montréal and Richard Sutton at the University of Alberta. Visionaries, they each played a crucial role in developing neural-inspired computing. The theory underlying machine learning and "reinforcement learning" is that computers can "learn" in much the same way that children do: through experience, rather than by following rules handed down from on high. In other words, feed a lot of data into a computer, without explicitly instructing it to interpret or sort the data in a particular way, and it will figure out how to recognize patterns much more effectively and make progressively more accurate predictions based on what it has "learned."

In the 1980s and '90s, most mainstream computer scientists considered the whole idea of artificial neural networks as somewhere between unrealistic and deeply kooky. Nevertheless, Hinton, Bengio and Sutton persisted during the so-called "AI winter," thanks to funding from the Canadian Institute for Advanced Research and their own universities, developing the algorithms and machine learning techniques that, today, are reshaping not only the way we do business but the way we live. Their work has fuelled a tremendous acceleration in voice recognition, language translation, and computers' ability to recognize and classify visual images. The applications are countless, from Siri, Apple's virtual assistant, to tumour detection to smart cars that know to brake when a child's ball rolls onto the road. Machine learning is transforming fields ranging from banking to janitorial services, and none of that would be happening without the crucial contributions of Hinton, Bengio and Sutton—and their students, who came from all over the world for a chance to study with them.

The high quality of Canadian research matters, then, not just in terms of expanding our knowledge of the universe, grooming talent and attracting really smart immigrants. Sometimes it's also worth a lot of money.

But we are leaving a lot of that money on the table, and companies in other countries are all too happy to grab it and run—right to market, to commercialize research conducted on our campuses. And too many of our talented graduates reap the benefits of a heavily subsidized education and then leave the country. Many of the best AI people in Silicon Valley were trained right here in Canada. But if it was impossible for them to build companies here, and if Canadian businesses didn't spot their potential, who can blame them for emigrating?

"Google, Facebook, Amazon and Baidu, in China, realized really early that AI was going to be the future of their companies, so it was in their best interests to spend a ton of money to tie up the talent as quickly as possible," explains Shivon Zilis, an expat who's made a big name for herself in the Valley as a founder of Bloomberg Beta, an early-stage VC fund specializing in machine learning ventures. "You had these post-doctoral students at Canadian universities making $40,000 to $60,000 a year, and they were being offered ten times that amount—or more, in the case of the pioneering researchers—in the US. Of course they left." And they took billions of dollars' worth of potential equity value with them.

Canada's failure to benefit from the intellectual property (IP) our tax dollars have helped to fund is another one of those long-lamented problems that just keeps getting worse. Our OECD ranking in terms of business–university R & D collaboration is now nineteenth out of thirty-five countries, and falling. Sound familiar? It should, because it's the same old story: lots of talent, lots of hand-wringing and costly government initiatives, and distinctly underwhelming results. American universities are far better at commercializing research, generating about 35 licences per institution compared with about 16 per institution here. In 2015, our thirty-six most research-intensive universities earned a combined $62 million in licensing income from campus inventions, which, thanks to the low loonie, is less than the amount the Massachusetts Institute of Technology (MIT) alone generated: US$62 million. And while MIT got 288 patents last year, U of T usually gets fewer than 10. Our record versus Stanford is even more depressing.

Again, the issue is not lack of talent. Our universities are crawling with talented people who have great ideas. The failure to commercialize them is partly cultural, partly related to the way universities in general and research in particular are funded, and partly related to the fact that the infrastructure and support for commercialization is subpar in Canada, to put it mildly.

In terms of health sciences, for instance, Toronto should be a hub, like Boston, points out Igor Jurisica, a computational biologist at the city's University Health Network and one of the world's most frequently cited experts in his field. In both cities, top-notch hospitals and research institutes are cheek by jowl with excellent academic institutions. Jurisica's own lab is located at MaRS, where educators, researchers, entrepreneurs and business experts are meant to cross-pollinate in a beautifully designed mix of refurbished heritage structures and gleaming modern additions across from Queen's Park. MaRS is all about turning inventions into innovation, and is billed as "a launch pad for start-ups, a platform for researchers and a home to innovators."

Among other things, Jurisica's research aims to shed light on the development of diseases and provide insight into why and how drugs work, and whether existing drugs can be repurposed to treat different conditions. For example, by using machine learning techniques to identify and analyze hundreds of thousands of different variables in tumour samples taken from thousands of different patients, his team has been trying to figure out why one person survives cancer but another dies—and how to use that knowledge to move a step closer to earlier diagnosis and customized treatments so that both patients survive. The ultimate goal is not only personalized medicine but, one day, prevention of diseases. Such complex projects are inherently multi-disciplinary, requiring collaboration with clinicians, biologists, chemists, engineers and mathematicians as well as massive computing power. (More than is actually available to Canadian researchers. Jurisica's team relies on the IBM World Community Grid: businesses and individuals all over the world donate their computers' idle time to perform computations on his data and send the results back to a central server.)

At a time when medical expertise is becoming ever more narrow and specialized, Jurisica's approach is pushing in the other direction, towards comprehensive understanding and treatment of an individual's whole biological system rather than one disease. A setting like MaRS is ideal for the kind of collaboration his work demands, but Canadian venture capital firms simply aren't robust enough, or forward-thinking enough, to support the commercial opportunities that arise as a result of all this collaboration. "We have critical mass in terms of people who can execute certain types of research as well as people who can validate the findings. So we have the potential," says Jurisica. "Why don't we have the financial resources to take this potential further, like in Boston or the Bay Area? We need to identify useful ideas and create capital around them so they can survive. Instead, what happens is that we kick-start something that has a lot of potential, then it goes south."

In the twentieth century, talented Canadian academics defected to the US because salaries were higher, research grants were more generous and some of the universities were more prestigious. In this century, they often cross the border for a very different reason: it's much easier to commercialize their research there. As we've seen, that's why Abe Heifets, one of Igor Jurisica's doctoral students, picked up and left after trying and failing to raise money in Canada. Atomwise promptly attracted US$6.3 million in seed funding.

Jurisica has watched his lab turn into something of a pipeline to the Bay Area. Kristen Fortney, another protege, is now CEO of BioAge Labs, a venture-backed company she started in Berkeley in 2015. BioAge Labs uses genomic data and machine learning to search for biomarkers that predict mortality; the goal is to help develop drugs that delay the onset of age-related diseases. After receiving her PhD in Toronto, where she learned the techniques that are crucial for her current work, Fortney headed to Stanford in 2012 for post-doctoral research on aging. She immediately noticed a big difference. In Toronto, academics are incentivized and rewarded for publishing papers; in California, it's all about founding start-ups. "I never even *thought* about starting a company until I came here," she says with a rueful laugh. "And really, commercialization is what all of us in health should care about— making sure that people can actually benefit from our research."

Fortney had left the University of Toronto feeling hopeful that, one day, someone would use machine learning to try to decode the aging process. At Stanford, surrounded by so many enterprising academics, she realized that she could be that someone. Once she turned her mind to founding a start-up, Stanford was there to help, with a certificate programme specifically designed to teach researchers entrepreneurial skills; in short order, she'd raised a two-million-dollar seed round. Life in the Bay Area is ridiculously expensive, Fortney admits, and the computational work her company is doing could be done elsewhere, but BioAge Labs won't be relocating to Toronto, at least not for the foreseeable future. For

Fortney, the "number one draw" of the company's current location is that it's surrounded by VC firms full of people who—even if they're fuzzy on the ins and outs of biotechnology—really "get" the potential of machine learning, and are ready and willing to pour money into her venture. "Everything just seems to move a lot faster here," she marvels.

That difference in speed will likely become even more pronounced because, in Canada, many top scientists seem to spend their days scrambling to find funding rather than carrying out the kind of groundbreaking research that is at the core of health science start-ups. "I'm just writing grants all the time," says Molly Shoichet, gesturing to a stack of papers on her desk. "This week I had two grant applications due. Two weeks ago I had five applications due at the same time." With close to five hundred publications to her name, more than forty major research prizes and whispers of a Nobel in her future, why is it so hard for a scientist of Shoichet's stature to find money?

"The grants tend to be small, and they don't last long enough. And part of it," she concedes, grinning, "is that I'm just always thinking, 'Oh, we could do so much more!' There is so much opportunity." Walking around her lab in Toronto, which is crammed with intimidating-looking equipment, she explains that half the thirty scientists there "are trying to grow cells, while the other half are trying to kill them off." Pausing at a microscope to inspect some breast cancer cells, she says, "We are asking really big questions, like 'Is it possible to heal spinal cord injuries using stem cell therapy?' In academia, it's our job to go after the biggest challenges, because if we don't, who will?"

But even when demonstrable progress is being made, researchers still spend a lot of time hunting for money to continue their work. Sometimes a grant expires, Igor Jurisica explains, "and there's nowhere to go and say, 'Look what we managed to do. We need continued funding.'" So projects stall and the possibility of translating and applying research to other areas—not just cancer, say, but diabetes—evaporates. When benefits from initial funding aren't maximized, he points out, money has been wasted. And there's already plenty of waste in terms of human capital: opportunities for collaboration—and innovation—are vanishing because a lot of researchers who have the expertise Jurisica needs don't have the resources to pay for additional personnel or equipment. "We're missing the potential of what we could accomplish," he says, "considering the capacity and calibre of the people here."

Canadian academics' record of punching far above their weight is especially impressive given that they've been doing so on a shoe-string. Unsurprisingly, however, an exhaustive federal review reported in April 2017 that Canadian researchers are losing ground; smaller countries such as Belgium, Australia, the Netherlands and Switzerland now outperform us on a per capita basis in terms of publications, citations, major prizes and patents. That may come as a shock to people outside the ivory towers, as for many years federal politicians and officials have bragged about the fact that Canada consistently ranks near the top of the OECD in terms of higher education R & D expenditures (HERD) relative to GDP. In fact, that boast was reiterated with great fanfare in the so-called "Innovation Budget" of 2017.

As it turns out, however, a great number of the dollars Ottawa reports as HERD come straight from the universities themselves, and therefore from sources such as students' tuition payments and provincial operating grants. The federal government chips in only about 25 percent, far less than governments in other countries with a strong record in research. In other words, Ottawa is not only shortchanging some of our strongest institutions, the ones we are counting on to help us catch up in the race to the future, it is also hiding its stinginess behind creative accounting. No wonder many

Canadians are not even aware of what is happening, and may be under the impression that this government really means business when it talks about innovation.

Molly Shoichet is courted by foreign universities "half a dozen times a year, probably," she says a bit sheepishly, as though a job offer every two months is no big deal. It is, of course, as is Shoichet herself, whose list of accomplishments and distinctions would fill up the rest of this book. To name just one, she's the only person in the entire country who's a fellow of all three national academies: the Canadian Academy of Sciences of the Royal Society of Canada, the Canadian Academy of Engineering and the Canadian Academy of Health Sciences. Like Jurisica's, her research requires extensive collaboration; the big questions they're asking cut across many disciplines. Nevertheless, she herself is something of a one-woman band, with deep expertise in engineering, chemistry and biology.

Lively and warm, Shoichet has the patient enthusiasm of a scientist who is routinely required to explain terms like *polymers*— "essentially long chains of hundreds or thousands of tiny molecules"—yet has never become immune to their romance. She is enthralled by science, and wants you to be too. Sitting at her desk in an unremarkable office in the Donnelly Centre for Cellular and Biomolecular Research at the University of Toronto, she produces a hypodermic needle filled with a blue substance—"so you can see it better, but also just because I like blue." The viscous liquid, which is made of hyaluronic acid (HA) and methyl cellulose (MC), has a somewhat magical quality: when pushed through a very fine needle, it emerges as a gel. She demonstrates, leaving a line of what looks like turquoise Jell-O on a piece of paper. That Jell-O, the result of more than a decade of experimentation, has won her a slew of awards and could be worth a fortune as a drug delivery vehicle.

"We wanted to be able to deliver drugs directly to the spinal cord," she says, explaining the genesis of her invention. "But if we just injected them into the fluid-filled cavity that surrounds the spinal cord, the drugs would flow away. Then we realized that if we dispersed the drugs into this hydrogel, the drugs would diffuse right into the spinal cord where we wanted them to, because the gel stays put."

When a drug is taken orally or injected intravenously, it doesn't just fail to deliver maximum therapeutic benefits to the intended destination, it also floats around the body and can be toxic for the tissues and organs that don't need it. Shoichet likens her quest for better delivery mechanisms to FedEx: "If you have something to deliver, you have to put it in a package, and you want it to get exactly where it needs to go at exactly the right moment." That's what her hydrogel can do, not only with drugs, it seems, but with stem cells too.

Figuring out how to successfully transplant healthy stem cells to the central nervous system so they stay alive in the human body long enough to stop or even reverse disease is the holy grail of regenerative medicine. Shoichet's team is trying to do that now, in collaboration with another University of Toronto research team led by Derek van der Kooy, who discovered stem cells in the human eye. "We are working on overcoming blindness—not slowing down the progression of a disease, but actually reversing it," Shoichet explains. "Our idea was to replace the photoreceptor cells at the back of the eye that are lost to blindness, but most cells transplanted to the nervous system perish, so we needed to find a way for them to survive. The hydrogel promotes cell survival and we also saw better integration with neural circuitry. There was some evidence of vision repair, in that pupils constricted when exposed to light, but . . . we're still working on achieving more repair."

In the meantime, Shoichet has been investigating the hydrogel's commercial potential. The daughter of two Toronto entrepreneurs, she worked for a small biotech firm in Rhode Island before going into academia, so the idea of building a business is second nature to her. She's already named her company: Hammock. Hammock? "The hydrogel is made of HA and MC, get it? Yeah, I know, I'm a marketing genius," she says, and laughs. It's her third biotech company, the one she really hopes will find traction, because otherwise it will almost certainly be years until patients benefit from her invention.

After weighing potential commercial uses of the hydrogel, she settled on the idea of using it to deliver analgesics, with the goal of providing pain relief while preventing opioid addiction. In the United States, unintentional overdoses from prescription pain relievers such as OxyContin and fentanyl have more than quadrupled since 1999 and are responsible for more fatalities than either car crashes or guns. Precise Canadian figures aren't available because deaths are investigated and recorded differently in every province, but at least 2,500 Canadians died from opioid-related overdoses in 2016, including from illegal drugs such as heroin, and that number will certainly rise.

Often, the path to addiction starts with a medical procedure. "Immediately after surgery, a doctor might inject analgesics to help with pain," says Shoichet, "and if you're in the hospital, you might get an intravenous pump so you can give yourself a little bit more of the drug to control pain. But being in the hospital, using a device, needing nursing care—that's all pretty expensive. The cheaper alternative is to send you home with a bunch of opioids."

Hammock would help in several ways. "You don't have to change the medical practice," says Shoichet. "You can still inject the drug post-surgery, but it would be encased in our gel. And since the gel just stays where you put it, you don't have to keep giving more and more drugs." Testing on animals has shown that when pain relief is delivered via her gel, it lasts a very long time. If it works the same way in humans, a single injection would deliver about three days of pain relief and patients wouldn't need to be sent home with bottles full of highly addictive pills. The gel has an added, unlooked-for benefit: it seems to prevent post-surgical adhesions, whereby internal organs and tissues stick to one another and can cause obstructions.

American researchers are also working on new drug delivery models for opioids, but judging by the data published so far, Shoichet's formulation appears to be significantly better because it lasts about five times longer. And there's another difference between her work and her competitors': they've been able to raise money and she has not. "Most investors just don't have the expertise to know if this is a good risk to take or not, and anyway, most of them either want to invest later in the development phase or they want an exit in two or three years. The timeline is much longer than that in health sciences because of the regulatory hurdles. We just can't get drugs to market that quickly, for very good reasons," she says.

"There aren't a lot of investors in Canada who've made money in life sciences, so finding capital is challenging. Biotech is outside their comfort zone," adds Ilse Treurnicht, a chemist like Shoichet, who, until June 2017, was also the CEO of MaRS. "Even though the aggregate investment going into Canadian health-related technologies is rising, I can't think of a recent substantial deal that was funded by a Canadian investor."

In other words, people like Molly Shoichet have to go to American investors in order to get funding for their companies. The regulatory pathway for Hammock will be shorter than usual because the analgesics and the components in the hydrogel are very well known to the FDA, and her team has already amassed an enormous amount of data. But the company still needs between two and ten million more dollars to enter the development phase, and that seems to be a non-starter in Canada. "It's really frustrating," Shoichet says, "because in Boston or San Francisco, we would've already raised money."

As it happens, her brother is also a professor who is trying to commercialize his research. "He comes up with new drugs, and I come up with the way to get them where they need to be," is how she summarizes their different areas. But while she's been knocking on doors looking for money for more than a year, her brother "walked down the street and met a venture capitalist, and the guy was like, 'Please, let me give you a million dollars, just go figure out if your thing works.'" The punchline, of course, is that her brother teaches in San Francisco. "It's a completely different mindset there," Shoichet says, "because there are people who've made an enormous amount of money in biotech, so they understand how to assess risk."

Would she move to the States to get funding for her company? She looks down at the squiggle of blue Jell-O on her desk, choosing her words carefully. "I love Canada. The University of Toronto has been fantastic, they're very supportive of my work. My mother is almost ninety years old and I'm very close to her, and my youngest son is still in high school here. But ..." She trails off. It's clearly not the first time she's weighed these pros and cons. "A lot of my brilliant students exit the country. I'm concerned about that—we've invested so much money in these people. Yet I understand why they go. They want to make a difference in people's lives. So do I. And in this field, if you have big dreams, you need big funds in order to achieve them."

———

Over the years, the chronic failure to commercialize the intellectual property created on Canadian campuses has launched a flurry of reports; you could spend the rest of your days reading them. If you did, you'd notice that economist Ajay Agrawal has written a few, documenting his discovery that although Canadian scientists have about as many inventions per capita as their American counterparts, our faculty and graduate students get many fewer patents and generate much less licensing income for their institutions.

It tells you everything you need to know about Ajay Agrawal that shortly after identifying this problem, he decided to correct it. Not by petitioning policy-makers or conducting more research or writing impassioned editorials, but by creating a mechanism for entrepreneurial-minded academics to start companies and raise capital. Although his manner is donnish and he's erudite enough to joust with the pointiest-headed of academics, Agrawal is fundamentally pragmatic. A doer. And what he did in 2012 was to start the Creative Destruction Lab (CDL) at the University of Toronto's Rotman School of Management. "Creative destruction" is a concept popularized by the economist Joseph Schumpeter, who argued that the process whereby old industries and companies are flattened and replaced by new ones is "the essential fact about capitalism." In other words, economic destruction is a necessary aspect of economic creation, and vice versa.

While CDL's explicit goal was creative—helping to get new companies up and running—it would be fair to say that Agrawal had a little destruction on his mind too. He wanted to shoot holes in the argument that sweeping systemic change would be required before anything could be done about our commercialization problem. He was of the mind that one determined person could make a big difference, even disrupt the status quo. Just as entrepreneurs do.

Agrawal himself is a serial entrepreneur of sorts, albeit one who trades only in futures. Whereas Next 36 is all about giving undergraduates the skills to become entrepreneurs, the mission of his second non-profit was "to facilitate the creation and growth of massively scalable, technology-based companies." In other words, CDL would help all those academics who were sitting on years' worth of research figure out how to spin it into gold.

To explain how he arrived at the conclusion that he could even do such a thing, Agrawal, a perennial winner of teaching prizes and "professor of the year" awards, goes Socratic. "Why," he asks, "does Silicon Valley have more successful start-ups per square mile than anywhere else on Earth?"

Um, the presence of ungodly amounts of capital?

He shakes his head: no. On its own, capital can't fully explain the disproportionately high success rate, he says. After all, in the heyday of labour-sponsored venture capital funds in the 1980s and 1990s, for instance, there was a huge surge in the capital available for small and medium-sized tech start-ups in Canada—but no real change in their levels of success.

"Do you think people in the Valley are smarter or hustle more?" he asks.

It's clear the correct answer is no.

"What about the scientific and technological breakthroughs at the core of those start-ups?" he continues. "Do you think they occur disproportionately in California?"

That one's easy: definitely not. Breakthroughs occur all over the place, including on Canadian campuses.

The phenomenal success rate of start-ups in the Bay Area, Agrawal believes, is related to the fact that so many VCs and angel investors there provide vastly superior strategic guidance. They're not just investors who know how to raise capital and deploy it to a company that's already showing evidence of market traction, they also have deep technical backgrounds and can recognize when a company is at the frontier of a field like computational biology or robotics. And, crucially, VCs in California know exactly what it takes to build, scale and sell massive tech companies, because they've done it themselves. Marc Andreessen, for instance, was one of two developers of Mosaic, the first widely used Web browser, and co-founded Netscape, among other companies; Ben Horowitz co-founded the enterprise software company Opsware. The two hired a bunch of people just like them, with deep experience in start-ups, and their VC firm, Andreessen Horowitz, now manages billions of dollars in assets and provided early backing for the likes of Twitter, Facebook, Airbnb, Foursquare and Buzzfeed. If a partner at Andreessen Horowitz or an equivalent firm in the Valley invests in your tech venture, you get incredible networking opportunities as well as introductions to other companies the VC firm is backing, whose technology may well enable yours to leap ahead, and vice versa. Most importantly, however, you will get far better advice on how to build your business into a global leader than you would from, say, a Toronto firm operated by people who have MBAs but no personal experience building a tech company.

Agrawal's shorthand for the element that makes all the difference is *judgment*. Start-ups in the Valley are more successful primarily because they have the benefit of their investors' expert judgment. "Once VCs write a cheque, they have an incentive to transfer their judgment," he explains. "They'll take a call from an entrepreneur on a Saturday afternoon and invest time helping her figure out whether to file a patent or how to set up a stock option plan. Without that transfer of judgment, the entrepreneur is making decisions in the dark."

And there are many, many decisions to make when you're trying to get a company up and running—so many that entrepreneurs can become paralyzed by fear of making a misstep. "It's very tempting to want to do things perfectly, and that can slow you down," says Mallorie Brodie, co-founder of Bridgit, the app for construction sites. "In the early days you don't feel comfortable making mistakes, but in order to move quickly, you have to make mistakes—a lot of them. Instead of running one experiment at a time, you need to run ten, simultaneously."

But which ones? The potential for experimentation is endless when you're trying to do something new. One of the biggest challenges first-time entrepreneurs face is simply trying to figure out what to do first. "Entrepreneurs wake up in the morning with a list of a thousand things they could do to build their businesses, and they don't know what to focus on," explains Agrawal. "So they pick a few things and work on them for a few months, and then they realize, 'Oops, those weren't the right priorities.' So they pick another few things, and after they do that a few times, they run out of capital, energy and sanity, and the business collapses."

Most tech founders are not stupid people. They tend to be quite smart in their own domains. But a robotics genius may not know the first thing about how to build and manage a successful start-up. The skills required to do that are very different from those required to succeed in a lab.

Tech entrepreneurs "desperately need judgment," is how Agrawal sums up the situation. But, outside Silicon Valley, "you can't just run down the street and buy five units of judgment."

Canada is not, however, a judgment-free zone. There *are* people who know how to build a prototype, raise capital, hire a team and scale a company up to viability—but they don't teach at universities, work at VC firms or run business incubators. They're building their own tech companies, not hanging around campuses looking for scientists to help. In Canada, the people who have judgment don't often transact with the people who need it. "In economics, we call that a market failure," Agrawal says, in the emphatic tone of a teacher who learned long ago how to make sure a message sticks.

He envisioned CDL as a market for judgment, connecting those who had it with those who needed it. It wasn't an incubator—start-ups wouldn't get office space, nor would the programme get an equity stake in the start-ups—or an accelerator either. Rather, it was a nine-month programme whereby large helpings of judgment would be served up in a room at Rotman. Every two months, a panel of seasoned entrepreneurs would convene for a full day to review each start-up's progress in detail, then offer founders specific advice on what to do next, spelling out three clear and measurable objectives to be achieved before the next meeting. Ventures that were not performing would be cut, so mentors could concentrate their energy on the ones that were most likely to succeed. In order for a start-up to remain in the programme, at least one mentor had to be willing to devote an additional four hours to helping the founders over the next two months, before the next CDL meeting rolled around.

The University of Toronto heard Agrawal out and then shrugged, more or less. No, he wouldn't get any teaching credit for organizing and running the programme, because it wasn't a traditional class. "The model was new and they didn't know what to make of it, so they decided to ignore it," he says. "It really was as difficult as starting a business, only instead of fighting market forces, we were fighting bureaucratic forces." He asked the big banks to get involved by donating resources to help build the programme, but received only blank stares. "Why would we do that?" they said. Canadian VCs too displayed little interest. (Today, the university, the banks and a few select VCs are enthusiastic partners of the programme.)

The entrepreneurs he approached to serve as mentors were more receptive. Agrawal knows a thing or two about twisting arms, but with this crowd, he didn't have to do much of that. Tech entrepreneurs Dennis Bennie, Fred Dawkins, Dennis Kavelman, Dan

Debow and Richard and Michael Hyatt wrote large cheques to help get CDL off the ground, as did retired steel magnate John Harris and John Francis, the former CEO of Trader Media.

And so did I, though Ajay's pitch did not start out well. "I'm asking for something far more valuable than money: your time," is how he began. It was the worst possible line to use with me, because though I'm happy to donate money, I am fanatical about time. When I was an undergraduate, I figured out that if you live to be eighty-five, you only have about 400,000 hours when you're not sleeping or eating. That's not a lot of hours if you're trying to accomplish something meaningful. Ever since, I've managed my time in half-hour blocks, and the prospect of wasting any of those blocks is really, really unappealing. I must have looked alarmed, because Ajay rapidly switched tactics: "I think this is really important for Canada, because we need more start-ups to scale. I know you agree. This is your chance to help make that happen."

He sealed the deal by mentioning that he was thinking of inviting some stellar academics—Igor Jurisica and Molly Shoichet—to serve as chief scientists to assess the merits of each venture. But it still wasn't quite clear to me exactly what CDL was, beyond a good cause. I had no idea that I was getting in on the ground floor of a start-up with enormous disruptive potential.

I am never more proud to be Canadian than when I am sitting in the stuffy room at the Rotman School of Management where CDL meetings are held. There aren't any windows, but it doesn't matter, because everything that's best about our country—talent, diversity, openness, humility—is on full display. The place is jam-packed with original thinkers, and the wide range of their perspectives and backgrounds is a huge strength of the programme. Founders and entrepreneur coaches fly in from all over—the UK,

France, the Bay Area, Boston—to get and give advice; from the start, Agrawal understood that a great programme had to be internationally oriented, so start-ups from anywhere in the world can apply to CDL. Canadian-style collegiality dominates, though. The camaraderie in the room, the sense that we're all pushing towards a common goal, is incredible.

Most of all, the spirit of decency and generosity, the *niceness* Canadians are known for worldwide, suffuses these meetings. A lot of very busy people volunteer whole days of their time—not just full days for the actual meetings, but time beforehand to read and digest dossiers of information about each start-up, and afterwards too, to coach founders, open doors for them, help arrange financing and help them to network. When you put up your hand at the end of a meeting to indicate support for a venture, you're pledging four hours of your time to help the founders, but it usually works out to be a lot more. Many of us put up our hands five or six times every meeting.

Mixed in with all this niceness, however, are two very strong flavours: ambition and competitiveness, which give the meetings an urgent, charged quality. No one will laugh if you talk moon shots here. Mike Serbinis, an honest-to-God rocket scientist who gave the world the Kobo e-reader, is one of the coaches. So is Barney Pell, CEO of Moon Express, who used to lead NASA's AI branch. In fact, founders are scolded when they aim too low or don't think about markets beyond their own backyards. It's difficult to get into the programme; of the 400 ventures that apply each year, only 75 are admitted, and of those, fewer than half will graduate. In the meetings, then, competition is both implicit—founders are very aware that some companies will be cut at the end of each meeting—and explicit: they're actively competing to get the established entrepreneurs and VCs in the room to give them time, or money, or both. In fact, the whole point of the exercise is competitiveness: to build companies that can compete internationally.

To that end, debate and action, not lectures and theory, are the order of the day. For that reason, Agrawal deliberately sidelined the tweedy types and put the coaches front and centre, where we can interact directly with start-up founders, who stand at the front of the room when their companies' progress is being reviewed. We're called the G7 Fellows because initially there were just seven of us coaching general tech ventures; now there are a total of thirty coaches, including lab associates and a group of seven other Fellows, called the ML7, who focus on machine learning start-ups. We are not a particularly impressive-looking bunch compared with the professors, tech experts and innovation officers from big companies who sit in the semicircular tiers of seats behind us. Many of them are in suits, while the closer someone is to the floor, the more likely he or she is to be wearing jeans and a hoodie. No one has shown up in gym clothes yet, but I wouldn't rule it out. There's a certain renegade ambience among the coaches on the floor, because to be there, you have to have defied the odds and built at least one very successful business from scratch.

There's Ted Livingston, founder of the chat network Kik and the driving force behind the Velocity Fund, a start-up accelerator at the University of Waterloo. And Sally Daub, founder of Toronto-based ViXS Systems, a semiconductor company, who's now a VC in the Valley but volunteers a huge amount of time to coach CDL start-ups. Shivon Zilis, the Bloomberg Beta co-founder who specializes in machine learning ventures, has done more to build the programme's ML stream than just about any other coach. Then there's Haig Farris, who pioneered technology venture capital in Canada and is the founding chairman of D-Wave, the Vancouver-based manufacturer of the world's first commercial quantum computer. He's mentored more student entrepreneurs and invested in more of their start-ups than anyone in the country.

"For a founder, having thirty brilliant people, with a combined net worth of more than three billion dollars, focused on solving your problems is invaluable," says Daniel Mulet, an associate director of the Creative Destruction Lab. "You just can't get that quality of judgment anywhere else in a condensed amount of time." And, he points out, the format is designed to encourage coaches to work their hardest. "We ask the mentors to introduce the companies—founders don't pitch—and then provide advice in front of an audience. That keeps the coaches on their toes, because they want to sound sharp in front of their peers."

We compete, in other words. "Competition with other G7 coaches is a key part of the dynamic," Ted Livingston says. "If you disagree with someone else, you're hell-bent on proving them wrong."

Yet the atmosphere is also curiously intimate. The room isn't that large and the semicircular seating means you can see the other eighty or so people in attendance. At times, you can sense everyone pulling for a particular company, willing its founders to succeed. At other times, it's as if everyone "gets" the potential of a start-up at exactly the same moment, and a current of electricity seems to pass around the room.

For an academic with such disruptive inclinations, Ajay, who moderates the meetings, is a stickler for preparation and order. Someone sitting beside him watches the clock to make sure that no start-up runs over its allotted ten minutes, and each coach is expected to check in with two or three founders before the meetings in order to prepare a concise introduction.

Last December it fell to Chen Fong, formerly the head of radiology at the University of Calgary and currently a tech angel par excellence, to introduce a Calgary-based company called Fredsense. I knew from the dossier that the term FRED stood for Field Ready

Electrochemical Detector, and that this start-up aimed to provide portable water testing for harmful chemicals. We've seen quite a few companies trying to remedy waterborne contaminants in the past few years—there have been a lot of long-lasting-battery companies too, and drone-related start-ups—and after a while they can start to blur together. However, Chen is God's gift to founders because not only does he roll up his sleeves and really help them network, but there's something droll about his manner, as though he's perpetually on the verge of a clever punchline, that makes people lean forward and really listen to him.

"So, these guys have genetically modified bacteria to be allergic, basically, to certain compounds," he began, gesturing to Fredsense CEO David Lloyd and president Emily Hicks, who stood at the front of the room trying to look as though they enjoyed being on display. "Let's say there's arsenic in the water—these bacteria will emit a protein that shows you it's there. In an hour. Which sure beats having to send the water to a lab and wait five to ten days for results. Last meeting, we asked them to get some letters of intent from companies to test their product. They got four. We also asked them to study the market and identify which sector would be easiest for them to get into, and they've come back saying that waste-water treatment is the one. Then money—we told them to raise some. They got a government grant for $150,000, but they need to raise more, I think. For the next meeting, I think they should have one pilot completed, or well on its way, with one of the four companies that signed letters of intent. And they really need to raise more money—$750,000—to unlock another government grant, and talk to more waste-water people to test the market."

"Do you have enough money to finish the pilot?" John Francis, a G7 Fellow and CDL founding partner, called out as soon as Fong had finished.

"Yes," David Lloyd answered.

"How are you going to demonstrate economic value? I think pricing this will be extremely complex," said Haig Farris. As often happens, his question kicked off a back-and-forth between coaches, which the founders watched like a Ping-Pong match, heads swivelling this way and that.

"I took them to see an environmental person who said he manages four hundred spills a year," Chen parried. "We only hear about it when a pipeline bursts, but apparently there are micro-spills all the time. That's good news—well, not for the planet, but for this company. It means the market's probably bigger than you and I see."

"But how do you put a dollar value on the product?" Haig asked. "Yes, your customer gets the information earlier, but what is the value of that?"

"It really comes back to this: what's the value proposition?" added Lisa Shields, founder of Hyperwallet. "Who's going to pay for this?"

Across the room, Andy Burgess, founder of Somerset Entertainment, a producer and distributor of specialty music, brought up a related concern. "Without a real idea of the target market, it's going to be difficult for them to raise money. Should we back off the $750,000 objective?"

Chen shrugged. "It's chicken and egg. They need government money to get a product to get the market to understand the value prop."

Time was up. The conversation had put a spotlight on the questions the company really needed to answer before we saw them again in February: who they were selling to, and how big their market would actually be. And they *would* be back. After approving Chen's three objectives, three of us put up our hands to take meetings in the afternoon with David and Emily, and start the clock on our four hours' worth of judgment.

Next came the Landmine Boys, a trio of Waterloo students who've built a robot to defuse and excavate land mines. Richard Yim, who came to Canada when he was thirteen, had a particular interest in the subject: when he was eight, his aunt died after stepping on one of the millions of land mines that remain hidden underground in Cambodia.

"They are going to autonomously excavate and neutralize land mines," Andy Burgess said, by way of introduction. "This method is safer, easier on the environment, and it's faster. Tomorrow, one of the founders is going to Cambodia to test the prototype digging up a land mine in a live scenario, which will be certified by a land mine removal expert, and then he'll meet with NGOs there to find out if they like what they see."

The new objectives for the next meeting all revolved around finding the answer to one question: was this going to be a company that sold robots to non-governmental organizations or one that provided a full, end-to-end land mine removal service?

"As far as I can tell, their competitor is a guy with a hand trowel," said Michael Hyatt, co-founder of BlueCat. "So it's valuable just to be able to dig up the land mine, extremely valuable to disable it, and insanely valuable if you can do all of that autonomously. I think anybody would rather send a machine into a minefield than a human being. But you have to validate that this thing works. How far are you from digging up *and* disarming?"

"A year," said Yim.

Don Tapscott, an innovation guru and adjunct professor at Rotman, weighed in. "I think you should have a complete service. If you sell someone this product and then they use it the wrong way and the thing gets blown up, you're out of business. This isn't a huge market, so I think you should take more of it if you can."

This kind of debate about what, exactly, a company is going to be or do is par for the course. Start-ups often morph radically during the CDL process, validating its founder's thesis: without access to judgment, most of them would almost certainly die. With it, they are able to pivot, as CDL itself has. In 2013, MBAs started sitting in on some meetings after a coach asked why, in a business school, business students weren't part of the programme. By the following year, students were getting course credit, and so was Ajay Agrawal: CDL now constitutes his full teaching load. In fact, CDL has become the most popular and therefore the most difficult course to get into at Rotman. It's definitely the most hands-on. Whereas the primary pedagogical tool in most business school courses is the business case, at CDL, it's the companies themselves, which are developing millions of dollars of equity value in real time—and the MBAs are expected to get their hands dirty and help.

Sometimes, it's a neatly wrapped-up win-win, as it was last year for Validere, a Boston company that was trying to commercialize a device its founders had worked on at Harvard. They could stick a probe into a liquid and figure out the key component on the spot, rather than having to take a sample to a lab (yes, another liquid-contaminant start-up). "They presented this and said they wanted to sell it to the luxury perfume industry, to be used to identify counterfeit perfumes," Ajay remembers. "The G7 said, 'Incredible technology, terrible market.' So the MBA students were asked to study about six different markets and meanwhile the company continued to try to raise money, and didn't get any." Then the MBA students came back and said, "You're not going to like this, but we recommend shifting from the sexiest possible industry, perfume, to the least sexy: hazardous waste detection." With that pivot, Validere was on its way. Between an introduction Chen Fong provided to oil executives in Alberta and a stint at Y Combinator, Validere raised US$3.3 million last year from investors in Canada and the United States. More than 10 percent of the MBA students who take the CDL course wind up joining the start-ups they work on; the rest leave the programme with a distinctly more entrepreneurial mindset.

CDL's biggest pivot, however, has been towards machine learning and, more recently, quantum machine-learning software companies. "Launching the machine learning stream in 2015 changed everything," says Ajay. "Before that, we were viewed as good in Canada, but no one was flying here from Silicon Valley. Now we have the greatest concentration of ML start-ups in the world, and VCs who won't even drive from San Francisco to San José are getting on a plane to come to Toronto five times a year."

Venture capitalists from Google and Bessemer are regulars at CDL meetings now, which is great news for start-ups. Ajay's initial goal of helping create companies with a combined equity value of $50 million within five years was surpassed long ago: in its fifth year of operation, companies that have gone through CDL have generated more than a billion dollars of equity value, and counting.

When academics have an efficient way to commercialize their research, they can create highly innovative companies that may be worth a lot of money one day, such as Blue J Legal. With Tax Foresight, the company's first subscription software product, lawyers and accountants feed in their clients' specific information and the software, which leverages machine learning, reviews a huge body of case law to identify hidden patterns and accurately predict how a judge will rule. It was a fluke that CEO Benjamin Alarie, who's also the Osler Chair in Business Law at the University of Toronto, even started thinking about how to apply AI to tax law. "I got a call from the dean's assistant in December 2014," remembers Alarie, who was associate dean of the law school at the time. "She said, 'Hey Ben, what are you doing? There's an event at the department of computer science and they're looking for someone to sit on a judging panel at 2:00.'" Alarie, who resembles an exceedingly lucid linebacker, rushed across campus to help select the U of T team that would compete in the finals of the Watson Challenge in New York, whereby students from different universities vie to come up with the most compelling commercial uses of IBM's supercomputer.

Watching the computer-science students present their ideas, Alarie immediately recognized that AI could be very helpful in tax law. "Taxpayers have a problem, because we have a self-assessment income-tax system where you're thrown on your own devices to assess your income, figure out what you can deduct and how much tax you have to pay," he explains. "The problem for government is that it's really hard to administer the system—they don't have an endless number of accountants and tax lawyers hanging around Ottawa to answer all the auditors' questions." Alarie's own problem, as a prof specializing in tax law, was that he was convinced that "as soon as they finish writing the final exam, 98 percent of my students forget what they've learned about tax law. It just struck me, 'I'm investing a lot of effort each year in this Sisyphean task of training people who immediately begin forgetting what they've learned. What if I concentrated that effort on creating a system that could serve as a common resource for professionals?'" Tax law, he reasoned, would be improved and clients would be better served if, instead of relying on a lawyer's memory and knowledge of case law, a tool existed that could synthesize previous court rulings in order to predict an outcome when given a new set of facts.

Along with two other professors from the law school and an enterprise software developer, Alarie helped create such a tool by training an algorithm, through a series of questions and answers, to understand existing rulings and what had driven the decisions. By the time Blue J Legal got to the Creative Destruction Lab in the Fall of 2015, its software could, when given the facts of a case it hadn't already "learned," accurately assess how the courts had actually ruled well over ninety percent of the time. I was impressed enough that I invested, as did several other CDL coaches, though it was clear that the team needed a lot of help to figure out how to fund and build a company. "The value of CDL is that you get an avalanche of feedback and then you're told the three most critical things to check off your list in the next six weeks," says Alarie. "If you've never started a business before, it's unbelievably helpful to be given really concrete goals, like, 'Your number one priority is to complete fundraising for your seed round, then develop a demo and hire two more developers.' We knew exactly what to do and how to divide responsibilities and just go for it." Today, partnering with Thomson Reuters, Blue J Legal sells Tax Foresight to Canadian accountants and lawyers, and has big plans to expand to other jurisdictions and other types of law.

"Law schools are not usually a hotbed of innovation," says Alarie, who took the risk of starting a company because he realized that if he didn't, someone else would. "There's no doubt that algorithms and data are going to transform the legal profession: the way that professional advice is offered, the way the courts work, the way individuals access justice and remedies for tort or breach of contract. If we don't have a hand in creating these tools, what sort of value are we providing to our students and to Ontario taxpayers, who pay a significant part of the freight of the law school?" Blue J Legal is a form of payback: U of T owns five percent of the company's non-voting shares. Alarie envisions a world where AI helps close loopholes in the tax code, makes lawyers better at their jobs, and provides clarity for the rest of us. "Legal answers will be very available, very quickly," he says confidently. "People in the future will wonder at the fact that anyone ever paid lawyers $500 or $600 an hour for their opinions and guesses about legal outcomes, whereas on their own iPhones, they can now get answers with a high degree of precision." The people best positioned to create that world are not software developers who don't really understand the law, or partners in law firms who don't want to risk their big paycheques, but academics who are encouraged to find ways to commercialize their deep knowledge and research. To become entrepreneurs, though, they need organizations like CDL.

One of the Lab's biggest success stories is a start-up that barely scraped into the programme in 2012 because its founder, Stephen Lake, had missed the cut-off date for applications. Those were still the early, flying-by-the-seat-of-our-pants days, and when Agrawal saw the late application, he recognized the name: Lake was a Waterloo graduate and Next 36 alumnus whose venture, an app to track healthy living, hadn't gone anywhere. But the guy's level of determination had impressed Agrawal, so he bent the rules and let him into CDL. In 2016, Lake's company, Thalmic Labs, which makes wearable bands that pick up electrical impulses from your arm and translate them to a computer, raised US$120 million. Dan Debow, their coach at CDL, is on the board, and Thalmic has decided to stay in Waterloo because, Lake says, "we have incredible access to loyal talent here, and we can offer them a higher quality of life since the cost of living is so much more reasonable than in Silicon Valley." But most of the money that's powering their expansion comes from Valley VCs such as Amazon's Alexa Fund.

"We really didn't have a choice but to go to the US for the last round. No one here can write that big a cheque," explains Lake. And, he says, the top-tier American VCs who've invested in his company are "strategic partners with the connections and networks to really help us grow. Our overarching goal is to build a great company here in Canada that's relevant on the world stage." He doesn't say it, but he doesn't have to: Canadian VCs don't yet have what it takes to help a company achieve global ambitions.

There are very few representatives from Canadian VC firms at CDL, scouting for great opportunities the way the Americans are. In the early days, most Canadian VCs didn't support the Lab and now they can't get in; competition for a seat in the room is fierce. But in any event, many still don't seem to have much of an appetite for the disruptive, early-stage companies that are selected to participate. "When Canadian VCs see traction, and they see customers buying something, then they'll invest and help a company grow," says Agrawal. "But most are reluctant to commit before customers do. Many don't have the background to look at the science and know if it's breakthrough or not, so they don't invest."

Perhaps that's why venture is "one of the worst-performing asset classes" in Canada, as Jim Balsillie, co-CEO of BlackBerry during its glory days, wrote in a piece in *The Globe and Mail*: "A 2013 study by Thomson Reuters and the Canadian Venture Capital Association reported a staggering divergence in ten-year pooled average returns between US and Canadian VCs. The American VCs' return was 13.5 percent, while the Canadian VCs lost 3.4 percent. A 2014 Cambridge Associates study of early-stage VCs was even more troubling, with US VCs reporting a return of 20.5 percent and Canadian VCs reporting a loss of 5.6 percent."

Possibly the increasing presence of foreign competitors will force Canadian VCs to up their game, but now they have to reckon with behemoths who can easily outgun them—and who are already poised to reap the greatest economic rewards from Canadian ingenuity developed with our tax dollars. This should be an object lesson for all Canadian businesses: if you don't compete, sooner or later you will probably lose—and so will the rest of us.

"It's quite unbelievable that our banks, with so much money under management, constantly miss opportunities to make a lot more money on companies like Shopify," says Dan Breznitz, co-director of the Innovation Policy Lab and Munk Chair of Innovation Studies at the University of Toronto. "Canadian banks are terrible at allocating capital, especially scale-up capital, for innovative activities."

Again, the lack of competition is a huge part of the problem. If you don't have to worry what competitors are up to, you don't have to scout out new opportunities. "Our banks were four years behind Google in terms of figuring out the significance of AI," Agrawal points out. If banking weren't an oligopoly, and competitive pressures were strong, "there would have been an incentive for the banks to be crawling around the universities looking for an edge, and they would have stumbled on this AI stuff." This AI stuff is already having a huge impact on their business, thanks to all the fintechs that are sprouting up, and may well prove the disruptive force that brings the sector to its knees. Belatedly, the big banks are now scrambling to pursue a variety of AI initiatives, and two have struck up partnerships with the CDL.

How can it be that a country with all our research strength, talent, diversity, openness to other points of view and, yes, niceness is not guaranteed to win in the knowledge economy? Why are our strengths not reflected in our biggest businesses? Why do we continue to squander the leads we have, and fail to support the people who are leading the way?

We do not have any kind of coherent plan in terms of productivity or innovation. "Canada has never had an innovation strategy," says Breznitz. "Economic growth policies and science and technology strategies aren't the same as proper innovation strategy. We have never defined what Canadian companies are supposed to *do*. We're obsessed with metrics—'we need more patents!'—but a true innovation policy focuses on the agents of innovation: entrepreneurs and companies. How should we influence them, and what do we want them to do? Do we want more

RIMs or more consulting or more manufacturing or . . . ? We don't even know. We just copy and paste what other countries are doing, and it doesn't work." In part, he says, that's because innovation is regionally specific: what works in the Valley probably won't work in China, and what works in Saskatchewan won't necessarily work in Nova Scotia.

Innovation strategy is tricky to devise because innovation can have negative side effects, as Breznitz points out. Portable water-contaminant detection systems are great—but not if you work at a traditional water testing lab. An algorithm capable of extraordinarily accurate tumour detection is a wonderful innovation—unless you're a radiologist whose services are no longer required. "Policies have to take into account that some of the technologies you develop will increase productivity, but they'll displace jobs. And no one really seems to be thinking about that."

Without awareness of these challenges we are facing, and the need to gear up for what's being called the Fourth Industrial Revolution, Canadians won't pressure the government to create such a strategy—and won't support it from one election cycle to the next. In the meantime, we are pissing away golden opportunities and failing to protect our advantages. As Jim Balsillie has pointed out, any tech company that does manage to struggle up to global significance is a sitting duck for patent trolls, because our government, so enthralled with regulatory excess in other areas, is only just now developing an IP strategy to protect Canadian businesses.

Unfortunately, they'll be trying to close the barn door after many, many horses have bolted. "Even in strategic areas, such as Artificial Intelligence, where Canada has been pioneering the research for over two decades, most of the patents, and with them the profits, revenues and monopoly rights, belong to foreign companies," wrote Dan Breznitz and Mark Fox, an urban systems engineering professor at the University of Toronto, in a recent *Globe and Mail* article. "To be blunt, Canadians operate in a world where the deck of cards is already dealt and our competitors have all the aces." And those aces are, very frequently, patents based on "our very own brilliant, publicly funded research." Ironic, given our junior-partner syndrome, that Americans understood the high value of our work, and we did not. Absurd that a small country, which should be more nimble, gave up a massive lead because we couldn't move fast enough to capitalize on it.

Advances in AI and machine learning, bankrolled with taxpayer dollars, should have been our passport to international markets. That's certainly what they've become for companies like Google, Amazon, Facebook and Twitter. It's infuriating when you consider all the dollars that have been squandered on SR&ED in order to coax companies to be a touch more innovative—all that time, we were sitting on wildly innovative technologies with endless commercial potential, but did nothing with them! Nor did we build a strong legal or regulatory fence around those key IP assets to try to protect them from being exploited by other countries.

And we simply waved goodbye cheerily while an entire generation of tech talent incubated on our campuses trooped across the border for salary hikes that, in the end, were infinitesimally small compared to the wealth that could have been created in Canada had they stayed. If the government had had an innovation strategy that focused on improving collaboration between businesses and universities, there would have been opportunities for commercialization. If that strategy had been comprehensive, and had focused on the need to remove barriers to competition in order to encourage innovation, maybe our telcos and banks would have been sniffing around the universities looking for advantages, the way Google and Facebook were.

We need to make sure nothing like this ever happens again. But it will, unless we have some sort of all-encompassing game plan of the sort Breznitz describes.

Every Canadian needs to understand that we are playing in a global game with extraordinarily high stakes. We are our own most dangerous opponents if we don't recognize our strengths or admit to our weaknesses, and if we don't have the will to win, much less a game plan. If we don't think like competitors, we leave ourselves open to the kind of IP leakage that is going on every day at our universities, where value is drained straight across the border. And if our biggest businesses do not have to compete—if they don't have to fight for customers and if they never look beyond our borders—they won't be creating any IP either. (As consumers, we could speed up this process by not being quite so polite and patient when we're overcharged and underserviced.)

We need a serious, meaningful competition policy that opens up the clubby Canadian business environment so that some of the innovative capacity that exists on our campuses has an outlet right here at home. I love the idea of companies scouring our campuses, looking for new ways of doing things; through CDL, I've learned how many incredible opportunities are just waiting to be discovered (and also learned that if we don't discover them, another country will). Government procurement policies that favour innovative Canadian companies—or even just favour innovation, regardless of the nationality of the provider—would also be a great thing, not only to support small companies but to spur competition. And government competition policies that open our markets and severely penalize anti-competitive practices by oligopoly players would save money for Canadian consumers and kick-start productivity and innovation like almost nothing else could.

But innovation can't be something that just government and businesses are responsible for. All Canadians have a responsibility, and fulfilling it starts with thinking differently about our capabilities, which are huge, and about what kind of future we want for ourselves and our children, and what we personally can do to help create it. One individual with a good idea and the drive to execute it can make a huge difference. And we need to start celebrating the Canadians who are doing that, whether they're creating programmes like CDL or simply coming up with a better mousetrap, in order to encourage others to follow their lead—and to let the world know that Canada fully intends to own the podium.

CONCLUSION

T rue story: There's a worldwide race to get a revolutionary
technology to market, and two Canadians are in the lead;
they've come up with something that lasts longer and works better
than anything that has gone before. There's a flurry of excitement,
and early investors back the pair's start-up. They secure patents,
but when they begin trying to scale their company to develop their
product and get it to market, their investors get cold feet and won't
give them any more money. Five years later, an American with
major financial backers buys out their patents, takes his own version of the invention to market and also receives all the credit for
this world-changing innovation. No one even remembers the
other guys' names.

That's the story of the light bulb, which, as every Canadian
schoolchild knows, was invented by Thomas Edison. Only it wasn't,
at least not in the sense that most people understand invention,

which is that one person or group of people works continuously on a project and comes up with something new. The creation of a commercially viable light bulb took almost seventy years, starting in 1810 in the UK, where a chemist devised something called an "electric arc." Over the years a lot of people played around with the concept, improving it incrementally, but no one came up with a reliable, surefire product. Then, in 1874, Henry Woodward, a medical student in Toronto, and Mathew Evans, who's sometimes described as a hotel doorman and sometimes as an innkeeper, patented a longer-lasting, nitrogen-filled bulb. Investors who heard about this incandescent creation provided seed funding for their company, but once they saw the first iteration of the bulb, they backed off. They thought the thing would never catch on. Without financing, all progress on Woodward and Evans's invention stalled. When a British inventor came up with something even more advanced in 1878, the two Canadians were probably beside themselves. Their lead was gone. The following year, Thomas Edison scooped up the British guy's patent and offered Woodward and Evans five thousand dollars for theirs—not an inconsequential sum in those days, and they were likely relieved to get any money at all. Edison added some important incremental improvements of his own to the light bulb, namely the addition of a thinner filament—and the rest, as they say, is history.

Or not, since the same kind of story is still playing out here: Canadians do important research, start promising companies and then can't scale up. But today, entrepreneurs have options that Woodward and Evans did not. They can easily pack up and move to the United States, or they can stay and accept American investment, as 44 percent of Canadian start-ups do. In the latter case, at least more jobs are created here, but either way, the biggest economic rewards leave the country. And the moral of the story is still the same as it was in 1879: Canadians do not get credit for innovation—even from other Canadians. It's just not how we think of ourselves, and therefore, unsurprisingly, it's not how the rest of the world sees us either.

As far as countries go, Canada has the best reputation on the planet, according to the Reputation Institute, which surveys people around the world to see what they think of iconic brands and companies, and how they rate whole countries too. Canada tops the list: We've been ranked number one in the world four times in the six years since the institute started rating countries, including 2017, and in the other years, we were number two.* We Canadians also have a higher opinion of our own country than the inhabitants of any other nation on earth.** Who could blame us? The Reputation Institute's surveys show that the rest of the world views Canada as a safe place to live and also one where ethics matter; they admire our progressive social and economic policies, and think that our country is a responsible participant in the global community. According to those same surveys, however, most people don't associate Canada with technology, high-quality products and services, culture or well-known brands. When it comes to business and innovation, we don't have much of a reputation at all.***

But we could, if we were better at marketing our country. We're known for maple syrup, but we could also be known for machine learning. One of the reasons we're not is that a lot of us are simply

---

* Sweden topped the list in 2016 and Switzerland was number one in 2014.
** This may not be a particularly reliable measure of anything other than self-regard, though. Russia is in second place.
*** The US is in the exact opposite position, trailing countries such as Poland, Malaysia and Indonesia to take thirty-eighth place overall in the RepTrak rankings in 2017. But that's because the rankings don't weight innovation- and business-related items—whether, for instance, a country is known for technology, high-quality products and services, and well-known brands— nearly as heavily as whether it's known as a safe or beautiful place.

unaware of our country's track record in terms of innovation. Many of us can easily name at least a dozen internationally famous actors, athletes and musicians who are Canadian. Very few of us could, without the assistance of Google, come up with a list of a dozen names of internationally famous scientists, entrepreneurs and business people who are Canadian.

In most elementary schools in the US, innovation is woven into the history curriculum. Kids don't have to take a special course on entrepreneurship to hear about Andrew Carnegie and Henry Ford, and they grow up in a culture where Martha Stewart, Steve Jobs and Elon Musk (a Canadian!) are brand names. They learn that their country's founders were innovators who rejected the status quo and came up with a whole new form of government that enshrined individualism (genius marketing, given the actual track record on slavery and social mobility). Canadian children grow up learning different lessons because, of course, our history is different. They learn about what it means to be a colony, an offshoot of a great power. They learn about the compromises required to hold our fractious federation together and about our kinder, gentler values (genius marketing, too, given our actual record on Indigenous people's rights and our legacy of regional pettiness). They learn too about our abundant natural resources—but very, very little about our abundant entrepreneurial talent. Maybe kids in Montreal learn about John Redpath, the sugar magnate who helped build the Lachine Canal, but do kids in Saskatoon? In Winnipeg classrooms, teachers may mention Keith Downey and Baldur Stefansson, the agricultural scientists at the University of Manitoba who originated canola, but what about educators in Charlottetown? And what kid anywhere in our country knows that John William Billes and Alfred Jackson Billes founded a start-up by the name of Canadian Tire in 1922?

To rebrand Canada as a place where innovation and

entrepreneurship thrive, we need to be aware of our history as well as our present-day strengths. To believe that we can innovate, we need role models, from the past and from the present. And we also need to make it possible for innovation to thrive in every corner of the country.

First and foremost, we must eliminate the barriers to domestic competition that discourage our biggest companies from seeking to do things better, cheaper and faster. If Canadian companies cannot compete within our own small, cozy market where they already have brand recognition and every advantage, they have no hope whatsoever of competing internationally. The goal here is not to destroy the incumbents but to smash the regulatory firewall that protects the oligopolies from having to innovate and become more productive—and from having to care about consumers. Let's face it: if exposure to more competition spells the end for a hugely profitable company because customers flee, it doesn't deserve to survive. Exposure to increased competition would help strengthen good companies, weed out the bad ones and allow promising challengers to emerge. The biggest winners would be Canadian consumers, who pay far too much for far too many things, and, ultimately, the entire Canadian economy.

We also need to ensure that innovative entrepreneurs really *can* thrive here—making sure they have a better shot at getting the funding they need to scale up. Many of the potentially disruptive technologies that Canada has helped to develop have been snatched away by massive corporate players in other countries, who have the money and the brains to know how to run with them. That will keep happening if our biggest institutional investors continue to have commitment issues when it comes to Canadian companies, and if the government continues to spread taxpayer dollars around rather than concentrating funding in areas of strategic importance where we have an opportunity to win. It is nuts, given the challenges we are facing, to continue come-one-come-all funding via tax credits in some vague hope of encouraging innovation, with no real game plan. And if the government is serious about promoting innovative Canadian ventures, it would be crazy not to revamp its own procurement procedures to give such companies a better shot. We do not need more studies and expert panel reports—we need to dust off the ones that already exist and start implementing their recommendations. Now, because there's no time to waste.

To encourage the investors in control of our deepest pools of capital to back Canadian companies and help them win, we need to train a spotlight on the ones that already are winning in order to show what's possible. Too often, it seems as though the spotlight is only switched on when a company is in trouble. In 2011 and 2012, when RIM, then Canada's most iconic and innovative enterprise, started laying off thousands of people, Brenda Halloran was the mayor of Waterloo. It was a time of high anxiety in the region, not least because RIM was the city's biggest commercial property owner and it was unclear whether Waterloo was going to rise or fall in the aftermath. "It was eerie," she remembers, "because streets that had been teeming with people were suddenly empty." Even more troubling to her was the fact that the media clearly took delight in the fall of the once-mighty company. "I don't think you'd see that anywhere else in the world—the media attacking our only giant company. Gleefully," says Halloran. "I think there's a kind of bullying mentality here. If anyone gets too ambitious, or too big, the knives come out." Tall poppy syndrome, with a vengeance.

Canada needs entrepreneurs with global ambition. While we don't have to worship them uncritically, we should celebrate the people behind the gazelles that represent our best hope of achieving three percent GDP growth every year and preserving our social safety net. I'm talking about entrepreneurs like Alex Barrotti, the co-founder of TouchBistro. You may be familiar with his company's product but unaware of the fact that it's a Canadian innovation, proving my point about the need to spotlight and support home-grown successes. If you've ever been to a restaurant where the server takes your order on an iPad, chances are good that the restaurant uses TouchBistro.

Barrotti came up with the idea, he says, when he was "basically a stay-at-home dad" in the Turks and Caicos, where he'd retired at the age of thirty after selling his second company, an online storefront creator called INEX, for US$45 million in 1999. Barrotti is a down-to-earth, friendly guy who still can't quite believe his own good fortune and who's never forgotten how bad it felt to be called stupid when he didn't speak English. When he was six years old, his family moved to Toronto from Uruguay, looking for a better life, but his father, a mechanical draftsman, could only find work as a manual labourer while his mother babysat relatives' kids. At thirteen, Barrotti fell in love with computers and taught himself to program—so successfully that, three years later, he was setting up computer networks for all the Catholic schools in Toronto. He didn't bother with university. No sooner had he received his high school diploma than he was making more money than his dad did, setting up computers for all kinds of people—and, while his high school friends were toiling over essays and working towards their degrees, Barrotti was actually *teaching* data-based design at the University of Toronto's school of continuing studies. A decade of non-stop hustle and two start-ups later, he was ready to spend the rest of his life looking at the ocean and going to his daughter's school on Wednesdays to serve pizza to the kids at lunch.

He'd been doing that in the Turks for quite a few years when, one day, the owner of the sushi restaurant where Barrotti liked to eat lunch approached him with a problem: Tourists preferred to sit on the patio to enjoy the weather, but he couldn't make sushi in the sun—it would spoil almost instantly. And it was difficult to keep the interior of the restaurant cool enough for the locals, who always chose to eat inside, because the servers were forever running in and out from the patio. "You're a software guy," Yoshi, the restaurant owner, said. "Can't you come up with some way to transmit orders from the patio so the servers don't need to go in and out so much?"

A solution already existed: install one of those big, stationary, custom computers you see near the kitchen in big restaurants, where servers punch in orders on a touch screen. But those units cost thousands of dollars and come with expensive service agreements— not an option for a small sushi restaurant in the Caribbean.

In April 2010, not long after that conversation with Yoshi, Apple came out with the first iPad: portable, wireless and roughly the size of a restaurant menu. Barrotti took one look at the thing and realized that if it was loaded with the right software, a server could take an order at the table and transmit it instantly to the kitchen. There would be fewer errors—no more writing on a pad and then punching an order into a machine—and service would be faster, so customers would be happier, servers would make bigger tips, and restaurants could "turn" more tables every night and make more money. A lot more money, as it turned out, because when TouchBistro was introduced in 2011, all a restaurant owner needed to do was download the app and shell out $69 a month for a subscription, as opposed to about $2,500, plus an ongoing service contract, for one of those big stationary units (most big restaurants have several of them).

Barrotti, who'd moved back to Toronto by then and joined forces with a young software developer named Geordie Konrad, found it easy to disregard potential investors who blew him off by declaring that the iPad was a gimmick and his company would never go anywhere. After all, when he was getting INEX up and running, he was routinely informed that people would never buy stuff online. I invested in TouchBistro partly because it was clear the company could disrupt the makers of those stationary custom computers in ways that were good for restaurateurs and customers, and partly because it was clear that Alex Barrotti intended to conquer the world. He had an aggressive plan to enlist restaurants in New York, for instance, and he'd figured out how to connect new establishments—about four thousand new ones open every month in North America—with credit card processors in return for a percentage of the processors' cut on transactions. Today, TouchBistro also helps restaurants automatically track inventory and meets a host of other industry-specific needs, and has become the number one iPad-based point-of-sale system in thirty-seven countries.

There are so many great Canadian entrepreneurial stories like that one. There's Hubba, which aims to be the LinkedIn for brands. Purpose Investments, which offers lower-fee investment products. D-Wave, makers of the world's first commercially available quantum computer (inexplicably, Google and NASA own one but the Canadian government does not). I know the founders of these companies, so I'm not unbiased, but I also know there are many, many other examples that have nothing to do with the tech world; you've read about a few of them in the preceding pages.

There's endless room for incremental innovation and "innovative enough" companies that can goose Canadian productivity and also, therefore, our economy. There's a ton of opportunity for convergent plays where what matters is not earth-shatteringly novel research but the ability to bundle ideas or processes in a creative way. But those companies too need access to growth capital in order to scale up to significance. Otherwise, there's a big risk that new enterprises that have what it takes to go the distance will stall instead and become also-rans, like Woodward and Evans's company did. If, that is, they don't relocate to the US first.

———

The US has built its business culture around survival of the fittest and rugged individualism. Sometimes this has meant that a few people get filthy rich and, along the way, many others get crushed. The idea of crushing the people who don't win, or of labelling anyone a loser, is anathema to most Canadians. Our problem with the American version of success is that it's not nice. It doesn't feel very Canadian.

But traditional Canadian businesses aren't aligned with our values either. They're not inclusive, progressive or diverse. They're not about innovation, and giving everyone a chance, and taking care of the little guys. They're not open to or even curious about the rest of the world. And they are not, therefore, equipped to guarantee Canadian prosperity, preserve our social safety net or foot the bill for our most costly values, such as the notion that we have a moral responsibility to offer shelter to people from war-torn countries. Continuing with business as usual could therefore destroy our country because, as I hope I've shown definitively, we are currently not positioned to succeed in a global economy where change is accelerating faster than ever before. As Kevin Lynch has written, "Reaching 50 million consumers—the definition of a mature breakthrough technology or product—took the telephone 75 years, radio 38 years, television 13 years, the internet 4 years and Angry Birds 35 days."

For Canada to find a place on the global economic stage, we need to build companies that are rooted in our values and reflective of strengths the world doesn't even know we have. We need to start leveraging our incredible international reputation in order to create incredible, internationally viable companies. Think about the iconic brands that derive some of their strength from national stereotypes: Mercedes benefits from Germany's reputation for superior engineering, Porsche is emblematic of Italy's reputation for style, and Toyota is a standard-bearer for Japanese efficiency. What would a Canadian car look like? The fact that it's difficult to visual-ize such a thing, even though car parts and automotive assembly are so vital to our economy, is our problem in a nutshell—especially when you consider how strong Canada is in terms of the technol-ogy that will be required to build fully autonomous vehicles. That's why Uber (co-founded by a Canadian!) has set up shop at the MaRS Discovery District in Toronto and hired Raquel Urtasun, a brilliant professor and machine-learning expert at the university, who is also one of the scientists affiliated with the Creative Destruction Lab.

Businesses that are aligned with our cultural values will reso-nate internationally because they will reinforce our reputation, which is already superlative. And building companies that take advantage of our strengths just makes good business sense. Multiculturalism and tolerance, for instance, should not simply be values we feel proud of and the world admires—they should be business strengths that we take full advantage of, the way Allan Lau has with Wattpad, the free story-sharing app he started with fellow engineer Ivan Yuen in 2006. Their concept is simple: anyone can write a story or even a whole book and upload it, one short chap-ter at a time, accumulating followers who post comments and some-times even original art and videos, depending on their degree of devotion. Wattpad is disruptive—consumers control the content—and, because most members of the online community use their mobile devices to read and write stories, it's transforming storytell-ing itself, making it a social, on-the-go experience.

With 45 million Wattpadders all over the world, the company needs a multilingual team that can communicate with users in more than fifty languages. But Lau didn't want to set up offices around the globe. "One, it's not cost-effective," says Lau, a soft-spoken engineer with a wry sense of humour. "And two, the team can share experiences and knowledge more easily if we're in the same place."

Toronto, then, is an ideal location. Half the city's population was born outside Canada, so it's easy to find people who speak Tagalog, Tamil or Turkish. If they're first-generation immigrants, so much the better, says Lau, who emigrated from Hong Kong more than twenty-five years ago. "People who grew up elsewhere are able to see things from two perspectives, and that's important when we're making decisions about product design, sales, how we approach marketing—anything, really. Our audience is global, so we have to be sensitive to cultural nuances. For instance, a tweet that's culturally acceptable in Western culture might be offensive in more conservative countries. A diverse team helps eliminate blind spots."

Another Toronto advantage: ready access to skilled technical talent, which is crucial for a mobile app that's constantly expanding its features in order to keep the community engaged. Recently, for instance, Wattpad added "tap stories"—narratives in the form of text messages—the perfect genre for millennial readers and writers. "We can hire from Waterloo and University of Toronto, and there are amazing incubators and accelerators in both places," says Lau, who's become something of a one-man PR agency for the Toronto–Waterloo corridor. He smiles and shrugs. "There aren't many other cities in the world with the combination of ingredients we need."

Without a diverse team actively building the brand in countries around the world, the company probably wouldn't have formed a partnership like the one it has with a television network in the Philippines, which turns Wattpad contributors' stories into miniseries. It's the polar opposite of the Hollywood model: fans, not networks or studios, drive the bus. Wattpad's international manager for the Philippines, based in Toronto, "understands the cultural nuances and what would be popular there," says Lau, and selects stories that should work as TV shows. "Of course, we have data too, telling us how many times a story has been read, but for this type of creative idea to work, you need a combination of data and human input." The Filipino network's ratings are up 30 percent, because "our stories have a built-in audience that wouldn't exist for an original, scripted show," Lau explains. "Some have [already had] tens of millions if not hundreds of millions of reads." It's a good deal for writers, who are paid when their work is adapted, and for fans, who get to see exactly the kinds of programmes they want to see on television. Wattpad is replicating the idea in North America, forming strategic partnerships with Paramount Pictures and others to bring Wattpad stories to TV. By leveraging one of Canada's signature cultural strengths— diversity—Lau has created a business that probably wouldn't have been as successful if it had been built in, say, Silicon Valley.

When "made in Canada" synchs with our strengths and what we already stand for internationally, it will be an incredibly powerful brand—if we open our markets, and our minds, to competition and if all of us are looking around for opportunities to do things a little better and a little differently than anyone else does.

The fact that Canada is relatively small, population-wise, can be a huge advantage in this regard: one determined person with a good idea can, pretty quickly, enlist help and get something new rolling. David Alston, for example, a veteran of numerous tech start-ups, was concerned about the state of STEM education in New Brunswick schools. Specifically, his kids were bored out of their minds by their tech courses. "I started looking into it and found out the curriculum was twenty years old. It had been updated in the nineties, to move to applications like Microsoft Suite, which seemed like a great thing because then you taught kids to use computers but they didn't have to learn to program," says Alston. To him, that didn't seem like a great thing at all, because most kids had already figured out those applications on their own, at home, before they were six years old. "Instead of inspiring them, the school system was repelling them, teaching them that tech is boring."

Alston found himself nostalgic for the good old days, when computers were more primitive and kids were forced to program, the way he and Alex Barrotti had been, so they learned to look for problems and figure out how to solve them—the key skill required in the knowledge economy. When software like Microsoft Suite didn't exist, "there would always be that moment when something was flashing on the computer screen and I'd think, 'Okay, *now* what do I do?'" Alston remembers, laughing. "You were forced to create and of course you failed, but that was good, because then you figured out how to succeed. A lot of great entrepreneurs are people from that Commodore 64 generation where you had to program and build things from scratch, and you were just constantly at a loss and getting knocked out of your comfort zone."

Kids in the New Brunswick school system weren't having those kinds of experiences. "I looked around and thought, 'These kids are not going to be able to compete in the digital economy,'" says Alston. But he knew better than to complain. "If I'd banged my fist on the table and said, 'Government, I'm a taxpayer, you need to fix this'— nothing would have happened. All people hear is 'Blah blah blah' and then they sleepwalk in the other direction." Change, he believed, had to come from the outside in. "You have to be entrepreneurial, roll up your sleeves and use whatever resources you can scrape together to create momentum. There's no government programme that changes things—government is about orderly systems, and change is usually a little chaotic and happens organically. It's always people believing they can make a difference, and then, if you start to create positive change, the government will come on board."

He kept his day job as chief innovation officer at Introhive, which automates customer-relationship management, but along with René Boudreau, Alston co-founded Brilliant Labs, a non-profit programme in Fredericton that makes tech education available in every school in the province. Enlisting "a motley crew" of half anglophone, half francophone teachers, principals, parents and tech mentors, Alston and Boudreau raised funds to put together portable "maker carts" filled with things such as miniature 3D printers and sewing machines, as well as robotics and wearable electronics kits. Schools borrow the carts and tech volunteers are available to help teachers figure out how to coach kids to create with, rather than simply consume, technology. They automate Lego villages, build and program robots, and invent shoes for the visually impaired. Some New Brunswick schools now have dedicated "maker spaces" and regularly summon help from the tech experts at Brilliant Labs, including help with ideas about how to fund-raise to buy more equipment when they need it.

"As with any start-up, it was all about getting this up and running fast, fast, fast," says Alston. "We realized we didn't need to convert a whole school. We just needed one or two teachers who were open to the idea, and hopefully we'd get the principal on board, and then it would take off." In the end, it was easy to get meetings with key government people who could provide funding. "People bemoan the fact that New Brunswick is small, but it can be a huge plus because we're one degree of separation and therefore can move very quickly." Brilliant Labs is now available in Nova Scotia too; friends of Alston's and Boudreau's heard about the programme and set it up there.

Sometimes, being small means you can think bigger because it's easier to get things done. Sweden, Denmark, Finland and Israel—some of the most innovative countries in the world—all make small population size work in their favour. Being small should make Canada more nimble too—and speed, especially when you don't have scale, is a significant competitive advantage.

When we take advantage of our size, rather than thinking like junior partners who won't ever amount to much, we can win. Witness Resson, an agritech company in New Brunswick co-founded by Rishin Biehl. Biehl, who grew up in a small town near Mumbai, could live anywhere in the world; a brilliant student, he won the international science and engineering fair when he was sixteen. He chose to study at the University of New Brunswick because, he says, "I wanted to live in a beautiful, uncrowded place." After finishing his master's in mechanical engineering, he had six job offers, including one from Bombardier and another from the Indian government, to work on their nuclear programme. But he had an idea for a drone-mounted technology so sensitive it could detect the movement of a single beetle in a field, and someone he met through a friend of a friend—Nicole Leblanc from the Business Development Bank of Canada; Fredericton is like that—convinced him to try starting his own company. First, he needed to be able to test his technology, so he had the idea of dropping by McCain Foods, unannounced, and asking if he could try it out on their fields. "Sure," was the answer, "go ahead." When McCain saw that Resson's technology worked so well that potato blight could be detected the moment it began to develop, the company invested (as did Rho Ventures in Montreal) and helped introduce Biehl to Monsanto, which chipped in millions of dollars. The company, still located in Fredericton, raised an US$11-million seed round in 2016 and is on its way to becoming a big player in agritech. It's an "only in Canada story," says Biehl. "In India, I don't think this would have happened, because it's too big. You'd never get in to see the right people who could help you."

We need to think like David—like scrappy upstarts, not junior partners—and use the strengths we have instead of worrying about Goliath's size. "To me, Canada is like a kid who has great genetics but doesn't exercise, so he can't run fast," is how Rishin

Biehl puts it. "Canada has everything going for it: low population density, lots of water, and when climate change happens, Canada will actually benefit from it. There are so many smart people, and such a willingness to help other people. All Canada needs to do is get up off the couch and move. Exercise. Train."

And we need to do that now, because the world isn't standing around waiting for us. The race to the future has already begun, and we're late getting off the mark. We have the talent, but we can't win without a game plan—one that clears away the obstacles we've put in our own path so that we can go hard and compete as though our future depends on the outcome.

Because it does.

ACKNOWLEDGEMENTS

This book began as a straightforward snapshot of the business landscape in Canada. Then we started deciphering statistics and realized that there's no such thing as "straightforward" when it comes to Canadian business. We are very grateful to the following people for sharing their thoughts with us: Lorne Abony, Ben Alarie, David Alston, Andreas Antoniou, Chris Arsenault, Kelly Ballance, Alex Barrotti, Rishin Biehl, Scott Bonham, Dan Breznitz, Mallorie Brodie, Craig Campbell, Alain Cohen, Chief "Keeter" Corston, Dan Debow, Sameer Dhar, Cam di Prata, Terry Doyle, Haig Farris, Joelle Faulkner, Barbara Fennessey, Chen Fong, Kristen Fortney, Brendan Frey, Jeff Grammer, Lauren Haw, Abe Heifets, Dave Henderson, Steve Irvine, Peter Kalen, John Kelleher, Bilal Khan, Katya Kudashkina, Stephen Lake, Allan Lau, Nicole Leblanc, Mara Lederman, Victoria Lennox, Kevin Lynch, Dion Madsen, Andrea Matheson, Laura McGee, Joe Mimran, Mike

Murchison, Aidan Nulman, Brian Ritchie, John Ruffolo, Tricia Ryan, Som Seif, Mike Serbinis, Molly Shoichet, Angela Strange, Razor Suleman, Ilse Treurnicht, Don Walker, Kingsley Ward, Ben Zifkin and Shivon Zilis.

At Next 36, all the participants and staff were very helpful, especially Jon French and Alexandra McGregor, and so was everyone involved with the Creative Destruction Lab, particularly Dawn Bloomfield, Jennifer Lee and Daniel Mulet. Thank you also to Megan Dover, who helped us with research, as did the resourceful Rachel Rafelman, who also transcribed many taped interviews.

Several people we interviewed went above and beyond, giving us many hours of their time and ongoing help: Brenda Halloran, Brett House, Igor Jurisica, Nobina Robinson and especially Brice Scheschuk.

Reza Satchu, without whom this book would not exist (and whose name we therefore cursed on more than one occasion), kindly allowed us to observe Next 36 interviews and final deliberations. Ajay Agrawal, an early supporter of this project, was unstintingly generous with his time. Simon Lockie's sharp memory and smart suggestions greatly improved the first chapter. And we were exceptionally fortunate to have David Naylor on speed-dial to provide expert commentary, cheerful disagreement and a raft of helpful suggestions.

At Penguin Random House Canada, Kristin Cochrane and Brad Martin championed this project from day one. Many thanks also to John Sweet, for careful copy editing; Scott Richardson, Five Seventeen and Terra Page, for designing and typesetting the book beautifully; Brittany Larkin and Deirdre Molina, for making sure there was something to typeset; and Robert Wheaton, Charidy Johnson, Beth Lockley and especially Shona Cook and Matthew Sibiga for getting behind the project in a big way. But we'd be nowhere without the vision, talent and editorial genius of

Anne Collins, whose passion for this book never wavered, even when we were well past deadline and she probably felt like strangling the one of us whose fault that was (hint: not Anthony).

Kate: So many thanks to Wendy Dennis, Kejda Trungu, Kim Tremblay Mercer and especially Jodi Cape for friendship and practical help, and to my mother, Elinor, for transcribing tapes (again!) and for never letting me win at board games when I was growing up, so I learned how to compete. "Thank you" doesn't cover all I owe to Chas. and Tristan, who bear the brunt of every book, but thank you to the most fun, lovable and funny kids in the world. Writing about the kind of country I hope they inherit made me hugely grateful for the uncompromising teachers and demanding coaches they have had: Cayleigh Murtaugh, Bill Simmons, Galia Shaked, "Bruiser" Ambrose, Alvin Noel and the incomparable Rudy Talarico. By insisting on excellence, they're building the podium not just for kids, but for all of us. My deepest gratitude goes to the most lovable adult I know, Peter Leinroth, who shaped this book in a hundred ways, from discussing it endlessly to researching Canadian tax law, a task that no New Yorker who's routinely subjected to zone five seating on Air Canada should ever be required to undertake.

Anthony: Building a successful business requires the support and collaboration of hundreds if not thousands of people, and I have many, many people to thank for helping me build Globalive—and for helping me understand the challenges Canada faces as well as the incredible advantages we have. Mark Rider, Mitchel Smith and Robert Torokvei believed in me when I was twenty-four years old, and provided the start-up financing that helped get Globalive's early companies off the ground. I owe a big debt of gratitude to them and the rest of our initial investors, as well as to the first big customers of our early companies, especially Rafael and the team at BBG Communications, and the teams at Canadian Pacific Hotels and Canada Payphone.

Many thanks also to Michael O'Connor and everyone else at Orascom Telecom who was involved in the Globalive Wireless start-up financing and spectrum auction, especially Naguib Sawiris, who invested hugely in Canada's wireless industry and was punished for his faith in our country's potential. I hope this book helps ensure that no other investors in our country are treated the way he was. I am deeply grateful to him for his faith in me, and for everything he taught me about the importance of competition.

Though in the preceding pages I'm sometimes critical of our banks, I have excellent reasons to thank the bankers at TD, CIBC, BMO and National who supported Globalive's acquisition of Yak Communications in 2006, and Daryl Johnston, who, while at CIBC, helped us secure the first credit facilities that drove our portfolio companies' growth. Thank you also to Cam di Prata, then at National Bank, and Kerry MacNeil at BMO, as well as all the advisers who, over the years, worked with us on various start-ups and financings to bring real competition and innovation to the telecommunications industry in Canada.

Many thanks to my co-founders of OneConnect, Pragmatic, Enunciate, JTC and Globalive XMG, among other Globalive portfolio companies: all of you helped introduce innovation in legacy industries, as did all the incredible executive teams of those companies.

To all of my friends and colleagues at Globalive: we challenged the status quo, together! Thanks especially to Gianni Creta, Anthony Cozzi, James Baskin, Peter Spinato, Rishi Bahall, Bhavin Shah, Mark Palma and Ash Brar, and the rest of the outstanding software developers and engineers on the early technology teams who helped create systems and business models to disrupt an industry that no one believed would ever change. And thank you to the team at Globalive Capital, including Brice Scheschuk, Simon Lockie, Dave Roff, and particularly Milanka Glisic and Florence Au, who have been at Globalive since the very early days. Thank you to Sujy Paran, Melanie Smith and Samaira Knol for all their support, and to Michael Bancroft at Bloomberg TV Canada for his belief in me.

For her support, encouragement and friendship, a special thank-you to Kimberly Underwood. Most importantly, I need to express my deepest gratitude to the people who know me best. My incredible family has always challenged me, stood by me and loved me. I'm the luckiest man on earth to have a mother like Donna Lacavera, a sister like Catherina Lacavera, and a father and best friend like Al Lacavera.

Over the years, the federal government has convened a number of expert panels to study Canada's competitiveness and our long-standing innovation problem. Every taxpayer would do well to read them, or at least their executive summaries, because they provide a detailed portrait of Canada's challenges, opportunities and missed opportunities. Though commissioned by governments of very different political stripes, they reach many of the same conclusions and include sensible recommendations, many of which have never been implemented. We relied heavily on a number of these reports, especially *Compete to Win*, also known as the Wilson report, and *Innovation Canada*, which is commonly referred to as the Jenkins panel report, as well as excellent studies by the Council of Canadian Academies and the DEEP Centre at Waterloo.

CHAPTER 1: Exhibit A

For facts, figures and detailed background information on the telecommunications market in Canada as well as the reasoning behind the government's decision to hold a spectrum auction, information about the set-aside for new entrants and the press release announcing the decision, see:
Industry Canada. "Government Opts for More Competition in the Wireless Sector," Government of Canada, November 28, 2007,
https://www.ic.gc.ca/eic/site/smt-gst.nsf/eng/sf10021.html.

For more information on the importance of a modern and innovative telecommunications infrastructure to Canada's overall competitiveness in a global economy, see:
Industry Canada, "Policy Framework for the Auction for Spectrum Licences for Advanced Wireless Services and Other Spectrum in the 2 GHz Range," Government of Canada,
http://www.ic.gc.ca/eic/site/smt-gst.nsf/eng/sf08833.html.

For an outstanding overview of the ongoing lack of competitiveness in wireless, and a good snapshot of how Canada compares to other OECD countries, see: Michael Geist, "Canadian Wireless Reality Check: Why Our Wireless Market Is Still Woefully Uncompetitive," MichaelGeist.ca, March 10, 2013, http://www.michaelgeist.ca/2013/03/canadian-wireless-reality-check/.

"The Canadian wireless market is hopelessly behind":
Michael Geist, "iPhone Shines Spotlight on Our Wireless Flaws," *Toronto Star*, May 5, 2008.

Canada's descent from ninth place worldwide in wireless networks and information technology in 2002 to nineteenth in 2007 and twenty-fifth in 2016 was tracked by the ITU:
International Telecommunication Union, *Measuring the Information Society: The ICT Development Index* (Geneva: ITU, 2009), table 4.2, p. 21, http://www.itu.int/ITU-D/ict/publications/idi/material/2009/MIS2009_w5.pdf.

. . . two of them, Telus and Bell, actually share a single network:
Even Rogers has complained about this arrangement from time to time. In the course of arguing that the CRTC should set caps on roaming costs at double the average retail price, Ken Engelhart, vice-president of regulatory affairs at Rogers, complained that Telus and Bell share a network and told the CRTC, "You should require both Bell and Telus to offer roaming across the entire country. That will make the wholesale market even more competitive." Christine Dobby, "CRTC in 'Strange' Bind: Ottawa Has Already Set Roaming Rate Caps," *Globe and Mail*, October 1, 2014.

In 2007 Rogers characterized newcomers as "all time corporate welfare bums" and Telus insisted the market was "vigorously competitive":
Michael Geist, "The Canadian Wireless Market and the Big 3: It's Always Been a Matter of Trust," MichaelGeist.ca, October 6, 2014, http://www.michaelgeist.ca/2014/10/canadian-wireless-market-big-3-always-matter-trust-2/.

A quarter of a million Americans wrote to the FCC . . . in Canada, exactly four consumers weighed in:
Michael Geist, "Spectrum Auction Has Plenty on the Line," *Toronto Star*, June 18, 2007.

Three facts made the investment appealing: ARPU, similarity of Big Three's pricing, low rates of wireless usage:
Ranji Bissessar and Alex Yeung, "The Billion Dollar Bet: Examining WIND's Sure Thing," *Ivey Business Review*, December 2010.

In 2007, Naguib . . . was actively scouting for a new place to invest his "war chest":
Cable News Network. "Face Time with Naguib Sawiris," CNN.com,
December 21, 2007,
http://www.cnn.com/2007/BUSINESS/12/20/sawiris2.interview/index.html.

The auction was a bonanza for the federal government . . . $4.8 billion:
Canadian Spectrum Policy Research, "Auctions,"
http://canadianspectrumpolicyresearch.org/auctions/.

One oligopoly executive tweeted about "King Tut":
Michael Hennessy, Twitter, December 11, 2009, quoted in
http://www.cbc.ca/canada/calgary/story/2009/12/11/clement-crtc.html

. . . another prominent Canadian telecom executive joked about camels:
Iain Marlow and Jacquie McNish, "Shaw Faces Heat over Orascom Comment,"
Globe and Mail, April 13, 2010.

"Consumers will vote with their feet and their pocketbooks and that's the way the market works":
Susan Taylor and John McCrank, "Canada Opens Mobile Market to Globalive,"
Ca.reuters.com, December 11, 2009,
http://ca.reuters.com/article/businessNews/idCATRE5BA1UB20091211.

The federal government's Competition Bureau . . . fined Rogers $10 million:
Canada (Competition Bureau) v. Chatr Wireless Inc., 2013 ONSC 5315 (CanLII)
http://canlii.ca/t/g04cv.

The Competition Bureau successfully insisted Rogers pay a $500,000 penalty:
Competition Bureau, "Court Orders $500,000 Administrative Monetary Penalty
in Rogers-Chatr Matter," Government of Canada, February 24, 2014,
http://www.competitionbureau.gc.ca/eic/site/cb-bc.nsf/eng/03675.html.

Although the CEO of Telus told reporters that "Blacks' premium locations" etc.:
CBC News, "Telus Snaps Up Black's [*sic*] Photo for $28m," CBC.ca,
September 8, 2009,
http://www.cbc.ca/news/business/telus-snaps-up-black-s-photo-for-28m-1.784512.

In 2015, when the telco finally pulled the plug on Blacks:
Marina Strauss, "Blacks Photography Falls Victim to Digital Industry,"
Globe and Mail, June 9, 2015.

In 2014, the CRTC finally reviewed incumbents' domestic roaming agreements:
Canadian Radio-television and Telecommunications Commission, "Telecom
Decision CRTC 2014-398," Government of Canada, July 31, 2014,
http://www.crtc.gc.ca/eng/archive/2014/2014-398.htm.

For more background on that decision:
Competition Bureau, "Notice of Consultation CRTC 2013-685—Wholesale
Mobile Wireless Roaming in Canada—Unjust Discrimination/ Undue Preference,"
Government of Canada, January 29, 2014,
http://www.competitionbureau.gc.ca/eic/site/cb-bc.nsf/eng/03648.htmC.

See also:
Christine Dobby, "Wind Cuts Roaming Rates Following Ottawa's Price Caps,"
Globe and Mail, August 21, 2014.

"When we complained, nothing happens":
CBC News, "Wind Mobile Backer Regrets Canadian Launch," CBC.ca,
November 17, 2011,
http://www.cbc.ca/news/business/wind-mobile-backer-regrets-canadian-
launch-1.1013522.

"The ultimate impact is likely higher churn of customers":
Michael Geist, "Why Verizon's Entry to Canada Would Reduce Consumer
Wireless Prices," MichaelGeist.ca, August 8, 2013,
http://www.michaelgeist.ca/2013/08/verizon-impact-on-pricing/.

As the Competition Bureau reported . . . the Big Three have "market power":
Competition Bureau, "Submission by the Commissioner of Competition before
the Canadian Radio-television and Telecommunications Commission—Telecom
Notice of Consultation CRTC 2014-76—Review of Wholesale Mobile Wireless
Services," Government of Canada, August 20, 2014,
http://www.competitionbureau.gc.ca/eic/site/cb-bc.nsf/eng/03786.html.

In 2017, the OECD again sounded the alarm:
OECD, *Policies for Stronger and More Inclusive Growth in Canada*,
Better Policies Series (Paris: OECD, June 2017), pp. 17–18,
https://www.oecd.org/about/publishing/better-policies-series/Policies-for-
stronger-and-more-inclusive-growth-in-Canada.pdf.

It's worth adding that in 2014 the OECD published a research report on
the outcomes when a country adds a fourth telecommunications provider.

The results were conclusive: four is a bit of a magic number, increasing the likelihood of innovation and driving down prices for consumers. In countries where mergers had occurred and the number of wireless competitors had decreased, the effects were negative:
OECD, *Wireless Market Structures and Network Sharing* (Paris: OECD, November 6, 2014),
http://www.oecd-ilibrary.org/science-and-technology/wireless-market-structures-and-network-sharing_5jxt46dzl9r2-en.

CHAPTER 2: **Going for Bronze**

For a good thumbnail sketch of Canada's rate of real economic growth, and why it is slowing, see pages 20–21 of the following report, which is also where we found the two graphs on corporate profits that are reproduced on page 64:
Andrei Sulzenko, *Canada's Innovation Conundrum: Five Years after the Jenkins Report* (Montreal: Institute for Research on Public Policy, June 2016),
http://irpp.org/wp-content/uploads/2016/06/report-2016-06-09.pdf.

. . . automation will wipe out as many as 7.5 million Canadian jobs:
Sunil Johal and Jordann Thirgood, *Working Without a Net*, Mowat Research #132 (Toronto: Mowat Centre, November 2016),
https://mowatcentre.ca/wp-content/uploads/publications/132_working_without_a_net.pdf.

For information on the global trade boom, and Canada's declining exports:
Deloitte, "The Future of Productivity: Smart Exporting for Canadian Companies," Deloitte.com,
https://www2.deloitte.com/ca/en/pages/deloitte-private/articles/the-future-of-productivity.html.

Also see the Economic Advisory Council's report on trade, which points out, "Although China's share of world trade has nearly quadrupled since 1995, Canada's share of that trade has fallen by about 25 percent. . . . We are currently at a competitive disadvantage to nations that have trade agreements with China" (p. 7):
Advisory Council on Economic Growth, *Positioning Canada as a Global Trading Hub* (Government of Canada, February 6, 2017),
http://www.budget.gc.ca/aceg-ccce/pdf/trade-commerce-eng.pdf.

For a good summary of Trevor Tombe's research on Canada–US trade:
Steven Chase, "How Much Trade Leverage Does Canada Really Have with the US?" *Globe and Mail*, February 13, 2017.

Two publications by the Council of Canadian Academies were extremely helpful in terms of understanding Canada's role in North American value chains, our failure to translate research excellence into business innovation, and our ongoing productivity problems:
Expert Panel on Business Innovation, "Innovation and Business Strategy: Why Canada Falls Short," Council of Canadian Academies, 2009.
Advisory Group, Council of Canadian Academies, "Paradox Lost: Explaining Canada's Research Strength and Innovation Weakness," Council of Canadian Academies, 2013.

Unless indicated otherwise, all direct quotes summarizing the CCA's findings, as well as all historical information about successive governments' failed attempts to spur innovation from 1916 onward, come from an article by Peter Nicholson, the inaugural president of the CCA:
Peter Nicholson, "Canada's Low-Innovation Equilibrium: Why It Has Been Sustained and How It Will Be Disrupted," *Canadian Public Policy*, November 2016, S39–45.

"Canadians traditionally have been conservative":
Kenneth M. Glazier, "Canadian Investment in the United States: 'Putting Your Money Where Your Mouth Is,'" *Journal of Contemporary Business* 1 (Autumn 1972): 56–68, as quoted in Seymour Martin Lipset, "Culture and Economic Behavior: A Commentary," *Journal of Labor Economics* 11, no. 1 Part 2 (January 1993): p. S337.

Statistics Canada tracks information on Canada's direct investment in the US and vice versa:
http://www.statcan.gc.ca/daily-quotidien/170425/dq170425a-eng.htm.

Since 2000, only one percent of Canadian exits have had a valuation of $500 million or more:
Advisory Council on Economic Growth, *Unlocking Innovation to Drive Scale and Growth* (Government of Canada, February 6, 2017), p. 5, http://www.budget.gc.ca/aceg-ccce/pdf/innovation-2-eng.pdf.

. . . we need to start adding $20 billion to the economy every year:
Kevin Lynch, "The Other One Per Cent Problem: Using Innovation to Spur Growth," *Policy Magazine*, May/June 2016, p. 51, http://www.policymagazine.ca/pdf/19/PolicyMagazineMayJune-2016Lynch.pdf.

The historical perspective from 1916 onward is courtesy of Peter Nicholson, but the quotation from the Science Council regarding Canadian investors' reluctance to back innovative companies is from Seymour Lipset's article, p. S337.

. . . an annual infusion of almost $23 billion of taxpayers' money via 147 innovation-related programmes and tax expenditures:
Using publicly available data, Kevin Page and Helaina Gaspard of the Institute of Fiscal Studies and Democracy at the University of Ottawa, along with two economics students, reviewed the departmental spending performance reports of ninety-four federal departments and agencies to come up with those numbers. However, just over 60 percent of the $23 billion is going to skills development and training. More typically, experts estimate the government's spending on innovation to be closer to between $5 and $7 billion annually, but they usually exclude skills/training. One thing is clear: a lot of money is being spent, and it's not being tracked at all well. For a quick summary of the IFSD study, see: Helaina Gaspard, Kevin Page, Kevin Emmanuel and Emel Medinic, "Before We Spend on Innovation, Let's Make Sure We're Getting Value," *Globe and Mail*, March 9, 2017.

We're in fifteenth place on the annual Global Innovation Index:
Canada ranks even lower on the Bloomberg 2017 Innovation Index, placing twentieth:
https://www.bloomberg.com/news/articles/2017-01-17/sweden-gains-south-korea-reigns-as-world-s-most-innovative-economies.

. . . foreign-controlled multinationals are responsible for almost 40 percent of BERD spending . . . and 50 percent of merchandise exports:
Advisory Council on Economic Growth, *Bringing Foreign Direct Investment to Canada* (Government of Canada, October 20, 2016), p. 2,
http://www.budget.gc.ca/aceg-ccce/pdf/foreign-investment-investisseurs-etrangers-eng.pdf.

". . . business complacency, the low educational attainment of Canadian managers":
OECD, *Policies for Stronger and More Inclusive Growth in Canada*, Better Policies Series (Paris: OECD, June 2017), p. 20:
https://www.oecd.org/about/publishing/better-policies-series/Policies-for-stronger-and-more-inclusive-growth-in-Canada.pdf.

Canadian companies' investment in ICT . . . is going down:
Peter Nicholson, among others, has flagged this issue, which is particularly acute for small businesses. According to the June 2017 OECD report, "In 2015, only 13.4% of small Canadian firms used enterprise resource planning software, well behind their large Canadian counterparts (63.5%) and

much lower than small firms in Germany (50.1%) and Belgium (44.5%)." The OECD recommended "coaching programmes to extend digital literacy"—and also reducing "impediments to competition to allow firms to grow, as larger firms tend to be better managed" (p. 20).

Canada's eighty-seven biggest corporate R & D spenders are relatively cautious: Research Infosource Inc., "Canada's Top 100 Corporate R & D Spenders 2015: Analysis," ResearchInfoSource.com, https://researchinfosource.com/top100_corp.php.

Only 30 percent of Canadian firms consider innovation important . . . just 15 percent would assume significant financial risk to pursue it: Advisory Council on Economic Growth. *Unlocking Innovation to Drive Scale and Growth* (Government of Canada, February 6, 2017), p. 5.

"puts the cart before the horse. A firm must first decide . . . innovation . . . makes business sense": Council of Canadian Academies, "Paradox Lost: Explaining Canada's Research Strength and Innovation Weakness," Advisory Group, Council of Canadian Academies, 2013, p. 28.

CHAPTER 3: The Gazelle Shortage

For all statistics regarding the number of Canadian small and medium-sized businesses, the number of employees they have, the contribution of small businesses to overall employment and GDP, and the percentage of SMEs that export, as well as the government's definition of *gazelle* and a breakdown of the number of gazelles per sector, see:
Innovation, Science and Economic Development Canada, Small Business Branch, *Key Small Business Statistics* (Ottawa: Government of Canada, June 2016), https://www.ic.gc.ca/cic/site/061.nsf/vwapj/KSBS-PSRPE_June-Juin_2016_eng.pdf/$FILE/KSBS-PSRPE_June-Juin_2016_eng.pdf.

We relied heavily on DEEP's extraordinarily insightful exploration of the challenges facing small businesses in Canada, which was our source for the observation that their average size at inception has been shrinking, that most experience zero or negative employment growth, that one-quarter see no benefit to exporting, and also for the direct quotes on pages 74, 78 and 81:
Dan Herman and Anthony D. Williams, "Driving Canadian Growth and Innovation: Five Challenges Holding Back Small and Medium-Sized Enterprises in Canada," Centre for Digital Entrepreneurship and Economic Performance, May 2013.

The Scott Shane paper that is summarized and from which we include quotes on pages 78 to 80 is also the text of the prize lecture he gave in Stockholm as the 2009 winner of the Global Award for Entrepreneurship Research:
Scott A. Shane, "Why Encouraging More People to Become Entrepreneurs Is Bad Public Policy," *Small Business Economics*, vol. 33, no. 2 (August 2009): 141–49.

Although the World Bank rates Canada *the second-easiest place in the world to start a business* (page 72), it also ranks us twenty-second in the world in terms of actually *doing* business (page 89):
http://www.doingbusiness.org/rankings/.

The Global Entrepreneurship Monitor reports its findings online, and the 2017 rankings can be found here, with information on Canada and the US on pages 47 and 101:
Global Entrepreneurship Monitor, *Global Report: 2016/17* (London: GEM, 2017),
http://gemconsortium.org/report/49812.

For more specific information on Canadians' goals when starting a business, on pages 74–5, however, we relied on the most recent thorough analysis of Canadian statistics:
Cooper H. Langford, Peter Josty and Chad Saunders, *Driving Wealth Creation and Social Development in Canada*, 2015 Gem Canada National Report (Calgary: Global Entrepreneurship Monitor, 2015),
http://thecis.ca/wp-content/uploads/2016/04/GEM-Canada-Report-5.2015.pdf.

. . . *really good entrepreneurs have an unusually high "multiplier effect"*:
Advisory Council on Economic Growth, *Unlocking Innovation to Drive Scale and Growth* (Government of Canada, February 6, 2017), p. 3.

Two reports provide excellent analysis of the characteristics of Canada's existing HGFs. All our facts and figures regarding the connection between exporting, job creation and increased profits come from these reports, and the first also includes the 2015 survey of entrepreneurs' ambition:
Business Development Bank of Canada, *High-Impact Firms: Accelerating Canadian Competitiveness*, BDC Study (May 2015),
https://www.bdc.ca/en/Documents/analysis_research/high-impact-firms-accelerating-canadian-competitiveness.pdf.

Chris Parsley and David Halabisky, *Profile of Growth Firms: A Summary of Industry Canada Research* (Ottawa: Industry Canada, March 2008), https://www.ic.gc.ca/eic/site/061.nsf/vwapj/ProfileGrowthFirms_Eng.pdf/$file/ ProfileGrowthFirms_Eng.pdf.

As a percentage of GDP, exports dropped from 46 percent in 2000 to 30 percent in 2012:
Deloitte, "The Future of Productivity: Smart Exporting for Canadian Companies," Deloitte.com, https://www2.deloitte.com/ca/en/pages/deloitte-private/articles/the-future-of-productivity.html.

Almost all other countries in the OECD increased exports as a percentage of GDP:
Mike Moffatt, "Canada Needs to Confront Its Shrinking Exports Problem," *Canadian Business*, January 20, 2015, http://www.canadianbusiness.com/economy/canada-needs-to-confront-its-shrinking-exports-problem-mike-moffatt/.

Small Canadian companies are only 47 percent as productive as large ones:
John R. Baldwin, Danny Leung and Luke Rispoli, "Canada–United States Labour Productivity Gap across Firm Size Classes," Statistics Canada, January 2014.

For a detailed analysis of what the small business deduction costs Canada, see:
Benjamin Dachis and John Lester, "Small Business Preferences as a Barrier to Growth: Not So Tall After All," C.D. Howe Institute, Commentary No. 426, May 2015.

For a quick review of interprovincial trade barriers and what they cost Canadians, see:
Trevor Tombe, "A Stunning $7,500 per Household Is the Annual Cost of Unfree Provincial Trade," *Financial Post*, March 28, 2016.

For a comprehensive review of foreign investment, and why Canada needs a lot more of it, see:
Advisory Council on Economic Growth, *Bringing Foreign Investment to Canada* (Government of Canada, October 20, 2016), pp. 2–4, http://www.budget.gc.ca/aceg-ccce/pdf/foreign-investment-investisseurs-etrangers-eng.pdf.

Even Donald Trump welcomes such immigrants with open arms:
Trump's letter supporting Lorne Abony's application for a US green card,
reprinted with Abony's permission.

To Whom It May Concern:

I am writing this letter in support of Lorne Abony's application for a U.S. Visa under the category of "a person of exceptional ability".

I have known Lorne Abony for approximately two years. He and his wife are members of my club Mar a Lago in Palm Beach Florida. In this capacity, I have become friends with Lorne and his wife.

It is well known that Lorne was the Founder and Chief Executive Officer of Fun Technologies ("Fun"). Fun is the world's largest online games and fantasy sports provider with over 35 million registered games customers and 600,000 fantasy sports teams.

When Fun was listed on the London Stock Exchange and Toronto Stock Exchage, Lorne Abony was the youngest CEO of any company listed on either exchange. Fun was one of the fastest growing companies in the history of the Toronto Stock Exchange. In less than three years the company raised over $160 million in five of equity financings, including its IPO. Lorne Abony also led FUN in completing eight strategic acquisitions for a total consideration of $128 million. In my view, these are exceptional business accomplishments.

In March 2006, media and cable giant Liberty Media ("Liberty") bought Fun for $484 million. Lorne remained as Fun CEO until Deceember 21, 2007. When Liberty acquired Fun, the company employed over 475 people in 7 offices around the world. Liberty is a $47 billion enterprise run by U.S. billionaire John Malone. Liberty owns some of the world's most prominent media assets including, QVC, DiretcTV, Starz and Discovery Network. To sell a public company to Liberty and Malone for $484 million is a very complicated and sophisticated undertaking and one that could only be carried out by a person with extraordinary business skills.

I believe that Lorne Abony has exceptional business abilities. Accordingly, I recommend him for the "person of exceptional ability" visa and I believe that he will make a very positive contribution to the U.S. economy.

Sincerely,

Donald J. Trump

PALM BEACH, FLORIDA

1100 South Ocean Boulevard, Palm Beach, Florida 33480   (561) 832-2600   Fax (561) 832-2669

BC outperforms all other provinces in terms of VC investment per capita:
Conference Board of Canada, "Provincial and Territorial Ranking:
Venture Capital," ConferenceBoard.ca,
http://www.conferenceboard.ca/hcp/provincial/innovation/venture-capital.aspx.

For an extensive discussion of the lack of availability of early-stage growth
capital, see pages 17 to 21 of the Advisory Council's *Unlocking Innovation* report,
cited above.

*"What we found was a funding system that is unnecessarily complicated and
confusing"*:
Jameson Berkow, "Canada's R&D Funding System 'Unnecessarily Complicated,'
Panel Finds," *Financial Post*, October 17, 2011.

The most balanced analysis of SR&ED is in the Jenkins report:
Review of Federal Support to Research and Development—Expert Panel Report,
Innovation Canada: A Call to Action (Government of Canada, October 2011).

For the most entertaining and damning appraisal of SR&ED, and the abuses of
the programme, see:
Barrie McKenna, "Dubious Claims Diminish R&D Tax Credit," *Globe and
Mail*, February 6, 2011.

For a history and stinging critique of Own the Podium, see:
Thomas Hall, "The Wrong Track," *Walrus*, September 2016,
https://thewalrus.ca/the-wrong-track/.

*"Governments may be bad at picking winners, but overgenerous tax credits allow any
loser to pick the taxpayers' pockets"*:
David Naylor, "Innovation in Canada: Pitfalls and Potential," *Policy Options*,
August 1, 2012,
http://policyoptions.irpp.org/magazines/policy-challenges-for-2020/innovation-
in-canada-pitfalls-and-potential/.

*Forty-three percent of all public companies in the US founded after 1979 received
venture backing*:
Ilya Strebulaev and Will Gornall, "How Much Does Venture Capital Drive the
US Economy?" *Stanford Business*, October 21, 2015,
https://www.gsb.stanford.edu/insights/how-much-does-venture-capital-drive-
us-economy.

CHAPTER 4: **The Aspiration Gap**

For detailed information on Canada's performance on the OECD's tests and on our international ranking, see:
OECD, *Pisa 2015: Results in Focus* (Paris: OECD, 2016), https://www.oecd.org/pisa/pisa-2015-results-in-focus.pdf.

. . . the University of Toronto . . . has fallen to twenty-second place: https://www.timeshighereducation.com/world-university-rankings.

For excellent comprehensive reports on the strengths and weaknesses of Canada's academic research vis-à-vis other countries', see both the Council of Canadian Academies' 2013 report *Paradox Lost: Explaining Canada's Research Strength and Innovation Weakness* and the report of Canada's Fundamental Science Review in 2017, *Investing in Canada's Future: Strengthening the Foundations of Canadian Research.*

The concern about talented students leaving is real. According to a 2011 study cited in the Jenkins panel report, "Statistics Canada has found that up to a fifth of doctoral graduates intend to leave Canada following completion of their degrees" (pp. 2–15).

CHAPTER 5: **It's Not Rocket Science**

"*. . . 18 percent of R & D employees have PhDs*":
Jenkins panel report, pp. 5–6.

The Jenkins panel also conducted a survey of about one thousand companies, asking "What are the most important sources for your firm's innovation ideas?" Employees and clients led the pack; R & D research was way down near the bottom of the list. (pp. 2–13).

"*. . . this creates a core imbalance, whereby university faculty are paid to research but college faculty are not*":
The original mission of colleges and polytechnics was to educate students for employment. As applied research is a by-product of the industry-teaching mandate, and was not included in the original mandate, college faculty are not paid for it—though they do it anyway.

The 2016 survey on Canadians' attitudes towards innovation:
Impact Centre, *Thinking Inside the Box: Canadians Lag Americans in Their Attitudes to Innovation* (Toronto: University of Toronto, January 2016),

http://www.impactcentre.ca/wp-content/uploads/2016/01/160208-Thinking-Inside-the-Box.pdf.

"Innovation is best understood as a mindset":
David Naylor, "Innovation in Canada: Pitfalls and Potential," *Policy Options*,
August 1, 2012,
http://policyoptions.irpp.org/magazines/policy-challenges-for-2020/innovation-in-canada-pitfalls-and-potential/.

CHAPTER 6 : **Sometimes It *Is* Rocket Science**

Information on Canada's international rankings in terms of academic research comes from the CCA report and the Fundamental Science Review reports mentioned above, both of which include detailed analyses based on a range of measures (e.g., volume of output, number of citations by other researchers, international surveys, etc.). Also helpful were the "State of the Nation" reports issued by the Science, Technology and Innovation Council: www.stic-csti.ca.

Our OECD ranking in terms of business–university R & D collaboration is now nineteenth:
World Economic Forum, *Global Competitiveness Report 2014–15*, p. 147.

American universities generate about 35 licences per institution compared with about 16 here:
Advisory Council on Economic Growth, *Unlocking Innovation to Drive Scale and Growth* (Government of Canada, February 6, 2017), p. 4.

In 2015, 36 universities earned $62 million in licensing income . . . MIT got 288 patents last year, U of T usually gets fewer than 10:
Sean Silcoff, "Billion-Dollar Breakout," *Globe and Mail*, March 18, 2017.

Canadian researchers are losing ground: smaller countries now outperform us:
Canada's Fundamental Science Review, *Investing in Canada's Future: Strengthening the Foundations of Canadian Research*, ScienceReview.ca,
April 2017, p. 45:
http://www.sciencereview.ca/eic/site/059.nsf/vwapj/ScienceReview_April2017-rv.pdf/$file/ScienceReview_April2017-rv.pdf.

Venture is "one of the worst-performing asset classes in Canada":
Jim Balsillie, "Canadians Can Innovate, but We're Not Equipped to Win,"
Globe and Mail, May 8, 2015.

"Even in strategic areas, such as Artificial Intelligence . . . most of the patents. . . belong to foreign companies":
Dan Breznitz and Mark Fox, "Canada's Intellectual Property Strategy Must Play to the Country's Strengths," *Globe and Mail*, August 4, 2017.

CONCLUSION

To read more about Woodward, Evans and their light bulb:
Susanna McLeod, "The Canadians behind the Light Bulb," *Kingston Whig-Standard*, February 12, 2013.

For Reputation Institute reports, see:
https://www.reputationinstitute.com/research/Country-RepTrak.aspx.

"Reaching 50 million consumers—the definition of a mature breakthrough technology":
Kevin Lynch, "The Other One Per Cent Problem: Using Innovation to Spur Growth," *Policy Magazine*, May/June 2016, pp. 51–54.

"44 percent of start-ups receive funding from Americans":
Alexandra Bosanac, "Why Do Canadian Start-Ups Ignore Government Funding Sources?" *Canadian Business*, July 16, 2015.

Note: AL = Anthony Lacavera

Abony, Lorne, 83–89, 97
Advisory Council on Economic
    Growth, 57, 88
Aga Khan, 118
Agrawal, Ajay
    on Canadian school system, 116
    on competition, 116
    and Creative Destruction Labs,
        192–94, 195, 196, 197, 201, 205
    and importance of judgment, 191,
        192–93
    on innovation and productivity, 161
    and machine learning, 202
    and Next 36, 114, 120, 121
    starts Creative Destruction Lab,
        189–90
    and venture capitalists, 206
agricultural technology, 228
agriculture funding, 162–64
Ahong, Tim, 126, 127, 129, 130, 132,
    134, 136, 139
Alarie, Benjamin, 202–3, 204
Alexa Fund, 205
Alfred Sung, 55
Alignvest Capital Management, 114
Alston, David, 225–27
ambition
    importance of, 75–76

lack of and trade, 77
Andreessen, Marc, 191
Andreessen Horowitz, 57, 76, 191
angel investors, 89, 90
Area One Farms (AOF), 162–63, 164,
    166–67
artificial intelligence. *See also* machine
    learning
    and banks, 207
    development of in Canada, 177–78
    and loss of patents, 208–9
    and tax law, 202–3, 204
Atomwise, 98, 103, 181
AT&T, 14

Balsillie, Jim, 206, 208
Bannister, Janet, 120–21
Barrotti, Alex, 218–21, 226
Bell
    acquires complete Virgin Mobile, 32
    attitude to competition, 10, 11, 13,
        26–27, 32, 33–34, 37, 40
    average revenue user per month
        (ARPU), 17
    control of telecommunications
        industry, 2–3, 7–8
    disincentives to expand, 9–10
    response to entry of WIND, 26–27
    and spectrum licences, 11
Bengio, Yoshua, 177